The end of Ulster loyalism?

Manchester University Press

The end of Ulster loyalism?

Peter Shirlow

Manchester University Press
Manchester and New York
distributed exclusively in the USA by Palgrave Macmillan

Published by Manchester University Press
Oxford Road, Manchester M13 9NR, UK
and Room 400, 175 Fifth Avenue, New York, NY 10010, USA
www.manchesteruniversitypress.co.uk

Distributed exclusively in the USA by
Palgrave Macmillan, 175 Fifth Avenue, New York,
NY 10010, USA

Distributed exclusively in Canada by
UBC Press, University of British Columbia, 2029 West Mall,
Vancouver, BC, Canada V6T 1Z2

British Library Cataloguing-in-Publication Data
A catalogue record for this book is available from the British Library

Library of Congress Cataloging-in-Publication Data applied for

ISBN 978 0 7190 8475 1 hardback
ISBN 978 0 7190 8476 8 paperback

First published 2012

Typeset
by Helen Skelton, Brighton, UK
Printed in Great Britain
by Bell & Bain Ltd, Glasgow

Contents

List of figures and tables

Figures

Tables

Acknowledgements

There were many people who helped and assisted with the writing of this book from within loyalism and beyond. However, I hope that they are not offended if I do not name them here as I would like to take this opportunity to acknowledge the memory of David Ervine and Billy Mitchell – who are no longer with us. One only hopes that their positive and inclusive image of a new Northern Ireland/Ireland will be passed down the generations. These were men who took risks for peace and swam against many tides. Their courage was mixed with foresight, humanity and a true vocation for peace-building and conflict transformation. Neither wanted any of us to continue living on the narrow ground. As David once quipped, 'I don't want to wake up every morning and ask myself 'Am I British or Irish?' I want to think 'Am I late for work?'

Thanks to Michael McKeown for permission to use his dataset.

List of abbreviations

ACNI	Arts Council of Northern Ireland
ACT	Action for Community Transformation
AIA	Anglo-Irish Agreement
CJINI	Criminal Justice Inspectorate Northern Ireland
CLMC	Combined Loyalist Military Command
CLPA	Combined Loyalists Political Alliance
CO	Commanding Officer
CRC	Community Relations Council
CRJI	Community Restorative Justice Ireland
CSI	Cohesion, Sharing and Integration
CTI	Conflict Transformation Initiative
DSD	Department for Social Development
DUP	Democratic Unionist Party
FRU	Force Research Unit
HET	Historical Enquiries Team
IFI	International Fund for Ireland
IMC	Independent International Monitoring Commission
INLA	Irish National Liberation Army
IPLO	Irish People's Liberation Organisation
IRA	Irish Republican Army (also known as PIRA – Provisional Irish Republican Army)
IRS	Independent Research Solutions
LVF	Loyalist Volunteer Force
MACS	Mediation and Community Support
MLA	Member of the Legislative Assembly
NIA	Northern Ireland Alternatives
NIHE	Northern Ireland Housing Executive
NIO	Northern Ireland Office

OC	Officer Commanding
OFMDFM	Office of the First Minister and Deputy First Minister
PACT	Pupils and Communities Together
PBNI	Probation Board of Northern Ireland
PMFP	Politically Motivated Former Prisoner
POW	Prisoner of War
PSNI	Police Service of Northern Ireland
PUP	Progressive Unionist Party
RAP	Restorative Adult Practices
RHC	Red Hand Commandos
RHD	Red Hand Defenders
RIC	Re-Imaging Communities
RUC	Royal Ulster Constabulary
SCC	Shared Communities Consortium
SDLP	Social Democratic and Labour Party
SOLACE	Society of Local Authority Chief Executives and Senior Managers
UDA	Ulster Defence Association
UDP	Ulster Democratic Party
UDR	Ulster Defence Regiment
UFF	Ulster Freedom Fighters
UPRG	Ulster Political Research Group
UUP	Ulster Unionist Party
UVF	Ulster Volunteer Force
UWC	Ulster Workers' Council
UYM	Ulster Young Militants

My greatest wish would be for an end
of the organisation and for people to
get into helping their communities
(UVF respondent)

Introduction

Ulster Loyalists are generally viewed as a 'dysfunctional' and ethno-sectarian abnormality dispossessed of meaningful value and positive intent, with their investment in conflict transformation and peace-seeking largely unknown or unappreciated (Shirlow and McEvoy 2008; Shirlow and McGovern 1997). The general perspective concerning Loyalists is that their actions and deeds mark them as being on the negative side of both moral opinion and ethical value. Loyalists are usually bounded into a homogeneous group of atavists and criminals within a putative judgmental frame that stretches across the ethno-sectarian divide. Much of what is opined about them is tied to an unshakeable prophecy of invariant stereotyping or, as Fintan O'Toole notes, they are an 'idiocy that comes with a fragmented culture that has lost both memory and meaning' (cited in Howe 2005:4).

There is no denial of senselessness within parts of loyalism and organisations such as the Ulster Volunteer Force (UVF), the Ulster Defence Association (UDA), the Red Hand Commandos (RHC) and the Ulster Freedom Fighters (UFF).[1] C Company[2] championed the title the 'Godfathers of (Ruthless) Kitsch', with a reputation for brutal sectarian actions, perniciousness and insidious beliefs. Moreover, the sheer brutality of the Shankill Butchers[3] narrowed the terrain upon which a positivist account of Loyalists could be centred. Yet, Howe notes:

> To say that Loyalist culture is *only* about sectarianism and supremacism – as commentators … have repeatedly done – is, bluntly, a lie. (Howe 2005: 3)[4]

Howe is correct in that there has been insufficient space for the presentation of those Loyalists who have engaged in transition, more reasoned and rational understandings of conflict transformation and who delivered decommissioning (BBC 2009a). Somewhat predictable is that positive Loyalist practices, codes and attitudes, which have uplifted and sustained the peace process, are generally dismissed via the regular narrative that:

In contrast (to Republicans), Loyalist paramilitaries in Northern Ireland, while also being non-State organizations, have constructed their purpose as being to bolster and protect the UK State and to protect Protestant people from the security threat posed by Irish Republicanism. They occupy an uneasy pro-State British nationalist or sub-national ethnic position and have not aimed at being revolutionary or liberatory. (Alison 2004: 448)

Such a perspective appears to ignore the existence of a positive and non-sectarian loyalism, a very evident case of failing to locate an accurate reading of internal and competing cultures (Bhabha 1994). The Progressive Unionist Party (PUP)[5] is the only political party in Northern Ireland that is pro-choice and which has had a sustained record of advancing ideas and policies regarding sexual and gender equality[6] (Purvis 1998). Loyalists who aim to raise consciousness in class and identity terms and in so doing question the lack of equity and social justice for working-class communities also remain generally imperceptible in such commentary. Within unionism, progressive Loyalists are also categorised negatively when invoked as communists/socialists or as those who are either too close to Republicans or who involve themselves in community development so as to expand their 'criminal power-bases'. Loyalism in whatever guise of Irish nationalist or Unionist interpretation is often objectionable because it is either, and somewhat confusingly, regressive/hegemonic according to Republicans, or radical/anti-hegemonic according to Unionists. Whether involved in conflict or peace-building it would appear that Loyalists should not be viewed as possessing any place that is not 'beyond the pale' of both Irish nationalist or Unionist tolerability and esteem. Even when considered within a more sympathetic contextual frame, loyalism is generally located within a landscape of fracture, despair and social grievance (Combat 2003; McAuley 1996, 2000, 2002, 2003).

As with all groups generally condemned by blunt subjectivity, the enactment of judgment aims to maintain a fiction of blamelessness upon those who wish to maintain a propaganda-conditioning perspective that only non-State combatants are at fault for conflict and criminality (Gormally et al. 2007). That perspective omits other factors that caused violence and criminality such as poverty, political economy, sectarian asperity, historical materialism, State collusion, symbolic violence and the social production and consumption of meaning (Bourdieu 1984; Mitchell 2002, 2003, 2008). In any instance information and opinion-forming is both assembled and understood via culturally assigned meaning and tropes, which are allied to purposeful statements within which non-State combatants are charged not as the product of conflict but somewhat erroneously as its grand architects and engineers. With regard to Loyalists that generally assumes the additional idea that their acts and deeds are based upon self-victimisation and an inherent flaw in their character and discursive construction. Evidently we are supposed to think of Loyalists as existing within an unethical vacuum constructed by self-destructive performance, and as a group that is hermetically sealed by its own ideological, criminal and violent enclosure.

Media attention, particularly from local tabloids, serves up a perpetual diet of stories concerning the involvement of paramilitaries and former political prisoners in crime (McDowell 2001; Parkinson 1988). What gets lost in such narratives is that over a decade since the early release of prisoners began, following the Belfast Agreement, a mere twenty-three, or 5%, of those released have had their licences suspended and have been returned to prison (Northern Ireland Prison Service 2010). By way of comparison, the recidivism rate for non-political prisoners, in Northern Ireland, is 48% within two years of their release (Northern Ireland Prison Service 2003). Despite this and other positive contributions made by Loyalists towards peace and stability, McGrattan (2009)[7] has challenged previous work by the author and others as being obsessed with labelling Loyalists and Republicans as political when this 'obscures the fact that the Republican and Loyalist campaigns were fundamentally sectarian and terroristic and undoubtedly criminal' (2009: 7). That perspective omits those who have also reacted positively to Loyalist transition and community activism including the Justice Oversight Commissioner (2004, 2005), the Criminal Justice Inspectorate (2007a, 2007b) and the Independent International Monitoring Commission (2009).

In part, these experiences of negativity and criminalisation can be traced to the 'problem' of pro-State terrorism (Bruce 1987, 1992; Crothers 1998; EPIC 2004, 2005). As outlined by Bruce (1992, 1994a, 1994b), the nature and 'awkwardness' of 'pro-State' groups means that they are in competition with and vulnerable to criminalisation and disassociation from the State and the forces which they purport to defend. For Unionists, the emphasis upon law and order and loyalty to the State meant that (in public) primacy was awarded to State agents. McEvoy (2001) has captured this distinction in an alternative light, focusing on the differing interpretations of the conflict as criminal versus political for Unionists and Irish nationalists respectively. According to this interpretation, Unionist politicians claimed terrorism was driven by a small number of 'men of violence' with criminal and psychopathic tendencies, rather than in response to any wider structural or ideological contexts. Therefore, Loyalist combatants in Northern Ireland were consequently much less socially acceptable than Republican 'political prisoners' who suffered less from stigmatisation from within their community. This has generally meant that Loyalist ex-combatants have found it more difficult to 're-integrate' politically and gain due recognition of their valuable work in transforming localised cultures of violence (Darby 1976; Mitchell 2002, 2003, 2008; Shirlow et al. 2005). Ultimately, loyalism is divided between progressive and regressive elements with the latter achieving greater note and attention when in fact the former have affected more significant shifts within the Loyalist body politic. As Gallaher (2007: 219) states, 'within loyalism it is clear that political Loyalism's identity politics is substantially different from that proffered by revanchist Loyalism'.

Despite obvious splits regarding the nature, direction and motive of various forms of Loyalist activity and representational variance in concepts and value systems, Loyalists remain labelled as a 'social threat' (Cohen and Young 1981). As Cohen notes the label of criminalisation is not merely a process of tagging but one that is both driven and reproduced:

> A condition, episode, person or group of persons emerges to become defined as a threat to societal values and interests; its nature is presented in a stylised and stereotypical fashion by the mass media; the moral barricades are manned by editors, bishops, politician and other right-thinking people; socially accredited experts pronounce their diagnosis and solutions; ways of coping are evolved or (more often) resorted to. (Cohen 1972: 9)

The issue at hand is not that certain Loyalists are not a risk to others through crime and violent enactment, but instead that the manner in which they are cast purposefully submerges those who offer alternative readings, actions and suppositions. Criminalisation is a tenaciously driven narrative construction that resolutely aims to represent Loyalists as insular and discredited. Such an approach is dangerously myopic and subverts the capacity of Loyalist conversion both in real and potential terms. Such casting of deviance would have some semblance of worth if it was accompanied by acts that aimed to uplift communities beleaguered by conflict, championed the cause of poverty reduction, aimed for a voice for the socially marginalised and pinpointed the manner in which conflict-related harms could be eased. Instead, as with all forms of moral indignation and labelling, there is no exploratory mechanism for community renewal and optimism advanced by those who label, but instead a symbolic ghettoisation of communities of disadvantage and social pessimism (O' Malley 1983; Wilson et al. 2003). When criminalisation is merely an act of discrediting and labelling and is without alternative ideas and models for inclusion its central purpose is thus more viciously driven at excluding the voice and actions of those aiming for social justice and inclusion. In the context herein the rise of increasingly positive Loyalist-led interaction is ever more countered by a more determined desire to produce the deviant Loyalist. Ultimately criminalisation is a process that highlights 'truth' at the cost of reason and societal emancipation.

Loyalism: contested readings

Loyalist antagonism has habitually been viewed as feral-like apolitical aggression. There is no doubt that Loyalist violence was pernicious, but to view it as without source or material underpinning and as reactive to fear and threat is to concede only to conceptual laziness or propaganda-seeking. In particular,

Loyalists are depicted as sectarian and in identity terms shorn up by an immoveable discourse that is tied to mythic notions and embodied idealism. In Cairns' (2000) summation the term Loyalist is collapsed into narratives of Orangeism which thereby fails to separate Loyalist discursive independence and the reality that many Loyalists view Orangeism as decaying, unthinking and imprudent.[8] As he notes:

> The events of Williamite history, above all others, connote and convey the Loyalist mentality which sees continually vanquishing the Irish nationalist – or 'Catholic' – enemy as a fundamental necessity; their heroic narrative ably embodies the ideal beliefs, values and attitudes to which the Loyalist aspires: a form of loyalty to the British Crown, a code of conservative moral values and, most problematically, anti-Catholicism. The presence of this discourse also effectively predetermines the Ulster Loyalist's political future, being continually reiterated in Orange speeches and writings. (Cairns 2000: 438)

Irish Republican analysis usually views loyalism as inseparable from wider narratives of Unionist domination. Within that worldview the collapse in Unionist hegemony in 1972 merely meant that Loyalists became directed by British State securocrats (Stevenson 1996). Despite developing conflict-amelioration initiatives Loyalists, within Republican discourse, remain a misguided arm of State collaboration that lacks social and cultural credibility. As confidentially noted by Jim Gibney, a senior Republican thinker:

> They don't have an independent existence in terms of determining what they do and where they go politically but in fact their future is bound up with how the British securocrat system sees the future. Up to this point the British securocrat system has been using Loyalists throughout the peace process and before that to achieve their objectives. (Cited in Shirlow and Monaghan 2006: 2)

In denying Loyalists any role other than as agents of hegemonic regulation they are further denied a symbolic order and alternative spheres of material reference (Finlayson 1997, 1999). As Gallaher has observed, academic analysis is rarely constructed around those who are not viewed as 'members of traditionally oppressed groups' (1997: 256–257) even though Loyalists felt repressed by the notion of Irish unification, super-grass trials and viewed Republican violence as a mode of symbolic and material oppression. To reject such a sense of implied subjugation is to suggest that loyalism is unthinking, unemotional and cataleptic. That does not mean that such senses of oppression are acceptable in terms of launching ethno-sectarian violence, but to assert that loyalism was without a sense of subjugation and repression is mistaken.

Loyalism is also understood as 'clearly and unambiguously ... groups on the fringe of society attempting to exert control over certain areas with 'their current motivation ... to do with criminal activity, racketeering and drug-dealing and so on. Any claim to have a political motivation has more or less disappeared' (David Ford, Leader, Alliance Party, interview 2005). When questioned on the meaning of transformative loyalism Alex Attwood, a Social Democratic and Labour Party (SDLP) Member of the Legislative Assembly (MLA) (interview 2005) stated that 'it is not correct, if this is what you are suggesting, that at its core it is now different, I don't believe so, I just think it is targeted, for want of a better word, differently'. Interviews with DUP Councillor and Policy Officer Clive McFarland (interview 2005) reiterated the general idea of 'a greater development of the criminal element within those groups' and that 'the feuds over recent years have just thrown that into very sharp contrast, it has kind of evolved into criminal-based empires'. Even when questioned on the role of transformative loyalism with regard to reducing violence, the perspective held that '... positive things which have come out of Loyalist paramilitary groups are few and far between' (Richard Bullick, Director of DUP Policy, interview 2005).

As Rankin and Ganiel (2008: 116) suggest, 'the story of an imprisoned Loyalist paramilitary bemoaning the day that he ever listened to "that man Paisley" has become apocryphal'. A substantial body of documentary and anecdotal material exists which provides evidence of an active association between certain Unionist politicians and Loyalist paramilitary organisations (Bairner 1996; Bruce 1992, 1994a, 1994b, 1995a, 1995b; McIlheney 1985; O'Callaghan and O'Donnell 2006). The current and former leaders of the DUP, Peter Robinson and Ian Paisley, are generally singled out by Loyalists for particular attention (Gallagher 1981; McIver 1987). Both played a role in Ulster Resistance, a paramilitary movement established in opposition to the Anglo-Irish Agreement (AIA) and a number of inflammatory speeches designed to lure and raise Loyalists into action were made by Paisley, including his declaration at a recruitment rally for Ulster Resistance that 'there are many like myself who'd like to see the agreement brought down by democratic means, but wouldn't we all be fools if we weren't prepared' (cited in Bruce 1994a: 33). Yet within certain sectors of unionism, literal denial of any associ-ation with Loyalist paramilitarianism has remained and has (arguably) biased attitudes towards the involvement of Loyalists in community work and other conflict transformation initiatives. In 1981 Andy Tyrie[9] explained a commonly held position among Loyalists concerning manipulation of them by Unionist politicians:

> The politicians never provide the necessary leadership, because when the crisis does come about they hide and leave it to the people. We provided the soldiers because we thought the politicians would be the officers and they would have the courage of their convictions. In private they gave us their blessing but in public they would not come out and be the officers. So we did all the things that were expected of us and got deeply involved in violence. We are seen as the thugs and the gangsters, the bully boys, but if you have a look deep into the situation you realise who the thugs and the gangsters and the bully boys really are ... You also

have to remember that because we're not controlled by the politicians, they are now trying to create their own paramilitary organisations.[10] They bring them out every six months to scare the life out of the Provos and every time they do it the Provos plant more bombs and shoot more people. (Rowthorn 1981: 27)

More positive external views emanate from those who have been working with Loyalists and aiding the transition into more peaceful means and strategies. As noted:

> I think loyalism is more positive than unionism to a certain extent in that at least it does focus on identity issues and issues around citizenship and stuff like that. Now it doesn't necessarily always do it in a particularly articulate manner but at least it does look at those issues. Whereas unionism tends always to be this thing of 'oh well our economic benefit is in the Union' and increasingly that's becoming more questionable. So actually by engaging in stuff around the whole Somme Centre and stuff like that, I mean I think that is potentially positive. Because at least if they then take step number three which is to then engage in saying 'where does this identity fit in any post-national circumstance in the island of Ireland or British Isles or Europe?' they have something with which to negotiate. The thing is then to continue with that work so that they do get to a stage where they feel they can negotiate a position. (Avila Kilmurray, Director Community Foundation for Northern Ireland, interview 2005)

In terms of depictions of itself the rejection of negative and hostile commentary is centred on presenting political practice as a guide to Loyalist transition. David Ervine, former leader of the PUP, constantly presented the idea that loyalism was fundamentally far more ahead than unionistm, in terms of the exploration for accommodation, than at the time of both the ceasefires and up to and beyond the Belfast Agreement (Ervine 1995, 1998, 2000, 2002a), thus indicating a positive developmental position. Ervine also offered a strong challenge to judgements that were directed against the communities in which Loyalists lived:

> I did a television programme with an Alliance MLA and one would have sworn blind having listened to the Alliance MLA that our streets are in absolute mayhem, there's punishment beatings in every street, that there is a drug house in every street, there's a prostitution ring in every street which just isn't true. (David Ervine, interview 2005)

A key desire for those who are involved in Loyalist transformation is the rejection of hegemonic-style leadership and the need for Loyalists to assert their own discourse and identity. As Tom Winstone, a former Loyalist prisoner and restorative justice worker, surmised:

> I think there is too many people within loyalism, especially what I said earlier about principled Loyalists, who will not allow us to be duped again. They have woken up and have called the bluff of those who would manipulate them.

> Principled Loyalists smell the coffee and call a spade a spade and rather than being used all the time. (Interview 2005)

A similar sense of usury is explained as follows:

> We recognise that over the past, Unionist parties in many cases have had ambivalent attitudes to Loyalist organisations. Have used and abused in many cases; have been quite happy to have the issue of the Loyalist threat or Loyalist backlash in their arsenal when they met prime ministers and secretaries of state; that there have been many cases where people have stood on platforms and castigated Unionist paramilitaries but at the same time they have whispered behind closed doors and behind the backs of their hands. At the same time the UVF have a higher agenda; the UVF don't wish to be seen as vengeful against those things that have happened in the past. (UVF respondent, West Belfast[11])

A fundamental feature of the problem with the term 'loyalism' is the wide-ranging manner in which it is used. It seems peculiar that a vociferous DUP member is determined as being a Loyalist but so too is a life-sentence prisoner who had engaged in armed violence; the latter may be influenced by leftist interpretations and the former allied to more religiously constructed and fundamentalist propositions. Todd (1987) aimed to formulate a two-fold typology between the Ulster British and the Ulster Loyalists, with the former more likely to adopt identity change and the latter, depicted as populist and rigid localists, driven by notions of self-determination and the 'right to action'. In fact it was from within sections of the Ulster Loyalist bloc that more nuanced forms of identity-based interpretation were to emerge, especially with regard to inter-community recognition and practice. The capacity of Loyalists involved in conflict transformation reminds us that identity is multiply constructed and is less contingent than proposed, given that it is both experiential and discursively driven (Boulton 1973; Bourdieu 1984; Cohen and Arato 1992; Jehn and Mannix 2001). Identity construction in Northern Ireland has been more fluid than assumed and in many instances is based upon the rejection of an extreme rendition of 'self'. Within this context Loyalists are understood as those who have been involved in paramilitarianism and/or Loyalist-inspired political and community-centred activity. The act of engaging or having engaged in violence sets such persons apart from a wider notion of loyalism that stretches across a series of ideas, aspirations and commitments.

A further part of the problem when studying loyalism is that it does not fit neatly within the identity-oriented literature that generally omits groups that are not viewed as challenging hegemonic power, cultural authority and State-driven ideology (Gallaher and Shirlow 2006). The work of Laclau and Mouffe (1985) is relevant in that they considered the need to explore fully conflict and its relationship with the material conditions of the the cultural, class and political. As noted:

it is impossible to specify *a priori* surfaces of emergence of antagonisms, as there is no surface which is not constantly subverted by the over-determining effects of others, and because there is, in consequence, a constant displacement of the social logics characteristic of certain spheres towards other spheres. (Laclau and Mouffe 1985: 180)

The actuality of events, episodes and conditions should always foreground theoretical elucidation, what Laclau and Mouffe refer to as 'the indeterminacy of the social'. The fluidity of social relationships and the manner in which hegemony is itself a site of changing power relationships pinpoints how all units of social, political and economic reference are shifting and constantly re-assembling. In accepting the fluidity of such relationships it is possible to produce a more grounded understanding of groups such as Loyalists, whose construction and practices waver from being embroiled in maintaining an ethno-sectarian status quo through to questioning the rationale of having done so. In both material and symbolic terms any understanding of progressive and transformative loyalism must appreciate that it has precluded deterministic statements and is aiming to produce a more multifarious account of past, present and future Loyalist action and motivations.

As Laclau and Mouffe (1985) argue, the sense of threat or the undermining of identity is the point at which social antagonism emerges. Within the Northern Ireland context non-State combatants entered into confrontation with variant understandings of threat and discrimination in which Republicans aimed to achieve equality through the removal of the British State and Loyalists aimed to maintain the constitutional status quo. However, throughout the conflict transitional Loyalists reconsidered the nature of threat, calling on several occasions for ceasefires, and argued that social antagonism had to be constructed around challenging the nature of status quoism via the building of community activism backed by notions of social justice that were contrary to previous assertions of ethno-sectarian asperity. However, the capacity to do so was ultimately undermined by the defenderist/aggressive role Loyalists constructed against the Irish nationalist/Catholic community and the failure to develop a Republican-style movement whose agency included armed conflict, politics, cultural 'awakening' and anti-State critique/action. Their fundamental failure, thus far, was their insufficient capacity, compared with Republicans, to shift into a discourse of legitimacy and political radicalism given that within the Unionist community they were publicly despised or viewed as an adjunct of State forces. A further problem for Loyalists was their dependence upon the Irish Republican Army (IRA) to remove itself out of armed conflict. As Andy Tyrie contended when interviewed:

You get caught up in the violence thing. Then you start to think what that has led to and all that, the violence and the hatred and all. Then some start to think of a way out, but there are few outs as the war is rumbling on. So you try new ideas and ways ah thinking but you can't move out of what you are in, if the IRA are still about. So you want to go somewhere, but you have thrown your hat in the ring and you are going to be there at it until the IRA go. You still try to build a different loyalism, a different type, that has learned that the people have to share this place. It's that, but when you know where you want to take people, you just can't because peoples being killed in them streets.

The desire to engage in anti-Catholic violence was not a 'concrete' social relationship given that transformative Loyalists had appreciated, in some form since the mid-1970s, the need for fluidity in thinking and the contingency of political settlement. The role of agents embroiled in conflict changes if the interests that they serve are achievable via other mediums or if the logic of conflict itself becomes untenable or is interpreted differently. With regard to progressive Loyalists, their role is as much based upon self-critique as it is upon reacting merely to the end of conflict more generally. For progressive Loyalists their preconstituted design and assembly of thought is now open to re-interpretation and it is evident that the role positive Loyalists have played in the peace process has largely been sustained by challenging the 'predictability' of self. One aspect of that is the conclusion of those Loyalists involved in conflict transformation that Republicans do not understand the nature of transformation but instead approach their actions via a narrow frame that is tied to an unshakeable destiny. For such persons conflict transformation artic-ulates change and rereading and is open to many conclusions. Unfortunately, and as discussed in Chapter 4, constructive and inclusive intent was not shared across the Loyalist body politic.

One characteristic of loyalism, unlike other paramilitary organisations, is the public nature of introspection, and the acceptance of many of the criticism made against it. Loyalists have a history of condemning those within its own ranks as ethno-supremacists and those who have engaged in criminal activity. As early as 1977 Gusty Spence asserted that:

> We in Northern Ireland are plagued with super-Loyalists ... If one does not agree with their bigoted and fascist views then one is a 'taig[12]-lover', or a 'communist' ... Unfortunately, we have too many of these people in our own ranks. No fascist or bigot can expect sympathy or understanding in the UVF compounds ... The sooner we realise that our trust has been abused, and the so-called political leader-ship we followed was simply a figment the sooner we will attempt to fend for ourselves politically and to commence articulation in that direction.[13]

Moreover, such persons also argued that there was validity in a desire for Irish unification, if pursued via democratic means. Through invoking democratic accountability such Loyalists took one of the first steps towards Loyalist transition.

Forms of resistance and fears of domination

The conflict in Ireland was centred upon variant forms of resistance and domination. A feature of Loyalist practice was evidently tied to resisting the Republican/Catholic 'other' via the invocation of 'protecting' the Unionist/Loyalist community and undermining the capacity to create a united Ireland. That is well known and has been explained in detail elsewhere (Aughey and McIlhenney 1984; Boulton 1973; Finlayson 1999; Gillespie 2001). However, less evaluated and understood is that loyalism, especially after the ceasefires of 1994, was also driven by forms of resistance between peaceniks and those who rejected peace accords (Finlayson 1997; Gallaher 1997). Loyalist resistance has been both internal and external (Miller 1978). There is also an evident external issue that impedes conflict transformation as noted by Billy Hutchinson, the former PUP MLA, in an interview with the author:

> Republicans don't know what conflict transformation is. I tell them this all of the time. They do not see anything beyond what is Republicanism. They always tell me we cannot talk about being oppressed as we weren't oppressed as they see it by the State. If you can't even understand that we were oppressed then how can they work towards transformation? They just don't see that we can produce art and ideas and move people on. The problem is that they tell us who we are instead of trying to understand, from our ideas, who we are and why we did and do the things we do.

It would appear that the general rejection of loyalism, within a framework such as that of resistance and domination, is based upon notions of ideological 'defectiveness'. A reminder that academia is riddled by subjectivity and that the selection of certain groups as worthy of study has more to do with their anti-State and anti-capitalist rhetoric than with studying conflict and agency more generally (Karanga 2000; Nordstrom et al. 1992; Sack 1998). Here the author is motivated by the ideas of conflict transformation, irrespective of the source, and argues that a great deal of what constitutes criminology and conflict studies fails to complete a proper analysis of what conflict is concerned with, especially when authors subjectively pick sides and fail to appreciate the depth of resistance-centred narratives, even among those who assert the hegemonic order.

A central aspect in studying conflict is the theoretical framework of resistance and domination that has been based upon determining how hegemonic constructions present counter-hegemonic sites as marginal and deviant (Kellerman 1996; Keith and Pile 1993; Massumi 1993). Irish Republicanism fits more neatly into such a model as it operated and developed out of the realities of discrimination and the oppression of Irish cultural identity. In challenging the hegemony of the Unionist State and British authority Republicans built a narrative of resistance tied to their subordination and marginality and therefore their violent action is presented as the dismissal and rejection of a submissive role (Gallaher 1997; Girard 1979; Whyte 1983, 1991). However, both Republicans and Loyalists were the product of the outplaying of State and nation-building by the two states in Ireland. Those states aimed for alternative ideological frameworks and in so doing made each unattractive to its minorities or possible, through unification, future minority (Follis 1995; Wood 2006).

In terms of their original discourses of resistance Loyalists assumed that their actions were a response to Republican threat and that this was linked to a belief that their violence, even if ethno-sectarian, was based upon resistance to the imposition of Irish State hegemony. Such resistance was not only sectarian or driven by national identity but also approximated ideas that challenged a form of hegemony which, it was imagined, would occur through incorporation into the Irish State. As noted by a senior UDA member:

> I'm not denying that we were sectarian but we also had our own ideas. The Republic [of Ireland] was a backward place, no contraception, no divorce and lots of censorship: It was hardly Disneyland. The country that executed more IRA men that the Unionists did. Did you know that?
>
> So are you telling me that if Northern Ireland was a better place to live, not just because we were the majority, but because the Irish State was rotten to the core and a backward place with no real welfare state, like we had? Was I was supposed to roll over and say 'Ok, let's have a united Ireland and live in a more conservative country that was just as sectarian'? Yeah right! A lot of southerners back then used to tell me the North, as they called it, was a better place than where they lived. (UDA respondent, Newry and Armagh)

In conceptual terms senses of defenderism are located within the framework of resistance and domination, irrespective of how imagined, as it reminds us that social antagonism and conflict, notwithstanding the source, is centred upon resistance not only to (Unionist) hegemony but also to the formation of a different (Irish nationalist) hegemonic order. We can open up the context of studying conflict if we consider that it can be both reactive or liberating when based upon challenging hegemony in whatever form. In interpreting loyalism within the resistance and domination framework it must be accepted 'that resistance can involve resistance to any kind of change whether positive or negative' (Pile 1997: 4).

In developing and sustaining conflict non-State combatants produced support bases and developed acts of resistance in the name of place-centred communities (Burton 1978; Horowitz 1985). The UDA's emergence out of groups such as the Woodvale Defence Association pinpoints the corralling of violent purpose around the 'protection' of residents who were constructed as victims of a rampaging 'other', and who aimed at undermining that community's constitutional construction. In sum, resistance by Republicans and Loyalists was directed at a community 'other' that was deemed insufferable, abhorrent and whose ideas and discursive agendas required rejection

(Douglas and Shirlow 1998; Graham 1998, 2004). Therefore, for both Loyalists and Republicans violent enactment was linked to opposing forms of spatialised resistance and the 'rationalisation' of violence as defenderist and protecting (Bourke 2003).

Given the territorial nature of conflict and the capacity to invoke the imagined community of 'self' as congruous but also fraught and imposed upon it, it is evident that violence was assembled around divided forms of socially constructed phenomena between the State, Republicans and Loyalists through differing values and aspirations. The entrapment of violence was based upon the certitude that the discourses of suffering, loss and human rights denial were endured by the community 'self' and was therefore more 'real' than the consequences of violence upon the 'other'. The difference lay in what each side wished to maintain or achieve. Interestingly, in terms of the Belfast Agreement which eased that entrapment, 'each side' had to drop, pause or dilute certain ideological demands and certitudes. Republicans accepted the principle of consent, agreed to the Northern Ireland Assembly within a partitioned Ireland and the Irish State, and rewrote Articles 2 and 3 of the Irish Constitution, which had laid a constitutional claim to Northern Ireland. Unionists had to uphold power-sharing, cross-border bodies and the reform of public policing. For all sides the Belfast Agreement was schizophrenic in that it was both ideologically sulfurous and identity sustaining. Interestingly for those former Loyalist combatants involved in the Belfast Agreement's foundations and design, the latter was invoked and the former understood as a reality of living within a contested society, a position that heralded those Loyalists involved in peace-building as more visionary than most Unionists, and aware of the need to undermine the perniciousness of conflict on behalf of civic society through taking political risks.

For Loyalists the initial ideological space into which the project of violence was reproduced was tied to monolithic and restraining practices that negated Irish Republicanism and the desire for Irish unity and even, at times, power-sharing via devolved political structures, although the position on power-sharing was to change (Hall 1994, 1996, 1998). Transformative Loyalists were those who rejected the label of supremacists and understood that ethno-sectarian construction and the enactment of violence was tied to outdated notions of State fealty and constitutionally led and status quo-driven asperity. Thus resistance, in the form of what was to emerge in the early 1970s, was internally generated, judged and prescribed upon.

Within transitional loyalism it is evident that it was not enough simply to view the 'politics of opposition' to the ideological 'other' as requiring the use of violence, if that violence could be removed through a cognitive investment in dialogue with armed Republicans. It would also appear that a motivation for transformative loyalism was linked to challenging mainstream unionism (McIntosh 1999; Walker 2004). The attempted removal of ethno-sectarian asperity and violence rendered transformative loyalism as Loyalist only in the sense of its history and the maintenance of loyalty to the constitutional link to the United Kingdom. As illustrated within this book, the fluidity and assembly of knowledge during conflict can be actively driven by a desire to resist the confinement and durability of practice, in this case ethno-sectarianism, through the production and reproduction of multifarious ideas that are guided by the principle of conflict alteration.

There are still those Loyalists who would wish to return to war, who feel embittered by the peace process and sense betrayal at every turn, but their capacity to rekindle conflict has failed due to the role played by transitional Loyalists. For transformative Loyalists resistance is not simply based upon opposition to the imposition of Irish unification but also to those agencies and groups who have aimed to relegitimise ethno-sectarian violence. The expulsion of Billy Wright from the UVF, and the feud with the Loyalist Volunteer Force (LVF), indicated a division between those who wished to resist via democratic structures and those who resisted the 'right' to do so (Anderson 2002). Internal forms of resistance are evidently vital when the reason and legitimacy of group action and authority is challenged. A seemingly important aspect of loyalism, after 1994, was the contestation over what resistance was to mean.

For regressive elements the desire was to resist the delivery of an 'objectionable' peace process whereas for transformative Loyalists resistance was against those, who Spence had earlier referred to as 'super-Loyalists', who opposed the potential for peace and who would drag sections of the Protestant community back to war. For the latter resistance, via politics and community activism, sought to challenge Unionist political leaderships that were deemed untrustworthy and disinterested in the social and material needs of deprived communities. In the post-1994 period, after the calling of paramilitary cease-fires, resistance to and for peace-building was located within the Loyalist bloc. That division was performed in its most extreme form via feud-centred violence.

Despite these general and time-specific readings, as well as the obviously inherent instability therein, it would appear counterintuitive that Loyalists have become actively involved in inter-community partnership, anti-racism/sectarian work, violence amelioration activities, social justice campaigns and restorative justice programmes. Evidently the negative aspects of loyalism, as evidenced by ethno-sectarian actions and ideological incoherence, has been, to some extent, paralleled by a process of transition that has shifted significant sections of loyalism (especially at leadership level) into a more sophisticated and articulate identity that is centred upon maintaining and delivering a post-conflict existence centred upon community, cultural and political activism. Positive Loyalist shifts are an indication of how conflict transformation is possible, not only among more articulate, grounded and politicised groups, but also among those who were pejoratively understood as being beyond the remit of reconciliation and transformation. Ultimately, the arguments presented within this book are not merely a guide to conflict transformation in Northern Ireland, but are additional to the wider international ideas and examples of conflict transformation, especially with regard to pro-State activists/militias (Kaldor 2001; Woodworth 2001).

Understanding the capacity of 'reactionary' militants to respond positively to peace negotiations and to shift beyond intransigent ideas and influences is an important development in the capacity required to move beyond stale and repetitive ideas concerning pro-State terror and in so doing opens up a field of inquiry that has remained submerged by simplistic ideas that such positive developments remain the preserve of those engaged in anti-colonial or 'liberation' struggles (see Carey 2007; Clapham 2005; Marti et al. 2007; Poole and Renique 1992; Silber and Little 1995 for analyses of pro-State militias). The Loyalist shift into progressive idea-building was based upon the adoption of a role that resisted mainstream Unionist and certain internal practice. That shift was formulated around reconceiving the conflict and rejecting the rhetoric of 'non-violent' Unionist politicians and those voices that told Loyalists that they were the fortified and embodied Protestant 'people'. It was as a result of the idea that the embodiment of the 'Protestant people' was mythic, that unionism was divided along class and sectarian lines and that Loyalist fealty was publicly unwelcome, that certain Loyalists aimed to redefine motivational acts (Chapter 3). This was not based on a rejection of Britishness/Ulsterness but instead was designed around an evolving contemporary situation (McMichael 1999). The capacity to lead positively was based upon a form of resistance to the 'self' through de-imagining cause, community and meaning, a mode of discursive shifting from 'we are the people' to 'who are the people?'

Without doubt, transformation-led Loyalists see themselves as 'dupes no more' and define loyalty in its immediate sense towards the Protestant working class. Gone, for such people, is a blind sense of faith linked to the State, political unionism and an uncritical analysis of Britishness or devotion to Ulster. If anything this form of loyalism had its starting point in questioning the rationale of loyalty and the post-colonial sense of itself. Again as Howe suggests:

> Crucially, some influential ex-gunmen came to feel that 'respectable' Unionist politicians had manipulated them by first inciting their violence, then indignantly disclaiming it. The people of the Shankill and other poor Protestant districts, so it was ever more assertively, even bitterly said, must no longer act brutally at others' behest, but start thinking for themselves. (2005: 3)

It is in the rejection of the 'certainties' of faith in institutions that had welded together Unionist solidarity that emergent and positive loyalism was engendered, stimulated and provoked. Provocation was linked to the rejection experienced by the adoption of the idea of self-help and the removal of guidance from a Unionist leadership that was deemed as non-liberatory and incapable or unwilling to serve working-class communities in terms of their material and social interests. In rethinking the essentialist ideas of pan-Unionist unity certain aspects of Loyalist identity were divorced from cultural absolutism and 'the core beliefs, values and symbols of what it means to be a Protestant' (Bruce 1986: 264). In essence, progressive and transformative loyalism was sought through less conventional cognitive and socio-emotive frameworks.

Transformative loyalism

In defining progressive or transformation-led loyalism it is obvious that it has certain tenets, proposals and objectives. These are generally tied to a leadership role and ideas constructed around a social capital approach dedicated to 'creating the social glue derived from 'residents' active participation in local social networks that benefit the whole community' (Innes 2004a: 152). This in turn is linked into modes of capacity building and the development of and realisation of community potential (Murtagh 2001; Robson 2000, 2001). Conflict transformation is also interpreted within loyalism as a process of contestation within and beyond in that conflict is also set within a social arena that encompasses suspicion, mistrust and the desire by others to restrain human rights development. Additional interpretations of conflict transformation include:

- The need to transform via an interpretation of equitable social, cultural and political definitions;
- That identity construction can both facilitate and undermine the deliverance of democratic accountability;
- That conflict can only be resolved when adversaries understand the capacity for transformation and the part that they can play in resolving conflict (Shirlow and Monaghan 2006: 4).

The desire to prevent future occurrences of violent disunity has been divided into two general perspectives. First, a conflict transformation perspective encourages an analysis of the antecedents of conflict as a way out of disagreement. Second, the seeking out of better ways to represent loyalism within a process of capacity-building and moral re-imaging has also emerged. Additional features include:

- Lifting loyalism out of insularity and into a host of civic and inter-community based relationships;
- Developing better relationships with government and statutory agencies;

- Promoting restorative justice schemes;
- Creating alternative community narratives which link loyalism into a post-ceasefire process;
- Challenging the mythic status of violence and in so doing diverting youth attention away from paramilitarianism and sectarian violence (Shirlow and Monaghan 2006: 4).

From this perspective, former paramilitaries involved in community work and restorative justice programmes seek to reduce tensions and/or promote reconciliation. There is a sense of the need to create an intersection between agency and structure via the shift from a military to a negotiator-defined leadership role. Academic and funder-led evaluations of Loyalist engagement have been affirmative, optimistic and assenting. In particular, they have commended the endorsement of values of non-violence, human rights and inclusiveness (Gormally et al. 2007; McEvoy and Mika 2001). Moreover, when other sections of unionism would not publicly meet or endorse Republican representatives, transformative Loyalists were working with Sinn Fein and the IRA on matters of social justice, interface violence and debates concerning attitudes towards truth recovery processes (Bean 1995; Eolas 2003; EPIC 2005). Loyalists have also campaigned on a vast range of issues on behalf of themselves and the Protestant and even Catholic communities, including:

- Improved social services;
- Facilities and rights;
- The establishment of local job-seeking and social capital schemes;
- Welfare, education, counselling, advisory and advocacy roles;
- The creation of advice centres, family projects, counselling services, children's activities and social activities;
- Campaigning for the rights of former prisoners and their families (Shirlow and Monaghan 2005).

This book, in examining transitions within loyalism, provides the capacity to challenge wider readings of such groups as merely apolitical, controlled by State structures and incapable of serious discursive and liberatory development. This is not to argue that the context of recent Loyalist activities can be transmitted to other arenas and pro-State militia contexts, but there is a requirement to pinpoint, illustrate and map out how such armed groups can shift into more meaningful activities and positive outcomes. It also does not indicate that there are no longer Loyalists driven by sectarian ideas and criminality, but what it does mean is that a robust inquiry into the ideas and actions of modernising loyalism produces information that is contrary to broader and public opinion (Miller 2004). In essence, the role and effect of transformative loyalism is both tangible and its role measureable.

Theoretical/analytical development

Beyond describing and articulating the context of 'pro-State' groups engaged in post-conflict recovery this book develops subject-led understandings of conflict and conflict transformation that stretches across criminology, political science, sociology and political geography (Jenkins 2003; Memmi 1990; Turk 1982, 1984; White 2003). In particular, there is a requirement to bring the study of political violence more firmly beyond a reflection upon the reasons for terror group existence and membership, especially with regard to the fashion of examining the structures of political conflict and legalism (criminal justice, human rights abuses/restoration and formal legal institutions) with regard to the understandings and dynamics of culture, agency and the overall interpretation of how conflict shapes conflict transformation (Della Porta 1992; Friedrichs 1998; Hamm 1994, 2002). However, as Mythen and Walkate note:

> Nevertheless, part of our understanding of, and reaction to, terrorism lies in its link with what is considered legal or illegal, whether such an understanding is constructed nationally or internationally. Moreover, we can certainly learn something about changing definitions and notions of what counts as crime, the criminal, the victim and 'fear', if current concerns around 'new terrorism' are given a more prominent position within the discipline of criminology. (2006: 380)

Without doubt political violence is linked to criminological and sociological definitions such as in this instance, praxis, the realities of State collusion, the seeking of order and for those involved in violence the learning and unlearning of motivations (English 2009). Despite the growth in the study of terrorism Silke has concluded that:

> Ultimately, terrorism research is not in a healthy state. It exists on a diet of fast-food research: quick, cheap, ready-to-hand and nutritionally dubious. The result of a reluctance to move away from the limited methodologies and levels of analysis of the past is that while the field may appear to be relatively active and energetic, growth in key areas remains stunted and halting. (2000: 12)

Studies of paramilitary groups have been concerned with the relationship with crime, which is an obvious venture especially when there is a requirement to gain funds for weaponry (Moran 2004; Morselli 2009). Such forms of analysis appear to discount ideological motivation and in some instance the reasons for engagement in paramilitary activity. Grabosky and Stohl (2010) have contended that States need to create a backlash against terrorist groups through stimulating community outrage without any acknowledgment that the State and its actions may be a catalyst for the assertion of non-State rendered violence (see also Pochrass 1987; Schmid 2004). The work of LaFree et al. (2009), with regard to backlash models and the impact of counter-insurgency tactics in Northern Ireland, produces a form of analysis that misunderstands the complexities of violence, the stimuli for it and that there was more to paramilitarianism than the performance of violence. A further failure is the failure to recognise that non-State combatants' disengagement from violence may be driven by internal analysis and the adoption of non-violent practices. Those involved in political violence in addition have relative cause for the legitimacy that they invoke, a matter that is also generally under-considered in terms of how the assertion of legitimacy can, somewhat ironically, also be turned towards peace-making (McEvoy and Shirlow 2009). If anything, counter-terrorism is more than security-driven and propaganda-led, as witnessed by the British State's evolution of a series of non-violent responses such as ending labour market discrimination and funding Republican and Loyalist transition. A key problem within forms of terrorism studies is that the discourses increasingly lack objectivity, replacing it with subjectivity and even advocacy (Miller 2004).

The work of Quinney (2000) and Pepinsky (1991) is relevant to the complexities of the Northern Ireland situation and their proposal for peace-making criminology. Their advocacy of more pluralist understandings of political violence appreciates the causes and foremost sources of violence and therefore a more nuanced and open interpretation is promoted by them as central to understanding the link between the adversarial underpinning of violence and the capacity to solve and root out the catalysts therein (Nic Craith 2002). In addition to interpreting a more complex appreciation of the causes of conflict, peacemaking criminology pinpoints a more positive advancement of the solutions and possibilities for conflict transformation. The promotion of more human and tolerant approaches to norm-breaking is linked to critically precise and forward-thinking perspectives on the manner in which social, cultural and economic relationships can be altered in order to encourage participation and the removal of the rituals and material realities of alienation (Cavanaugh 1997; Clapham 2005; Dunn and Morgan 1994). Or, as noted by Barak, 'this is to foster the development of a more holistic and practical approach to violence and nonviolence, war and peace, injustice and justice' (2005: 136).

Although not writing on Northern Ireland Barak (2005) constructs a relevant three-fold typology regarding how relationships can be organised in order to stimulate conflict transformation. First there is a requirement to 'understand where our adversarial and mutual responses come from' (137). Second is a requirement to 'assess our political, economic and social policies locally, nationally and globally' (137), and third a requirement to 'attempt to transform the social realities far and near with respect to a peacemaking realignment that struggles to maximize peace and justice as it attempts, simultaneously, to minimize harm and violence' (2005: 137).[14] Such a typology maps onto positive Loyalist-led transformation. The central strength within the promotion of peacemaking criminology is that it does not separate adversarialism and mutualism but instead conjoins effect and potential into an inclusive mode of academic analysis. In developing that approach within criminology and other subjects this book provides a more packaged account of Loyalist activity that stretches across motivation, collusion, transition out of violence and the impacts of imprisonment such as humiliation and masking and how such material collisions endure via the consequences of processes of criminalisation (Sappington 1996). Personal as well as societal norm-breaking behavior is an important variable in interpreting Loyalists when we appreciate that the vast majority who engaged in violence did not have criminal pasts. The use of social control violence to fill a policing 'vacuum' created by political conflict is also noteworthy, as are varied neutralisation techniques that motivated activity.

Analysing such factors is important in terms of developing understandings of the role of actors and the degree of agency in terms of stimulating collective action, but less well-studied is the reality that the vocabulary of conflict (i.e. justice, equality and the removal of threat) contains the same thematic concerns as conflict transformation (i.e. justice, equality and the removal of threat). Mobilisation is not simply paralleled by de-mobilisation and organisational disbandment but by processes of conflict transformation that seek the same ends as violence, but within which alternative methods and discourses are furthered and the rituals and symbols of violent motivation are recoded (McEvoy and Shirlow 2009). There is a need to understand how the knowledge and practice of conflict can create new comprehensions and concerns that do not undermine ideological objectives but promote their articulation and practice via new modes and means of conflict transformation-based practice. In broader terms this echoes Lederach's (1997) argument that violent conflict is not necessarily resolvable but can be transformed and cease when participants re-evaluate notions of legitimacy and the validity of motivational ideas and frameworks.

In so doing this book challenges reductionist theories and understandings such as 'mutually hurting stalemate' and the 'ripeness' (Zartman 1989) for conflict transformation that fail to understand the reasons why group identities that appear fixed, bounded and immutable are actually contextual and open to alternative and internal forms of re-interpretation with regard to experience, shifting political circumstances and the agentic potential to re-interpret senses of 'betrayal' and of having been 'duped' when engaged in 'pro-State' activity (Ballymacarett Think Tank 1999). How conflict transformation was fashioned around internal discussions and debates that aimed to reduce the imagined community of hegemonic orderism and shift into the articulation and practice of alternative identities, practices and codes (i.e. restorative justice/conflict transformation), is a vitally important aspect of meaningful analysis. It explains how shifting out of violence requires a re-analysis of perceived State-agent relationships and of having misread the level of community-based corroboration for violent activities. Shifting from what were imagined as 'concrete' relationships with the State and community and in so doing learning via the experiences of criminalisation and rejection can lead towards ideological and discursive re-assessment that is crucially led from within and is centred upon an organic rationalism. It is at this point that we can observe a significant difference between Loyalists and Irish Republicans. Republicans utilised criminalisation as a reason and justification for cause, while the Loyalists felt criminalisation as rejection and as a break in overall Unionist solidarity. For Loyalists criminalisation meant seeking a sense of 'self' and the development of internal inspection and re-analysis, and the consequences of criminalisation were both two-fold and contradictory. First, the immediacy of criminalisation and negative labelling led to forms of castigation and the rejection of loyalism and Loyalists which in turn initially drove such groups underground and reduced the capacity for Loyalists to do more than reflect upon their own sense of legitimacy. It is instructive that a central feature of the Sinn Fein and IRA peace strategy was to interlock those sympathetic towards a united Ireland, whether that was Irish-America, the SDLP or the Irish State, into a loose coalition that created the space necessary for the Republican movement to emerge away from having been felon-set and labelled as deviant and untrustworthy. That loose coalition created the *bona fides* that Sinn Fein was serious about peace-building as it illustrated that they had become engaged with those opposed to IRA violence and who represented forms of Irish nationalism that were hostile to them. In analogous terms the Republican movement was akin to the prodigal son who was reclaimed while Loyalists appeared as an unwanted prodigy for whom no one would claim parenthood or even any distant familial relationship:

Second, and somewhat paradoxically, the experience of criminalisation and rejection became the starting point upon which alternative Loyalist discourse was to be founded and reconstructed. It was in rebuffing criminalisation and the depiction of loyalism as apolitical and near-feral that key persons began the process of recasting their own sense of identity and grievance through actively challenging the mythic reiteration of 'self' that was centred upon a series of ideas envisaged around Unionist solidarity, notions of defenderism and Protestant hegemony. Those who have advanced the transitional form of loyalism have utilised senses and experiences of State, media and community criminalisation to redefine parts of that identity and the need to re-interpret conflict and define a post-conflict role that is linked to conceptions of conflict recovery and inter-community agency. Interestingly those who have remained involved in crime and violence have not become cognitively aware of the meaning of criminalisation and have remained fixated with the idea that they are 'beloved by their community' (BBC 2003). In redefining loyalism out of violence positive leadership styles have dealt with organisational splits in which wreckers (military/ideological) and spoilers (criminals) challenged the authority of parent organisations to reform and in so doing 'betray' the 'real' meaning of loyalism.

The shift away from such violence is contextual and driven not only by the decline in Irish Republican violence but also via the establishment of Loyalist ideas and authority that now promotes restorative justice programmes, the techniques of non-violent intervention, de-criminalisation approaches and the internal de-legitimisation of Loyalist violence. It thus displays how organic intellectualism and idea-building within such groups can subvert their own reactionary discourses and in so doing challenge from within as opposed to being merely led by external forces and pressures.

Loyalist violence was centred upon digging into what appeared to be an inescapable ethno-sectarian position. That position would have remained rigidified and ongoing if it was not challenged by a self-help ideology of intro-spection, value-seeking, re-orientation and ultimately the delivery of new ideals, vocabularies and ideas that redefined the meaning of cause. Espousing and delivering such change was tied to a process that was uneven and at times contradictory, but it has been a process that has led to the near invisibility of Loyalist violence, the creation of a community/voluntary structure that sustains a social interventionist approach and the creation of what is under-stood as a modern-day approach that is not attached to the certainties of Unionist conventionalism or the concept of majoritarianism. Instead progres-sive practice is based upon analysing the meaning of conflict and post-conflict through recognition of secularism and the plight of estranged communities generally cut adrift from the material benefits of peace. The issue here is not one of electoral success as Loyalist politics has had meagre successes, but one of influence and community activism. Therefore, the majority of such achieve-ments run against vilification, negative and hostile commentary and the supposition that the 'thugs' of loyalism had diminutive capacity or prospect. Moreover, the role, for example, that the UDA and UVF/RHC played in the peace process between the ceasefires of 1994 and the signing of the Belfast Agreement in 1998 appears to have disappeared in the accounting and analysis of that time (Dixon 2001).

In defining the transformative context of loyalism the remainder of the book focuses in detail upon the meaning and interpretation of violent enactment within a range of contexts (Chapter 1). Chapter 2 develops and explains Loyalist experiences and perspectives regarding collusion, a key ideological battleground in a purposeful (re)writing of conflict and harm. Chapter 3 analyses the ideas that progressive and transitional Loyalists presented, beginning in the mid-1970s; the novelty of those interpretations of conflict and argues that these shifts in perspective were key to later strategies of conflict transformation. It explains how present ideas and practices are both contrary to but also linked to the sense of injustice and insecurity that initially drove Loyalist violence.

This is followed by a chapter on intra-Loyalist feuding which was at its most extreme during the period of peace-building. This included the Shankill feud and the UVF's use of violence to settle an ongoing conflict with the LVF. The material presented indicates how variant ideas located within loyalism created tensions between progressive and regressive discourses. It also indicates that the idea of resistance and the appropriateness of 'resistance' were central to the struggles over the authenticity of Loyalist discourse and the future that was appropriate for loyalism. Unlike media reports that view such intra-Loyalist violence as merely criminal activity and the control of criminal empires, it is argued that the rise of those intent upon undermining progressive attitudes was driven by unreconstructed identities and also by those whose egos could not cope with the loss of 'status' that had been guaranteed by conflict. The acts of leadership and the importance of that leadership in undermining the return to violence is evaluated and explained.

The practice of conflict transformation is evaluated in Chapters 5 and 6. Through developing the theme of Loyalist transition evidence is provided regarding how Loyalists have presented and articulated conflict renovation (McAuley et al. 2010). This entails a detailed mapping of the extent and importance of conflict transformation initiatives and programmes and concrete examples of transitional work. That work is tied to restorative justice programmes and the removal of social control (punishment) violence and the development of wider ideas concerning social justice and the building of social economy initiatives. It also involves inter-community dialogue with Irish Republicans and Republican communities and the addressing of the legacy of the past. Some of this work, including interventions with youths to remove the desire to engage in sectarian violence is highly impressive and is studied by politicians/community activists from other conflict zones as a model of guardianship policing. It also explores how a UDA-linked initiative was undermined by external political machinations that were not based upon the validity of the work undertaken but via an act of censure. As Gallaher (2007) has shown, cosmopolitanism as a framework for conflict transformation simply provides a hollow signifier of tokenistic intent when in fact the reality of transformation from within loyalism is internally driven; Loyalists here being those who work to reduce tension and asperity through grounded signifiers of coping with and challenging the post-conflict mess that remains.

Chapter 6 examines the redrawing the past through exploring a significant part of Loyalist transition that has been centred upon the use of history in order to redevelop ideas of working-class cohesion. This has been achieved via public history talks and the redrawing/re-imaging of murals in order to create non-sectarian imagery and the location of working-class pride and the presentation of locals who have achieved fame via sport, writing and invention (Vannais 2001). The aim of such activity is to recast perceptions of the Loyalist 'self' and in so doing de-militarise images and notions that were centred upon

Protestant defenderism and simplistic notions of betrayal and Republican/Irish oppression. The mediums through which loyalism now operates (wall murals, plays, poetry, art and video) are multi-various but are centred upon narratives that positively reflect community congruity and senses of working-class worth and value. This chapter also assesses and presents examples of historical recasting and shows how the reconstruction of micro-histories aims to create wider non-threatening senses of history and loyalty. Such histories, especially those connected to the Battle of the Somme, locate shared events between Unionists and Irish Nationalists. The redrawing of the past has been a powerful medium in the wider strategy of Loyalist redefinition and conflict transformation.

Remaining challenges to loyalism are discussed in Chapter 7. Despite presenting a series of positive acts that are intent upon removing conflict and armed resistance there has been a failure by the media and significant section of society to recognise the positive attributes of transformative loyalism. This chapter also shows how wider readings of criminalisation in the press and a series of exposés regarding collusion between sections of loyalism, the police and British intelligence also undermined Loyalist transition. Constant depictions of crime and allegations of Loyalist criminality has tended to dominate media coverage and this has maintained a form of criminalisation that undermines wider Loyalist shifts. In addition, Chapter 7 explores how extensive forms of criminalisation have and continue to undermine the integration of Loyalists into civic society. High levels of ill-health, income-related poverty and even suicide pinpoint the effects of engaging in violence and also of criminalisation-based legislation and wider hostilities towards that community. Based upon extensive interviewing of former Loyalist prisoners, this chapter highlights the impact of criminalisation upon that community.

Ultimately this book aims to expand the discussion of groups such as Loyalists and their journey out of violence – a political, social and cultural expedition that has been uneven, incongruous and frustrating. There are obvious ways in which loyalism can be viewed as objectionable and even loathsome, but also ways in which it cannot. There are many episodes and events that are devious, pernicious and challengeable but there are also persons whose aim, for a significant period of time, has been to shift on to an alternative stage of positive motive and rationalism. In many instances such persons have undertaken the design of such shifts without external corroboration or assistance. Their consciousness and intent has been shaped by the realities of conflict and the shaping of alternative notions of belonging and identity attached to the experiential. This is not to simplify the harm caused and the burdens developed but provides a starting point for the analysis of non-State combatants to challenge a path that merely presents such persons as pathological. Conflict assertion is tied to senses, experiences or perceptions of exclusion that are conjoined with pre-existing texts of fear and signs of foreboding.

Political violence never emerges in a vacuum or in an asocial or apolitical manner. That does not render violence as judicious but the failure to seek solutions to divisive conditions is in itself a catalyst for violent conditioning. For some, the initial stages of violent engagement are also the first steps towards conflict transformation, although that is generally unknown during the early stages of conflict. With acknowledgment of remaining regressive and ethno-sectarian elements this book explores those who have aided the route of alternative consciousness-raising and the de-coding of the allure for violence. It is not an account that aims to validate anything more than the cause of conflict transformation and the goal of settlement.

The book concludes by asking whether we are viewing the end of Ulster loyalism. The conclusion summarises the future of Loyalist-based conflict transformation. It shows how the future of loyalism is dependent upon support from State agencies and other funders in order to maintain key interventionist work. It also shows that without transformative loyalism the capacity of sections within it to drift back to violence would be possible. In sum, the book will detail the complete package that forms conflict transformation within loyalism. This will cover the lineage of conflict transformation, the adaptation and adoption of peace-building strategies, the struggles over legitimacy between peace-builders and non peace-builders, the material realities and examples of programmes of conflict amelioration and the struggle to develop transitional loyalism within a society generally hostile to it. The book provides an analysis of transformative loyalism as it moves out of violence and the difficulties and complexities of such a process of change. Whether we are witnessing the end of Ulster loyalism cannot be surmised until we comprehend the journey taken by it thus far.

Notes

1 The two main Loyalist paramilitary organisations are the UDA and UVF. The Ulster Defence Association (the parent group of the Ulster Freedom Fighters (UFF)), was formed in 1973, largely due to what was perceived as an inability of the UVF and the State to respond to Republican violence. As Bruce (1992) argues, the UVF has always self-identified with the representation of a 'regimented' and 'justifiable' political army. The term UDA is used here to encompass both the UDA and UFF. Loyalism is here understood as Loyalist paramilitarism and the groups associated with it. It is acknowledged there are wider definitions of loyalism with regard to the imagined Protestant people of Ulster. See Arthur Aughey, 'The Character of Ulster Unionism', in Peter Shirlow and Mark McGovern (eds) *Who Are 'The People'? Protestantism, Unionism and Loyalism in Northern Ireland* (London: Pluto Press, 1997), p. 16–33.

2 A section of the UFF based in the Lower Shankill area.

3 The Shankill Butchers, led by Lennie Murphy, produced a frenzied and psychotic killing spree in the mid to late 1970s. They were renowned for killing through the use of torture. Around ten civilian Catholics as well as nine members of the

Protestant/Loyalist community were killed by them. Murphy was to be killed by Republicans with allegations that he was set up by Loyalists.

4 Andrew Finlay (2001: 3) in challenging the reductionist reading of Anderson and Shuttleworth (1994) and Susan McKay (2000b: 11) states that 'like Anderson and Shuttleworth, McKay does not offer any sustained analysis of the currents within unionism that seek to engage positively with Protestant fatalism and the need for change'.

5 The PUP was formed in 1979 and has links with the UVF and RHC (see PUP 1981, 1985a, 1985b, 1996a, 1996b, 1996c, 2003a, 2003b).

6 Information on the PUP available in the document 'What is the PUP?' available at www.pup-ni.org.uk/home/default.aspx.

7 McGrattan (2009: 2) has stated that many persons writing of restorative justice and Republican and Loyalist involvement therein are self-entitled conflict 'transformationalists' who produce a 'narrative understanding of the conflict that is exceptionally similar to that of Republicans'. With regard to my own work such a description is both erroneous and rejected.

8 It is common to hear some Loyalists refer to the Orange Order as OBs (Orange Bastards).

9 Andy Tyrie led the UDA from 1973 to 1988.

10 Here referring to the Third Force. In a *Time* article dated Monday 7 December 1981 a journalist wrote the following: '"Left, left, left, right, left." As the column of men approached, a hymn singing crowd of Protestants who had gathered in the main square of the community of Newtownards outside of Belfast grew silent. The militant Protestant leader, the Rev. Ian Paisley, had spoken of the "third force," his shadowy army of vigilantes, and now they appeared out of the night, marching three abreast, in ranks some 5,500 strong.' Copy held by author.

11 No respondents are named unless they approved to be so. The fieldwork for this book was undertaken in 1998–1999, 2003, 2005 and in 2010 and 2011. In sum, around 340 persons either as individuals or in groups were spoken to/interviewed. The designation used is the organisation belonged to and Westminster Parliamentary Constituency in which the interview was undertaken. There may be more than one person in each organisation quoted within any area but who have the same designation.

12 A derogatory term, akin to Fenians for Catholics.

13 Copy of Spence's 1977 speeches held by author.

14 Despite such a positive typology Barak (2005: 136) states 'the ideas and philosophies of contemporary peacemaking criminology have probably met with greater resistance and denial …' from those that advocate warmaking or adversarial justice than have, perhaps surprisingly, some of the actual peacemaking practices of 'restorative justice' that have been adopted worldwide'.

When people rejected me because I killed
others I wondered why. When I wondered
why I learnt to learn. When I learned new
things I wondered who am I. That is when
you realise that violence has to stop.
(UDA respondent)

1   The extent and nature of Loyalist violence

Loyalists felt threatened by any diminution in Northern Ireland's constitutional status as they viewed the United Kingdom both as a cherished unit of cultural reference and as a contrary society to the Republic of Ireland which they accredited as being socially, culturally and politically underdeveloped. The numerical decline and exclusion of Protestants within the southern State after partition also indicated to them the potential of a negative future (Hart 1996). When violence deepened in the early 1970s the reproduction of identity shifted from the mere reproduction of kinship to a redefinition and hardening of cultural practices and symbolic intent (Feldman 1991). Part of the psyche that upheld and rationalised a Loyalist response was the covenanter notion that 'the people' maintained the right to dissent from State direction if any State-driven course was antithetical to their interests (Aughey 1985; Aughey and McIlhenney 1984; Nelson 1984). In upholding their 'rights', Loyalists asseverated and legitimised violence though the conception of a beleaguered peoplehood.[1] In historical terms, the arming of the UVF in 1912 remains viewed as an act of 'necessity' that was re-invoked with the reformation of the UVF in the mid-1960s. As presented:

> It would appear that prior to 1912 there had been no long-standing ideological commitment on behalf of Unionists to the use of armed force. The inclusion of the words 'by all means necessary' in the Covenant together with the formation of the Ulster Volunteer Force were, therefore, acts of will rather than of ideology. They were acts borne out of necessity. The doctrine of necessity stands behind most revolutionary projects. (*The Principles of Loyalism* 2002: 40)

In broader terms Patterson (1982) observes that

> The political argument was that rule from Dublin would be economically and socially retrogressive and this was of particular importance in integrating the Protestant working class into the Unionist movement. A related factor often

ignored in analyses which dwell so much on Protestants sectarianism is the role played in unifying the Protestant community by the sectarian aspects of Irish nationalism then and since. (1982:27)[2]

Crenshaw (1983: 2) has shown that anti-State groups 'deny the legitimacy of the State and claim that the use of violence against it is morally justified' whilst those opposed to them 'deny the legitimacy of opposition and hold that violence in the service of order is sanctioned by the value of the status quo'. Loyalists adopted a value position regarding the constitutional status quo but challenged the 'validity suppositions' that the State was effective in dealing with threat (Crenshaw 1990; Habermas 1998). Such an invocation of State invalidity is similar to Habermas' assumption that political violence is a neo-populist reaction against the constraints of socio-political arrangements and senses. For Loyalists the 'failure' of the State to quell Republican assault signalled State 'insufficiency'. As with various combatant groups they believed that 'right' was on their side and that the 'other' must be coerced into yielding the very moral 'authority' or entanglements required for violent confrontation as proposed by Aretxaga:

> Our political imaginaries and the violence that accompanies them are character-ized by an entanglement of discourse and desire that needs to be examined rather than taken for granted, because it is this entanglement that constitutes political realities. (1997: 63)

Socio-political grievances, in whatever form, were a key part of conflict assertion and modes of objection were manipulated by those ethno-sectarian entrepreneurs who wished to displace the resolution of conflict through utilising objection into a mode of violent interaction (Innes et al. 2007; Sageman 2008; Vasquez 1993; Vasquez and Mansbach 1984). The 'right' to assert a legitimacy of violence was 'proven' by the enactment of a discourse of reaction centred against a subjectivised 'other', with the structural causes of emergent political violence being attached to the bifurcation of origin, cause, reproduction and meaning. Perception, threat and the experience of harm were not synonymous between antagonists and their respective communities, especially in terms of State violence (Ni Aolain 2000). This lack of synonymity aided the duplication of violent antagonism and provided competing discursive edges. The repetition of conflict is in itself a condition in the problem of political violence in as much as grievances uphold suspicion, mistrust and misgiving. In places of high conflict the choice to not engage was narrowed as the extent and durability of objection and assault coalesced around senses and experiences of persecution and alarm (Shirlow and Murtagh 2006; Keen 2001). In essence, the Loyalist invocation of constitutional protec-tion violence echoes Arendt's (1969: 155) contention that 'violence appears where power is in jeopardy ...'.

Therefore, serious acts of violence occur when 'normality' is severely challenged (Goffman 1972). The actors and agents involved in the genesis of conflict in the 1960s were those who occupied a social space that was highly ritualised not only by custom but also via a constant scanning for signs 'of' and 'for' alarm' (Goffman 1972: 241). Alarm was within a contested State and society more than a process of imagination but a reality linked to the nature of ethno-sectarianism and violent performance. The temporal nature of threat and therefore alarm meant that fear of subjugation was pre-established, within the Loyalist mindset, by the demands for Irish unification (Longley 1997; MacGinty 2004). When such alarms were linked to the presentation of an organised threat, Loyalists tuned 'their conduct to the requirements of the situation' (Goffman 1972: 242). In essence, there was no normality for either Loyalists or Republicans within a contested State and less so when there existed a cultural position of preparedness linked to reacting to menace through the energising of community-centred fright – what Nasar and Fisher (1993) understand as a reaction to fear and threat that is centred upon its very boundedness. Accompanying this was a suppression of commonly held senses and the adoption of violence-led temporality and discursive surfacing. The desire to feel part of the community 'self' also lead to a personal silencing of alternative non-violent voices. As Goffman asserts:

> Rather, each participant is expected to suppress his immediate heartfelt feelings, conveying a view of the situation which he feels the others will be able to find at least temporarily acceptable. The maintenance of this surface of agreement, this veneer of consensus, is facilitated by each participant concealing his own wants behind statements which assert values to which everyone present feels obliged to give lip service. (1959:10)

For those living in highly segregated communities, the places in which violence was most performed and reproduced, the reality of conflict initially drove a purposeful bonding of experiences into strategies for reaction and community cohesion (Shirlow and Murtagh 2006). This was akin to the signal crimes perspective in which the experience of disorder leads to communicative acts that were conjoined with notions of securitness and the appreciation that community space was insecure, violated and symbolically constructed around the identification of a threatening 'other' (Pickering 2001). What were considered as deviant acts of aggression against the community 'self' became more intensely symbolic as the enactment of violence shifted from seeking 'signs of alarm' to the experience of them (Billig 1995; Calhoun 2008; Elshtain 2001).

For Loyalists, pinpointing the source of threat was tied to creating a functioning communicative landscape of prejudice directed against 'deviants' whose acts led to Protestant encumberment. Signal incidents (Innes 2004a; Nasar and Fisher 1993), such as rioting and disorder in the late 1960s, thus released pre-arranged forms of reactive conditioning and as Nieburg states 'individuals and groups, no less than nations, exploit the threat as an everyday matter' (1962: 865). Certain Loyalist actions were aided and even directed by sections of the security forces but there was no exclusive State direction of Loyalists as they reproduced their own notions for the 'appropriateness' of violence. Loyalism is a complex and at times confusing identity formation. It is composed of those from both the ideological left and right and those who acerbated extreme practices of ethno-sectarian prejudice and those who did not. The only generalised identity site for Loyalists is that they were anti-Irish unification.

Therefore, violence came in its most extreme form during the collapse of the Unionist State in the early 1970s, and after the signing of the Anglo-Irish Agreement in 1985. Between these two periods Loyalist violence significantly dipped in terms of volume and it came as no revelation that those who upheld the Belfast Agreement did so around the standard that 'the union had been secured' (UVF respondent, Mid-Ulster). In substantial terms Loyalist violence peaked in the 1970s and has in recent years virtually disappeared. As Guelke (2000) has opined:

> Thus, the cease-fire called by the Combined Loyalist Military Command (CLMC), representing the main Loyalist paramilitaries, rested very largely on the assumption that the Republican movement's turn to an unarmed strategy was dictated by its recognition that the long war had failed.

Guelke exposes a key point in Loyalist thinking, as explained by Billy Hutchinson, who had attempted peace talks with the IRA as early as 1983 when he was imprisoned:

> In supporting the peace process the UVF followed two points. One, the Union was secure. Two, Sinn Fein's idea of a united Ireland had changed as they now understand that there are two power bases in Ireland and their goal is for two Sinn Fein ministers one in Northern Ireland and one in the Republic to meet for cross-border talks. They are a very different organsiation now. In the 1970s and 80s when we tried to broker peace they didn't have any ideas on peacemaking or conflict transformation. There was no Sinn Fein of any note and we were trying to broker peace with what were essentially militarists. (Interview wth author)

What is interesting here is the point held, for a long-period of time, that the Republican movement when it became progressively more led by Sinn Fein had undertaken a form of practical metamorphosis, the key issue being that Loyalists had come to feel less threatened by the likelihood of Irish unification unlike most Unionists who were less capable or even prepared to read republican shifts. The Loyalist reading seems to be based upon an earlier Loyalist perception that the IRA were not 'true' republicans but instead violent nationalists who would at some point accept less than what other modes of republicanism would have demanded.

Loyalist violence over time

Loyalist violence fell into three general forms: regime challenging violence, constitutional protection violence and anti-transgressive violence (Kriesberg 1982). Regime challenging violence, such as the bringing down of the Sunningdale Agreement,[3] was rare and centred upon upholding violence when it was considered that political elites may undermine the constitutional status quo. Constitutional protection violence, the main form of violent enactment, centred upon stepping beyond the monopoly of the State to operationalise and perform violent acts in order to subvert any attempt to destabilise or violate the boundaries of Northern Ireland's constitutional position, or what Rosenbaum and Sederberg (1976) would consider as establishment violence. That violence was linked to an avowedly ethno-sectarian framework that operationalised a desire to pinpoint the 'other' as 'deviant' even if their 'deviance' was merely a desire for Irish unification or, in more pathetic terms, their religion. Finally, anti-transgressive violence was based upon asserting violence against those who had or were perceived to have challenged Loyalist or community authority. That included harming those involved in transgressive criminal acts such as drug-dealing, thieving, paedophilia, rape and even racism, attacking those who were police informants or who publicly challenged loyalism and Loyalist activity, such as those who spoke out against Loyalist violence, as well as punishing Protestants involved in sexual or social relationships with Catholics. Loyalist feuding was also designed around the concept of attacking those Loyalists who had challenged Loyalist authority and fealty (Persic and Bloomer 2001). The performance of all forms of such actor-based violence has now virtually disappeared. As illustrated in Figure 1.1, Loyalist punishment shootings rose, especially after 1999, and generally fell after 2003. In the period of growth in such violence by all groups, after the ceasefires of 1994, it is evident that Loyalist violence was turned to internal community control based activity. It was without doubt a particularly brutal form of informal policing with victims who were generally young people living in marginalised communities and in some instances included persons with special educational needs. However, it would appear that the bedding down of restorative justice and internal debate within loyalism has led to the near disappearance of such activity. In sum, Loyalists have taken significant steps to reduce and remove very significant forms of violence enactment.

This has been a slow process, but in general most violence in longitudinal terms declined after the ceasefires of 1994. Furthermore, Loyalists have not, by June 2011, reacted to 'dissident' republican violence which they most certainly would have done previously. In particular, it is the case that the removal of key individuals has led to declines in Loyalist violence. As shown below, Loyalist violence had been performed and defined within specific territories and in many instances were tied to certain persons.

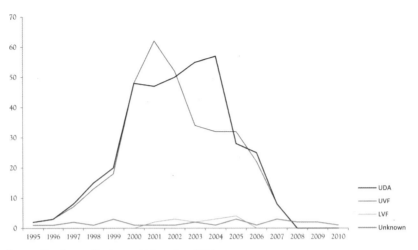

Source: Based upon Shirlow and Monaghan 2006.

Figure 1.1   Loyalist punishment shootings 1994–2010

Loyalists were involved in some 996 deaths between 1969 and 2005 (Shirlow and Monaghan 2006). There is no exact precision with regard to recording politically motivated deaths in Northern Ireland concerning both how we measure who the dead are, what categories of death to include and the group responsible. To argue otherwise is absurd and therefore we can only discuss the data available and with certain caveats. The Police Service of Northern Ireland (PSNI) estimate that there were 3,365 conflict-related deaths in Northern Ireland with a small majority of those being civilians (54.2%). Around 16% (the smallest share) of all deaths were Republican or Loyalist combatants compared with nearly twice as many who were members of the security forces. Nearly 60% of all conflict related deaths fell in the first decade of conflict followed by a decline to 23.2% between 1980 and 1989 and additional falls in the 1990s (15.1%) and 2000s (2.1%).

The reason for these falls in conflict-related violence seem obvious given the calling of paramilitary ceasefires in 1994. However, they do not explain why all violence generally fell from the highpoint of the 1970s (Figure 1.2 illustrates the peaks and troughs of Loyalist violence in Belfast). In addition, State-led militarisation, counter-insurgency tactics and the construction of interface walls between predominantly Catholic and Protestant communities undermined conflict (Jarman 2002; Ni Aolain 2000). The paramilitary leaderships after the mid-1970s engendered greater discipline via the sanctioning or otherwise of violent acts and began to consider political solutions. They were in addition destabilised by the loss of key personnel (especially bomb makers) due to imprisonment and were affected by the growth in military intelligence and group infiltration by State informants (Galliher and Degregory 1985;

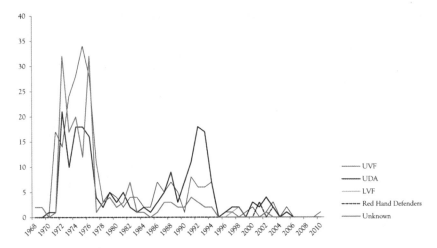

Source: Based upon Shirlow and Monaghan 2006.

Figure 1.2   All Loyalist deaths in Belfast 1969–2010 by organisation responsible

Murray 1998), as well as a decline being due to various attempted ceasefires and political initiatives undertaken by paramilitary groups. There was also an acceptance in the late 1970s that the policy of high-volume violence against the civilian Catholic community did not turn that community against the IRA and other republican groups. That did not mean that such violence was not to remain or even grow at specific points, but there was undoubtedly a series of tactical shifts that occurred.

Re-evaluations of tactics by paramilitary groups promoted greater 'precision' and 'tactical' use of violence. For Loyalists that meant mimicking the IRA's cell structure, training volunteers to be led by intelligence gathering, and to adopt more discipline and micro-leadership-based approaches. This approach appears to have sustained Loyalist violence in the Westminster electoral constituencies of North Belfast, West Belfast, East Londonderry and Upper Bann, areas in which those publicly alleged as being involved in collusion or questionable relationships with elements within the security forces were most active, notably Torrens Knight, Johnny Adair, Billy Wright and Mark Haddock.

Organisational shifts produced, in very general terms, two Loyalist combatant types: those in the 1970s who became embroiled in violence due to societal breakdown and the collapse of the Stormont regime, and a second generation who gained greater status and notoriety from a pronounced Loyalist upsurge in violence in the early 1990s, and who championed the erroneous notion that they had brought the IRA to the negotiating table. The earlier group consisted of those who initially were more generally committed to transformation, compared with the latter group who were overtly militaristic and status-seeking.

The majority of Loyalist killings (57.8% of all deaths) occurred during the 1970s, with the 1980s witnessing a very considerable decline (13.9% of all deaths). However, that share grew significantly in the succeeding decade – rising to 22.2% of all deaths – before falling to less than 6% of all Loyalist deaths in the 2000s. Loyalists are the only combatant group whose violence, in terms of deaths, declined so significantly in the 1980s and then drastically rose again in the 1990s. The growth in violence towards the end of the 1980s, due in part to the unfolding of the Anglo-Irish Agreement in 1985, was led by several factors. The main Loyalist paramilitary groups sensed that the IRA was going to call a ceasefire and 'reasoned' that a final push would ensure Loyalists would be able to gain a decisive role in any upcoming negotiations. Some Loyalists contend that groups such as the UFF's C Company, led by Johnny Adair (who himself has admitted to assistance from the British army), were manipulated by elements within the security forces into placing strain on the IRA to sue for peace. Others felt that the Anglo-Irish Agreement lead to a doomsday scenario of Irish unification and in reaction to this they sought to remobilise.

The decline in Loyalist violence in the 1980s was due to several factors. Imprisonment had removed key individuals and strategists. The fall in Republican violence was noted and reduced the nature of Loyalist reaction. Key individuals within loyalism, especially those coalescing around the PUP and elements within the UDA, had some impact in terms of re-analysing the nature of conflict via the conceptualisation of the conflict as a negative and unwinnable civil war. In an interview with the *Sunday World* in 1982, Andy Tyrie, the then Supreme Commander of the UDA, said that Loyalists should not react violently to the significant growth in the Sinn Fein vote in the recently held Assembly election, as such a rise was 'not … as big a threat as dodgy Unionist politicians'.

A further reason why violence declined in the 1980s is allied to the growth and part-formation of Loyalist politicisation (Chapter, 3). The rational for violence was being explored via the development of introspection among key individuals in the late 1970s. However, there are several reasons why Loyalist violence pertained despite efforts by key personnel regarding its cessation or redirection of Loyalist violence. First, in some instances there was no absolute division between 'hawks' (those against peace) and 'doves' (those for peace), with the latter espousing a refined version of violence (Bruce 1992, 2000, 2004). Second, in other instances there was too sharp a division between those who wished to take a political community turn and those who wished to maintain violence. Third, the early attempts to gain political representation failed to garner significant support as the Unionist community adopted a clear division between paramilitaries and politicians and the latter undermined parties such as the PUP through labelling them as crypto-communists and collaborators with Sinn Fein. Fourth, feuding between and within groups reduced the capacity to build the platform required for consciousness-raising and the branding of a non-violent identity. Finally, there was a 'constant "stirring" by the security forces, who used black propaganda vehicles ...' to drive Loyalist violence (Bruce 1992: 133). Nonetheless it would appear that the key personnel, who were eventually to lead loyalism into the peace process and beyond, had implanted ideas and perspectives that were gaining some currency among those involved in violence during the 1970s (Cusack and Taylor 1993). A decline in violence was obtained in the 1980s, but a complete cessation was unfeasible as long as Republican violence pertained. One interpretation of the fall in violence during this period is as follows:

> We were debating things inside about what way to proceed. We starts on about the rights and wrongs of killing and all that. I asked about say like just shooting some Catholic working on his car. Bent over the bonnet working at his car and should we whack him? We all agreed that was not the way anymore and this is what we came up with. We had to stop the sectarian thing as it just went round and round and no one benefitted. The Provies were slowing down and that was needed to be said. The UVF had to come up with ideas and ways ah thinking that would take us into looking after our own affairs. Not just killing and protecting, defending, but giving something back. We were a creed more then than about being an identity. That's the bit that was making me change. A creed is just a blind loyalty and you don't control that. I and the likes of the ones I was in with needed our own identity. I used to think all the time about how we could get beyond being a creed. (UVF respondent, North Down)

Much is also made of Loyalists outstripping Republican violence in the early 1990s and as noted by O'Brien:

> Re-equipped and re-organised Loyalist paramilitary groups, the UDA and UVF, in 1991, killed 40, compared to 47 by the IRA and in 1992, for the first time, Loyalist killings outstripped those of the IRA. (1997: 123)

The level of 'outstripping' when comparing Loyalist with Republican violence is accurate but hardly spectacularly so, with only ten more deaths in 1993 and seven more in 1994. In fact between 1990 and 1999 Loyalists killed eight more people than Republicans. Much of what is made of that period is linked to some Loyalists contending that they managed to grow their violence directly against the Republican movement, which in statistical terms is generally untrue, as their violence remained generally fixated upon Catholic civilians. With regard to the same period Republican discourses uphold that Loyalist violence, especially at that time, was being driven by State-Loyalist collusion, which is also not completely accurate, given the level of autonomy of Loyalist action, especially regarding revenge-seeking after key episodes of Republican violence. Ultimately, there was a momentous upsurge in Loyalist violence in the early 1990s and as noted by a UDA respondent from West Belfast:

> By the late 80s the new breed were on the run. Most of us had had enough and were working the other way for some sort of accommodation. I think by the late 80s most of us wanted it to simply stop while others wanted to push on. Some of us knew that those people were being manipulated into what they were doing, and that seemed dangerous to me. We knew the IRA were about to leave the stage and some thought that a big push would bring them to heel very quickly. I always thought it was just a lot of eegits who had got the run of the organisation and were just in it for their own benefits. Lads with big egos and not much loyalism or anything to offer about them.

The UDA's acquisition of weapons from South Africa in 1988 is seen as vital in terms of increasing their capacity, and that is accurate in terms of the Loyalist upsurge in killing at that time. However, the upsurge in the early 1990s was less significant than the volume of such violence in the 1970s – a sometimes forgotten but vitally important fact. As noted below, the targeting of members of the Republican movement did rise in the period running up to the ceasefires of 1994 but there was a relatively constant volume of such violence across each decade. Somewhat depressingly more attention has been paid to the deaths of Republican combatants and others (especially when collusion appears evident, such as the killings of Pat Finucanne and Rosemary Nelson) than to the vast majority of victims who were civilian Catholics (Lawyer's Committee for Human Rights 2002) – an object in propagandising deaths that fits into both the collusion-driven discourses asserted by Republicans or the eulogisation of Johnny Adair and Billy Wright by some Loyalists. In reality, the majority of Loyalist victims were less 'prominent' and innocent citizens killed in the 1970s (Sluka 1996, 2000, 2007).

The violence of the early 1990s may have been indicative of some power-shift with Republicanism in which the 'serve was being returned', but to construe that this was a predominate factor in the Republican movement pursuing peace is problematic (Crawford 1999, 2003; Taylor 2000). That movement had for several years been developing a peace strategy which worked to redefine the conflict through the growth in Sinn Fein's political mandate. Sinn Fein for some considerable time had been working on a strategy of internal de-militarisation and was aware of changing political circumstances that would permit them to follow a purely political path (Shirlow and McGovern 1997). If anything, the growth in Loyalist violence at that time probably put pressure on transitional Republicanism in the sense of slowing down their shift from military means, such as the community pressure put on the IRA to 'hit back' evidenced by the Shankill bombing in 1993.

Furthermore, the Republican strategy at that time was concerned with concessions and recognition from the British and Irish States more so than it was in any way concerned with building a co-joined peace process with Loyalists, which they purposefully represented as nothing more than as puppets of British securocrats. In 1993 the IRA bombed the Baltic Exchange in London and probably caused somewhere in the region of £1 billion of damages, or the equivalent financial burden of all the bombings in Northern Ireland since the conflict began. That event probably illustrated an increasing prioritisation for the British government to bring the IRA to the negotiating table. The symbolism of Gerry Adams in negotiation with world leaders provided the cache the Republican movement desired, whereas sitting around a table negotiating with Loyalists would hardly have had the same impact and would also have been symbolically dangerous in that Republicans would be deeming Loyalist as equivalent to them. This is not to deny that Loyalist violence did not condition some response, in that it reminded the Republican movement of the futility of ongoing violence. Loyalists also contend that as they got closer to key Republicans and their families this drove a sense of fear among them. Probably and more accurately the upsurge in violence meant that:

> Neither the Republican 'armed struggle' nor the Loyalist response was going to gain a victory. There had to be another way. (*The Principles of Loyalism* 2002: 72)

Civilian victims

The largest category of Loyalist victims were Catholic civilians. Loyalists[4] were responsible for the deaths of some 712 civilian Catholics – 71.4% of all deaths that they were accountable for (Table 1.1) between 1970 and 1999. Of these 61.9% were killed in the 1970s, falling to 13.3% in the 1980 and rising to 25.5% in the 1990s. In sum, Loyalists killed 441 civilian Catholics in the 1970s, dropping to 95 in the 1980s – a fall of 78.0%. The number of deaths among Catholic civilians nearly doubled in the succeeding decade but remained 59.8% lower than the number killed in the 1970s. The blunt assertion that Loyalist violence was unwavering and constant is unsound, unevidenced and invalid.

It is only though appropriately untangling the volume of violence within a temporal frame that it is possible to locate the causes and impacts of Loyalist violence. That is not to offer the contention that a reduction in the killing of civilian Catholics removes the stain of such violence, but it does illustrate that combatant groups contain members who are, with regard to intent and practice, divided on the use of violence and tactics and that variant approaches are adopted during the lifespan of conflict. There are ample examples of thoughtless killing and ruthless sectarianism, such as the murder of Margaret Wright, who had been 'mistaken' for a Catholic, in a South Belfast drinking club, and in 1992 the murder of Ann-Marie Smyth, a Catholic abducted from a football supporters' club in East Belfast. Ian Hamilton, a UVF member, was killed by his own organisation for involvement in a Loyalist 'own goal' when killing Margaret Wright, but only a warning was given to the man who killed Ann-Marie Smyth. The killing of the Quinn brothers, aged between eight and eleven, in 1998 during the Drumcree standoff, testifies to naked sectarian actions. Loyalist violence was thus a mixture of brutal revenge-seeking that aimed to counter Republican violence and/or autonomous sectarian acts. At times Loyalists drew back and attempted alternative solutions, and to their credit some rapidly recognised the perniciousness of such violent actions.

As shown below there is a spatio-temporal dimension to Loyalist violence. The Anglo-Irish Agreement and the resignalling of constitutional 'threat' was a prominent catalyst for growths in violence that led to the re-arming of Loyalists. However, this particular form of violence declined significantly post 1994, with some twenty-two Catholics killed (compared with 153 killed in the period 1990–1994) by Loyalists, of which thirteen were linked to C Company/Red Hand Defenders and the Mid Ulster UVF and its splinter group the LVF – the groups that objected to or tried to destabilise the peace process and perpetuated violence that was not sanctioned at leadership level. Gerry Adams had in 1994 predicted 'that Loyalist violence would not end even if the IRA "called a halt to violence" and if the Loyalists did not see a "sell out" in the background'.[5] In fact Loyalist violence was to slow dramatically and in particular was to become significantly less sectarian in terms of the deaths of Catholic civilians compared to the share of what were to become Loyalist victims. What Adams failed to appreciate was the role of those working within loyalism for peace and that Loyalists linked their 'legitimacy' for violence with 'countering' IRA violence. A failure by Loyalists to react to an IRA ceasefire would have sent out a hollow signifier that contested their claim to legitimacy as amphigoric.

As indicated in Table 1.1 the geography of Loyalist killings of Catholic civilians is relatively narrow, with 72% of such deaths occurring in the Belfast and Upper Bann Westminster constituencies. In several constituencies – North Down, West Tyrone, East Antrim, Lagan Valley and South Antrim – such killings peaked in the 1970s and there was no growth between the 1980s and 1990s. In Foyle, which covers the city of Derry, such violence stopped in the 1970s. East Londonderry, Fermanagh and South Tyrone and Upper Bann are the constituencies in which the rise in deaths in the 1990s was most statistically significant, yet the Belfast constituencies and Upper Bann constituted 65.9% of all such deaths in that period. In the vast majority of Westminster constituencies, as noted, Loyalist violence against Catholic civilians never paralleled that in the 1970s, even within Belfast where the total number of Catholic civilians killed in the 1970s was 299 compared with 96 in the 1990s, a difference of −67.8%.

In the period 1970 to 1974 the number of Catholic civilian deaths due to Loyalist violence totaled 227, falling to 210 in the period 1975–1979. Between

Table 1.1   Catholic civilian deaths by decade and Westminster constituency

Westminster constituency	Catholic civilian deaths 1970s	Catholic civilian deaths 1980s	Catholic civilian deaths 1990s	Total deaths by Westminster constituency
North Down	3	0	0	3
Strangford	2	0	2	4
West Tyrone	3	1	0	4
North Antrim	2	1	5	8
Foyle	10	0	0	10
East Londonderry	2	0	11	14
East Antrim	10	4	3	17
Mid-Ulster	3	4	8	18
South Down	6	4	8	18
Lagan Valley	10	5	4	19
South Antrim	22	0	4	26
Fermanagh and South Tyrone	20	1	6	27
Newry and Armagh	26	2	9	37
East Belfast	32	3	11	46
Upper Bann	23	4	20	47
South Belfast	22	13	22	57
West Belfast	92	20	28	141
North Belfast	153	33	35	222
Total by decade	441	95	176	712
Average per constituency by decade	24.5	5.2	9.7	39.8

Source: Based on Shirlow and Monaghan 2006.

1980–1984, the period of attempted political development within both loyalism and republicanism, the number of Catholic deaths fell to 39; the Hunger Strikes in 1981–1982 and the election of Republicans did not drive Loyalist violence, as had been expected. In the period 1985–1989, post Anglo-Irish Agreement, the number of Catholic victims rose to 56 before hastening to 153 between 1990 and 1994. In numerical terms, during the 1990 to 1994 period, the worst five constituencies for numerical growths in the killing of Catholic civilians were South Belfast, Upper Bann, West Belfast, East Londonderry and North Belfast. In ten of the eighteen constituencies the rise was either below five victims, no growth was observed or there were small declines. North Antrim and Mid-Ulster are the only Westminster constituencies in which the number of Catholic civilians killed in the 1970s was higher in the 1990s. Evidently Loyalist violence had significant geographic and temporal dimensions.

Table 1.2 Catholic civilian deaths by Westminster constituency
(1985–1989 and 1990–1994)

Westminster constituency	Catholic civilian deaths 1985–1989	Catholic civilian deaths 1990–1994	Total change
South Belfast	3	21	+18
Upper Bann	0	16	+16
West Belfast	12	24	+12
East Londonderry	0	11	+11
North Belfast	20	31	+11
Newry and Armagh	0	8	+8
East Belfast	2	10	+8
Mid-Ulster	2	7	+5
South Down	3	7	+4
Fermanagh and South Tyrone	1	5	+4
Strangford	0	2	+2
North Antrim	0	2	+2
East Antrim	1	3	+2
South Antrim	0	2	+2
West Tyrone	1	0	–1
Lagan Valley	5	4	–1
North Down	0	0	0
Foyle	0	0	0
Total by period	50	153	103

Source: Based on Shirlow and Monaghan 2006.

If we consider the same data (Table 1.2) via the half decades of 1985–1989 and 1990–1994), we can view the acceleration in violence after 1990. Furthermore, within the South Belfast, Upper Bann, West Belfast, East Londonderry and North Belfast constituencies the numerical rise in violence post 1989 was heavily influence by organisational response (Table 1.3). In East Londonderry all eleven Catholic deaths between 1990 and 1994 were undertaken by the UDA who had been dormant within that area during the previous five-year period. Interview work with Loyalists invoked the contention that the UDA in East Londonderry were better armed as a response to the Anglo-Irish Agreement and that a key figure, Torrens Knight,[6] who was involved in the 2003 Greysteel massacre, was an alleged police informant. The Greysteel massacre led to six Catholic and two Protestants deaths and was in reaction to the Shankill bombing in which nine Protestant civilians and an IRA combatant were killed. In the immediate period after the Shankill bombing sixteen Catholic civilians were killed in revenge attacks. In the previous year the killing of eight Protestant workmen at Teebane in Co. Tyrone led to the death of eleven civilian Catholics, of whom five were killed in an attack upon

Table 1.3 Catholic civilian deaths (1985–1989 and 1990–1994) by organisation responsible within selected Westminster constituencies

Westminster constituency	UDA 1985–1989	UDA 1990–1994	UVF 1985–1989	UVF 1990–1994
East Londonderry	0	11	0	0
North Belfast	10	21	10	10
South Belfast	2	18	1	3
Upper Bann	0	2	0	14
West Belfast	6	19	6	5
Total	18	71	17	32

Source: Based on Shirlow and Monaghan 2006.

a bookmakers shop in South Belfast. These two events led to nearly a fifth of all Catholic civilian deaths for which Loyalists were responsible in the period 1990–1994. There is an obvious pattern to Loyalist violence during this and other periods, with regard to revenge seeking.

The killing in February 1992 of Andrew Johnston, a Protestant civilian, led directly to three revenge attacks. Stephen and Kenneth Lynn were killed in 1991 by the IRA, who were seeking a previous Loyalist occupant of the home in which the attack occurred. This led to the direct killing of Des Rogers and Fergus Magee the next day. In the same year the killing of Thomas Gorman by the Irish People's Liberation Organisation (IPLO) led within a matter of hours to the death of William Johnston within yards of where Gorman was killed. Such a pattern of revenge violence is not as obvious within Republican groups, but Republican acts undoubtedly drove Loyalist violence, especially when the victims were civilian Protestants.

The areas influenced by C Company (North and West Belfast) also indicate significant growths in this period and the UDA in South Belfast undertook a substantial re-engagement in violence possibly due to the imprisonment of Jackie McDonald, the alleged area commander, in 1989. McDonald had been a restraining influence and had been temporarily replaced by a younger and more militant personnel whilst he was imprisoned. Within the same Westminster constituencies (as detailed in Table 1.3) UVF violence was less marked. In certain Westminster constituencies UDA violence quadrupled whereas the number of Catholic civilian victims of the UVF during the same period grew by fifteen, of which fourteen were due to the UVF in Upper Bann, a group influenced by Billy Wright. In West Belfast as UDA violence escalated the UVF reduced the number of civilian Catholics victims from six to five.

What was emerging was a landscape in which those who were to become the wreckers and spoilers after the ceasefire of 1994 were flexing their prowess while others who would support the peace process were aiming to reduce or control the level of violent engagement. It could be contended that of the 153

Table 1.4 Civilian deaths in Northern Ireland by group responsible

	Republicans	*Loyalists*	*State*	*Unknown*	*Total*
Protestants	487	155	26	24	689
Catholics	267	712	159	19	1157
Not from N. Ireland	23	12	4	1	40
% share	41.0	46.6	10.0	2.3	100
Total	774	879	189	44	1886

Source: McKeown 2009.

deaths of Catholic civilians that took place between 1990 and 1994, 103 were linked to the imprisonment of Jackie McDonald[7] and those who influenced the Mount Vernon and Mid Ulster UVFs. This is not to excuse such violence but instead to point to a heterogenous landscape of Catholic civilian deaths.

McKeown (2009) estimates that were 1,886 non-combatant[8] Catholics and Protestants killed in Northern Ireland by Republicans, Loyalists and State security forces between 1970 and 2005 (Table 1.4). Of these, 46.6% were killed by Loyalists, compared with 41% by Republicans. The majority (61.3%) were civilian Catholics and of these 61.5% were killed by Loyalists, 23% by Republicans and 8.4% by the security/State forces. The low State share would be challenged by Republicans who would contend that a much greater share of collusion-linked deaths are not detected within such a mode of inquiry and presentation.

Protestant civilians constituted 36.5% of all such deaths. Republicans killed 487 Protestant civilians or 70.2% of all Protestant civilian deaths. Loyalists were responsible for 22.4% of such killings and the State a mere 3.7%. The Catholic civilian population was more burdened by State violence, a situation that mimics the variant experiential contexts between civilian populations. In overall terms around 28.0% of all Republican victims were Protestant civilians compared with 71.4% of Loyalist victims who were civilian Catholics. Republicans and academic sources contend that the killing of Protestant civilians by Republicans was rarely linked to sectarian actions, noting that such non-combatant deaths included collateral victims during attacks upon the security/State forces, ex-service personnel and business people selling goods to the security/State forces. McGarry and O'Leary (1995) for example uphold the supposition that few Protestant civilian deaths were directly planned by Republicans.

In the periods 1970–1974 and 1975–1979 the number of Catholic civilians killed by Loyalists fell from 227 to 210, whereas Protestant victims of Republican violence rose from 124 to 166, with the percentage share of responsibility for Loyalist civilian killings falling to 44.2% between the two periods. In the 1980s Republicans were responsible for the majority (although by a small number) of such deaths (107) compared with Loyalists (95). This was followed, in the early 1990s, by an immense re-assertion of Loyalist ethno-sectarian violence, although the number of Protestant victims also rose. In overall terms and between 1970 and 1994 Loyalists killed 207 more Catholic civilians than Republicans killed Protestants and of these the majority of that difference (185) were Catholics killed within the periods 1970–1974 and 1990–1994.

Loyalists do not accept the interpretation that Republican violence was not sectarian and conclude that all Republican-related violence against the Unionist community and security/State force members was anti-British and thus prejudiced. For Loyalists there is virtually no distinction between civilian Protestants and members of the security forces (unless targeted by them) killed by Republicans. The death of security force members was viewed by Loyalists as an assault upon the wider Protestant/British community and its values and concerns. Any Republican violence was greeted as a general and illegitimate assault upon individuals who they included as part of the collective 'self'. The interpretation of violence is crucial here in terms of casting legitimacy and the primacy of the constitutional principle of consent to Loyalists. Republicans view Loyalist violence as ethno-sectarian in that it targeted civilian Catholics with intent, whereas they argue that their violence was rarely directed against Protestant civilians with purpose. Loyalists do not deny that this was the case regarding Catholic civilians, and would acknowledge the meaning of such violence. What they object to, as detailed below, is the denial of Republican sectarianism.

Without doubt Loyalist violence was driven by ethno-sectarianism[9] and the idea that Republican violence, especially when it created Protestant casualties such as at Kingsmills, Bloody Friday and the Shankill bombing would lead to revenge-seeking and in particular the targeting of civilian Catholics. Loyalists viewed conflict as based upon a civil war scenario and rejected the Republican sense that their struggle was essentially an anti-imperialist one. As noted in *The Principles of Loyalism*:

> Republicans claim that their war was against the British administration not the Unionist people. The fact of the matter is that the British administration is only here because the Unionist people want it to be here. The real British presence in Ireland are those of us who cherish our British citizenship. Thus, the real opponent of the Republican objective of a United Ireland is the Unionist community, not the British administration. Notwithstanding the rhetoric used by Republicans about British imperialism being the current obstacle to a United Ireland, they know exactly who the British presence in Ireland really is, and they know that to break the Unionist veto on a United Ireland they need to break the will of the Unionist people, not the will of the British government … No amount of debate

will convince Unionists that the Republican campaign was not directed against them. (2002: 30)

In advancing the idea of a fortified Protestant/British people whose legitimacy was based upon the principle of consent regarding the Union with Britain, attacks upon the British people whether civilians or State combatants was interpreted as an ethno-sectarian attack upon 'their' community, irrespective of whether or not the Protestant/British people agreed with the use of Loyalist violence or otherwise. In particular, the policy of Ulsterisation that led to greater security force activity based upon the increased deployment of the Royal Ulster Constabulary (RUC) and Ulster Defence Regiment (UDR) meant that when members of those organsiations were killed they were ultimately understood ever more so as the Unionist/Protestant dead (Graham and Shirlow 2002). There is a general opinion among Loyalists that the Republican claim that bombing economic targets led to unintentional civilian deaths is objectionable and is refuted by the oft-mentioned argument that:

> Republicans had to drive to Protestant towns and the question always is how many economic targets in nationalist towns and places did they drive past before they got there? The answer is lots. They would bomb the Protestant towns and knew fine well what they were after. (UDA respondent, East Belfast)

A central aspect in Loyalists explaining their violence as reactive is based upon specific events such as the first no-warning IRA bombing of the Shankill Road's Four Steps Inn in 1971 in which two Protestant civilians died. As explained within *The Principles of Loyalism*:

> The UVF was quick to adopt the IRA strategy and the 'no warning' bombing of civilian targets became part of its strategy as well. (2002: 29)

What is omitted within that narrative is the recognition of condemnation of that bombing by nationalist organisations and political representatives. The Northern Ireland Civil Rights Association, for example, described the attack as the 'work of madmen and an obvious attempt to stir up more sectarian hatred' (McKittrick et al. 1999: 103). This is an important point in that it undermines the Loyalist supposition that violence against civilian Catholics was somehow legitimate as the IRA was oppressing the Unionist people on behalf of the nationalist community, that the nationalist community harboured and morally supported the IRA and that even moderate nationalists benefited from Republican violence and Protestant flight, due to Republican violence, from predominantly Catholic areas.

Loyalists also killed around four times as many Protestant civilians as they did members of Republican movements. Some of that violence was based upon punishment killings and the killing of alleged informants. McKeown (2009) estimates that seventeen Protestants were either killed in accidents and attacks upon commercial property, that an additional sixty-seven killings were punitive/punishment based, and that fifty-four deaths were sectarian. These deaths can be placed in four broad contexts. First, direct association killings of Protestants who were in adult relationships with Catholics. Second, random sectarian attacks on Catholic bars, bookmakers and other premises that Protestants frequented. Third, sectarian attacks in Catholic neighbourhoods and the failure to recognise that the victims who lived in the homes attacked were Protestants, and finally sheer bullying and drunken rows that escalated into killings.

Alleged supremacism

A central contention deployed by Irish Republicans against Loyalists is that they were motivated and controlled by a discourse of supremacism and were effectively a State/Unionist militia driven by brutal and insidious supremacist acts that were linked to a culture which aimed to maintain the Unionist veto, undermine power-sharing and maintain a discriminatory power system (Farrell 1976). Gerry Adams' (1994) assertion that 'Loyalist violence is not and never has been reactive' and that to consider it as such is based upon 'trying to distract attention away from the reality of conflict in the Six Counties and the role the RUC plays in sustaining it through repression and collusion with the Loyalist death squads' denotes a sense that to think otherwise is to advance a 'perverted view of Loyalist violence'.[10] As stated in An Phoblacht (1998) loyalism is 'the bloody expression of a supremacist elite determined to protect its privilege'.[11]

Such perspectives appear counterintuitive when explaining Loyalist transition, the sometime declines in Loyalist violence and the desire of certain Loyalists to power-share with Republicans as early as the mid to late 1970s (Gallagher 1995). Furthermore, there is no sense within such commentary of the scale of supremacism, its temporality and also its contestation within loyalism. For Loyalists there was also a concern about Irish unification meaning an alternative form of supremacism. One of the fundamental flaws of Republican and Irish nationalist readings of loyalism is that it fails to remember the sectarian nature of State construction within the Irish State. What is meant by supremacism is generally linked to the idea of a dominant settler narrative and a rejection of the Unionist interpretation of the industrial-rural divide that was the island of Ireland (Clayton 1996; Hyndman 1996). Within the invocation of supremacism Unionists and Loyalists have been erroneously viewed as Afrikaners and Zionists in a crude and exaggerated form of comparison. There is no doubting that some Loyalists were conditioned by supremacist logic, but that does not equate fully with other and competing Loyalist perspectives. If anything it was from a dawning realisation that Loyalist violence against Catholic civilians was a misnomer that peace strategies began to emerge in the early part of the conflict. Or more accurately:

> Whilst inside I heard Republicans going on about us lot as supremacists. I had to laugh at that but it was a good lesson as those of us who started talking peace used that label to promote our ideas. If they said we were supremacists they were wrong, so we could say back 'no we are not and here is why'. Yes there were bigots but not ones who wanted to Lord it over Catholics. So knowing that allowed us to move away from the Unionist leaders, they were the ones they meant. So we debated it out and came up with the fact that we were anti-Republican and anti being forced into a united Ireland. So we were wanting to share Northern Ireland and that meant we was ahead of the middle[12] Unionists and the IRA. So the way they labelled us, the word you used, meant we developed ideas of our own. (UVF respondent, North Down)

Loyalists, via their own discourse, accepted their promotion of ethno-sectarianism as motivational through welding Catholics into a 'treacherous foe', as long as Republican violence remained. This point was openly, although erroneously, expressed as follows:

> The nationalist community was, in the eyes of the UVF, culpable. It was the enemy that stood behind the IRA's campaign of terror and it was the only visible enemy that could be targeted. Many UVF volunteers did not believe that there was any real difference between physical force Republicanism and constitutional nationalism. They may use different methods and may reject each other's methods, but they share the one core objective – the incorporation of Ulster Unionists into Catholic Nationalist State – and they share the spoils of war. (*The Principles of Loyalism* 2002: 31)

However, within the same espousal of the 'enemy within' there is no denial or desire to misrepresent the reality and conditioning that motivated Loyalist violence. The manner in which the author accepts responsibility for a 'dehumanising' and 'vicariously' driven violence pinpoints an acceptance of a violence based upon an ethno-sectarian logic. As stated:

> The UVF has never sought to hide the fact that its campaign was aimed at subjecting the nationalist community to a level of violence that would instil fear and terror in members of that community … It was a harsh and ruthless strategy that was dictated by the nature of the conflict. It dehumanised members of the nationalist community and reduced them to the status of scapegoats who were forced to suffer vicariously for the sins of its 'secret army'. There is no way that that strategy can be dressed up in fancy military terms to make something that was horrible look good. The objective was simple – subject the nationalist community to an oppressive force of violence as retribution for Republican violence. (*The Principles of Loyalism* 2002: 31)

The wall mural painted in a UFF wing of Long Kesh (HM Prison Maze), in 1998, that included cartoon figures from *The Flintstones* and heralded the caption 'Yabadabadoo Any Taig Will Do' presented a deeply sectarian understanding of loyalism and its intent. Among many Loyalists there was a strong and endurable anti-papism which linked cultures of Orangeism and Paiselyite anti-Catholic rhetoric into a maxim that Catholics were deficient, cruel, tyrannical, treacherous and committed to the spreading of Catholic canon and that the IRA was involved in a religious conflict which aimed to devastate Protestantism (Jordan 2001). That currency of thinking constantly reflected and promoted supremacist unionism and in so doing employed biblical literalism to advance the idea of 'supressing the heathen' (UDA respondent, North Antrim) and implant the idea that the IRA were 'ambassadors of Rome' who had been 'entrusted' with a sectarian campaign directed by the Catholic church and whose Cardinal (O'Fiaich) was described by Paisley in 1978 as 'the IRA's bishop from Crossmaglen'.[13]

There are ample examples of sectarian actions and the use of language in which Loyalists described Catholics as 'filth', 'scum', 'sewer rats' as well as other pejorative terminology that provides sufficient evidence that some Loyalists were discursively constructed along a repugnance for and detestation of Catholics. Without doubt there were many examples of a desire to keep Catholics in their place, as noted by a UDA member:

> I just hated Catholics, plain and simple. I'm not too keen on them now. It's nothing more than that. I just hate them and the way they get on. If that's what you mean by sectarian then that's what I am, I'm just a bigot. (UDA respondent, South Down)

The idea of an agreed unified supremacist Loyalist culture abounds and is probably the worldview held against them. However, there is a distinction between ethno-sectarianism and supremacism as far as Loyalists are concerned, with the majority rejecting the latter and those, such as William McGrath, who presented such ideas. McGrath, the leader of an avowedly sectarian group (TARA) called for the Catholic Church to:

> … be declared an illegal organisation. History proves that it is a conspiracy against the fortunes and liberties of mankind. For generations this evil thing has blighted our land. It must be destroyed, so that our fellow countrymen who have been deceived by it, will have an opportunity of entering into an eternal relationship with God through Christ and of discovering their common identity with us. The indivisible oneness of the Irish people will then become a reality.[14]

In general terms and in significant interviewing of Loyalists there was a strong rejection of the idea that the IRA were a conduit for the 'Church of Rome' or, as one UVF respondent noted, the rhetoric of Paisley and certain Loyalists was little more than 'biblical illiteralism and papist bogeymen nonsense' or ' the gibberish that the IRA were emissaries of Rome Rule' (UVF respondent, West Belfast). As stated by a UDA member:

> I am being honest and I want you to believe me. I don't need you to believe me, but it would be good if you did. I joined up simply because my mate's da was killed

by the Provies. I hated the Orange Order and thought that people like Paisley and Craig were a curse on the people.

It was simply that a decent man got killed for no reason. The person who wanted a united Ireland did that. So I thought of if that is, if they won we will all be for the high jump. Maybe that was stupid but that's what I thought. I was no bigot, I had Catholic girlfriends and mates 'n all that. It was what they did to someone who was a decent man and not a bigot or a Paisley man. No not like that.

I told a Provie that and he just sat and stared at me. I said to him 'you see, you made me'. He said that his way of thinking was that we were puppets of the State and that was what he still felt like. So that's it. I told him the truth of the matter and he couldn't say 'Oh I see what you mean'. I admit that I did things I regret but all he can say is 'yer a puppet of the State'. What's the point of that way of thinking to just think of me as some bigot's puppet or whatever he was saying? I know they (Republicans) didn't start the Troubles, and you might find it odd my saying that, but they did a hell of a lot ah bad things to get someone like me into it. People always think we are the stupid ones. At least we think for ourselves. They just have a script they read off sort of thing and that's very sad for them ones. (UDA respondent, Lagan Valley)

According to Loyalists it was the sectarian collectivisation of Catholics as a threat as opposed to any supremacist cultural identification that drove Loyalist violence. A common theme in rejecting surpemacism was the contention that Loyalist violence aimed to assault the pursuit of Irish unification and that early in the conflict Loyalists understood the imperatives of power-sharing. Furthermore, after the collapse of the Northern Ireland Parliament and the position of the Protestant bourgeoisie Loyalists argue that there was no actual structure of political economy from which to develop and sustain supremacist acts. As explained by a UVF respondent from East Antrim:

It's a lot easier than that. I lived in a poor place and the IRA lived in poor places too. I didn't hate them as a people and I definitely didn't want to keep them in their place for the big bosses. My community was under attack and that was all the motivation needed. The Provies used to say to me when I was inside that I was propping up the Unionist bourgeoisie. The mills and the shipyard had all but gone and I used to wonder what the hell are they on about? They just couldn't accept that people fight for lots of reasons. Some are afeared [afraid] and do it for fear of being seen as weak, some gets into it as they lost loved ones, some are mad bigots, some are bullied into to it. I could go on all day. They [Republicans] think someone was pulling the levers. But who was that? If I was defending the privilege of the elite why was I in prison? And more than that when was I aware of doing that? I never once thought I am going out there to prop up the elite and the big bosses. I was going out there to defend the meek and the ones under threat. That's a bit, a big bit different by my way of reckoning.

To embroil the threat of IRA violence into a representation of a wider threat from a community that generally rejected and was opposed to such violence, can be determined as sectarian when that threat was merely ideological and desirous of Irish unification. Rose's (1971) seminal work on attitudes in Northern Ireland conducted on the eve of conflict clearly showed that around a third of Catholics agreed with Northern Ireland's constitutional position and that the majority of Catholics stated that welfare payments were adequate. In addition, Rose found that 75% of Catholics agreed that the system of government provided a series of benefits and that 80% were against the use of force to achieve constitutional change. It is also important to note that when calling their ceasefire in 1994 the Combined Loyalist Military Command (CLMC)[15] reiterated and endorsed the desire for constitutional change in whatever form based upon the principle of consent and the non-use of violence. This was a reinstatement of Loyalists ideas that had broken a circuitous form of ethno-sectarianism positioning them as being opposed to any form of political, cultural or economic sharing or constitutional change. As explained by a UDA respondent:

> One day I met an aul [old] Catholic woman I knew when I was a wee lad. Her son had been killed by Loyalists. She asked me why he had been killed. I said that he was part of a community that wanted to have a united Ireland. She said 'Son, we all wanted that but would never have harmed anyone for to be getting Ireland joined together. So you killed us ones for a way of wanting something that was peaceful. I never brought my ones up to hate you but to be full of love for others. Is that it? He was killed for being a Catholic who would have never got involved in killing.'
>
> It hit me like a rock between the eyes! She was right, we was killing for people having an idea and that was not on. (UDA respondent, East Belfast)

The advancement of a purely supremacist logic, that accounts for Loyalist motivation, does not explain why many Loyalists developed and supported the peace process more so than did the wider Unionist community (Gallaher 2007). As contended by David Ervine (interview with author):

> If the Provisionals engaged in atrocities then it was my job to fight them. They think that we were naked sectarians. So if we reacted to Bloody Friday or Enniskillen or Le Mon and they say that it is not reactive but simply sectarian then I have to question that. I know because I was there and I know what motivated me. If you heard that something had happened then the question was how do we react? It was a pernicious cycle that we had to free ourselves from. But at the end of the day Loyalists would not allow themselves to be threatened.
>
> For them (Republicans) there is a fear that drives them when they simply identify us as naked sectarians. If they accept that we reacted to them and their violence then it means that we can verify the conflict as a civil war. I accept my part and can explain it and even though I can now say that my part was pernicious in that innocent people were harmed I can still say that a lot of what people like me did was based upon Republican violence.

In reality, Loyalist violence was more reactive than Republicans accept and less reactive than some Loyalists wish to remember.

Killing Loyalists

The rise in intra-Loyalist violence after the ceasefires echoes a definitive argument that the capacity to stop violence became a problem internal to loyalism, due factionalism and a rise in criminality. In the past, the main obstruction to 'thinking loyalism' was the activities of the IRA (Bruce 1992). In the post-1994 era the key hindrances and impediments were within. The peace 'spoilers' evidently came into opposition with former comrades and the reaction to them led to violence directed against the 'spoilers' due to a desire to eject and banish the potential for future violence and supplementary factionalism. Despite peace-building efforts militarists within the main paramilitary groups used the removal of regressive elements both to provide stability and more importantly assert peace-building strategies (Morrill et al. 2003). Such intra-Loyalist violence highlighted the ongoing atomisation of Loyalist identity and multiple reconstructions of it at 'intensely localized scale[s]' (Graham and Shirlow 2002: 881). The relevance of this fragmentation of loyalism was clear in that authority would not be challenged and the mainstream denied their chosen path.

During the course of conflict Loyalist paramilitaries have taken action against other Loyalist paramilitary groups. The feuds that occurred after 1994 were nothing new as, as Bruce contends, 'like any two competing organizations, the UDA and UVF have rarely been on good terms for long' (1992: 124). Early disagreements were generally limited to fist fights and brawling but by the mid-1970s this had evolved into several killings and bomb attacks between Loyalist groups. In the 1970s these divisions led to some twenty-one deaths with a decline to nine deaths in the 1980s, a situation that paralleled other declines in violence. However, after 1994 around thirty-eight Loyalists were killed by other Loyalists. Some 40% were either killed in internal feuds and 'punishments', with an evident peak in internal violence post-1999 as a result of the feuds between C Company and the UVF and the UVF and LVF (see Figure 1.3 for internal groups deaths 1973–2006). Feud deaths grew again after 2000 due to conflict between the UVF and C Company and the UVF and the LVF. Feud deaths in 2005 related directly to the UVF moving to 'obliterate' the LVF (Steenkamp 2008). Other deaths, it is alleged, such as those of William Stobie and Jim Gray[16] aimed to silence those who held key secrets regarding collusion and/or criminality. The death of Bobby Moffatt, a former Loyalist prisoner, in 2010 led to Dawn Purvis, leader of the PUP, resigning (Independent International Monitoring Commission 2010). Moffatt's death appears to have been linked to a complicated relationship between his family and the expulsion of a family member due to alleged anti-social behaviour.[17]

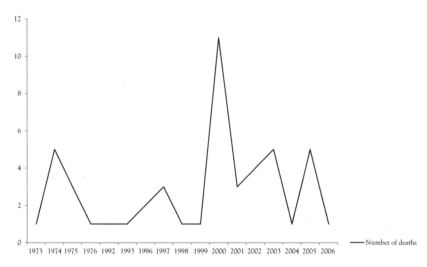

Source: Based upon Shirlow and Monaghan 2006.

Figure 1.3   Internal Loyalist deaths 1973–2006

However, it threw up the fundamental problem of violence remaining and or arms having been retained.

Again, as noted above, the rise of key individuals during the re-establishment of Loyalist violence in the early 1990s led to particular characters emerging who were understood by other Loyalists to be psychotic, self-indulgent figures encouraged by 'shadowy' figures within the security forces who were also opposed to the peace process. There is no doubt that the removal of Adair and Wright led to a decline in Loyalist violence. UVF violence against the LVF led to its disbandment in 2005 and Adair was expelled after the death of John Gregg in 2003 (Bruce 2004). Established leaders claim they struggled to steer a course between promoting non-violence and utilising violence towards these groups.

Furthermore, the removal of these elements was based upon debilitating the desire of others to join them. As a senior member of the RHC contended:

> In other words, if you were having to discipline someone within your own organi-
> sation, tactics became different because where you once would have expelled
> someone, you had to be conscious of what you were doing because them people
> would have run and jumped onto this other vehicle, so that vehicle had to be
> destroyed once and for all because the LVF, and there is proof beyond a shadow of
> a doubt, started five feuds and the last feud, people were adamant and determined,
> that this would be the feud to end all feuds. (UVF respondent, North Belfast, cited
> in Shirlow and Monaghan 2005: 6)

Killing Republicans and Nationalist political activists

The killing of Sinn Fein members and IRA activists as well as nationalist political activists accounts for around fifty-four deaths or 5.6 % of all Loyalist killings in Northern Ireland. In comparison Republicans killed around twenty-six members of Loyalist organisations. Some Loyalists exaggerate the number of combatant Republicans killed and Republicans have used these deaths to promote the idea of collusion, even though Republican and nationalist activists constitute the smallest category of Loyalist victims. Loyalists killed, in Northern Ireland, twenty-six Republican combatants, of whom seventeen were IRA members with an additional seventeen deaths of Sinn Fein activists and eleven nationalist and other Republican representatives. Across the decades there was not much fluctuation in the number of such attacks. But the most sustained period ran between 1988 and 1993 when Loyalists were responsible for the deaths of twenty-six Republican activists or combatants. The usual explanation for such low numbers is generally linked to Republican combatants being presented as a secreted army:

> There was no IRA headquarters, no uniform, no enemy saying 'here I am, come and get me'. It was easy for them to kill the security forces as they wore uniforms. They hid away and used Catholics as a shield to protect them. (UVF respondent Newry and Armagh)

In the period after 1986, and with regard to allegations of collusion, at least nine victims were former IRA prisoners and Loyalists contend that these persons were known to them. The death of some eleven Sinn Fein activists during the same period was accounted for by their greater visibility in local council chambers. 'Operations' such as the attacks on Boyle's Bar in 1991 led to the death of four active IRA members and resulted in the IRA killing UVF members John Bingham, Trevor King and Leslie Dallas. The killing of former IRA prisoner Larry Marley in 1987 led to his family stating that the RUC had informed him a few weeks before his death that he was under threat after they became aware that information on him had been passed to a local UVF commander in North Belfast. The issue of collusion is dealt with in Chapter 2, but Loyalists generally contend that the extent of such collusion, especially with regard to the death of active Republicans, was minimal. In an interview with a senior UVF respondent (Mid Ulster) the following was stated:

> If all this information on the IRA was given to us then why were so few Provos killed? If we had all this information from the peelers [police] and the army on the Provos then why didn't that lead to a lot of Republicans lying in their graves. So maybe that information was useless, there was only bits of it or it was not as accurate as Republicans claim. Or maybe we didn't get none of it at all. If someone had passed information to me on a top Provo, that Provo wouldn't be around now.

Conclusion

Many Loyalists view their appreciation of conflict transformation not just as a discourse-driven mobilisation of tactics but also as a learning process in which shifting away from violence appears like a personal journey. There is undoubtedly not the same unswerving loyalty that Republicans invoke regarding historical 'certitude' or anti-hegemonic countenance but instead there is a learning curve that was guided by consciousness-raising and the experience of violent performance. Most assert that their violence was revenge driven, contrary to Republican analysis, and ethno-sectarian in the sense that the 'other' community was positioned as a homogenous and therefore legitimate mass. If anything loyalism's fundamental problem was that it was constituted by rationalists and irrationalists and it was only when Republicans aimed for peace that the former could position themselves into a process of meaningful and asserted conflict transformation. That process has been slow and it took until 2007 for the UVF[18] and UDA to issue significant statements of intent to decommission.[19]

Ultimately, violence was driven by ideological purpose and competing constitutional discourses in which the collective 'self' was required to invoke and reproduce odium upon the collective 'other'. Identity was built upon the sum of social relationships experienced by living within a place-centred value system of imagined community congruity that led to a legitimation of harm caused when set against harm endured (Capoccia and Kelleman 2007). Violence initially intensified the discourse of 'threat' as it shifted from the imagining of it to the realities of harm and community-centred endurance (Shirlow and McGovern 1996). Violence was never complete and wavered through various cycles, forms and means. Republican violence did provide a proviso for Loyalist responses as did other signs of alarm, but much of Loyalist responses were already set in material, socio-political and cultural mediums that were pre-existing and were discursively linked to modes of intentionality and the defence of terrains of constitutional reference. Loyalists were pre-ordained to defend the boundaries of the United Kingdom as much as they were arranged to maintain Unionist hegemony. The onset of conflict and their public rejection by Unionism enhanced a raison d'etre increasingly driven by the centrality of constitutional desire. Loyalists in simple terms were repulsed by the idea of Irish unification and their violence was never simply a reproduction of the British State's or political Unionist desires and requirements. It was linked to acts of social and cultural production and significance that constituted a mixture of reasons and purposes and a development of power relationships that stretched from defence to assault and through to the cessation of violence. As Barak (2005: 141) upholds in a more general sense, Loyalist violence imitated the supposition that:

To begin, adversarial models of social intercourse assume that one engages in antagonistic behavior for three reasons: to overcome another, to achieve revenge and/or to arouse envy. Adversarialism also assumes that parties oppose each other's interests more than they share anything in common. Finally, adversarial paradigms assume that conflicts are the essence of life, and living consists of enduring them, winning as many as possible and learning how, when necessary, to live with losing them. Viewed from these vantage points, the adversary school of thought excludes all opportunities but antagonism and battle in one form or another. It also means that self, other and relationship are defined in terms of conquering and submitting.

A more interpretative and reasoned approach must be marked by sensitivity to the symbolic components and construction and mobilisation of Loyalist violence. That does not mean that such violence was not ethno-sectarian or a representation of narrow and prejudiced narratives of identity. However, to suggest that it did not operate in a context of threat and imagined imposition and only upon State edict undermines the nature and complex underpinnings of the package that constituted harm, violence and cultural impairment in Northern Ireland. In a general sense those who now uphold Loyalist transformation view past violence as anachronistic and not worthy of being dressed up in normative self-eulogising perspectives. Such a perspective is undoubtedly felt but is also part of a discursive jag at Republicans who, Loyalists contend, over-legitimise violence. If anything, there is among such individuals a sense of accepting sectarian motivation, and that there was a pernicious current within Loyalist 'logic'. It is generally within that form of Loyalist cognition that it was admitted that violence was driven by insidious, menacing and destructive tendencies. For those who later pursued conflict transformation the legitimacy for that violence remained but the certitude for it did not. As noted 'at times we just sounded like Paisley with guns and I never wanted that' (UVF respondent, West Belfast). The desire to cease violence was linked to an alternative social intercourse that stretches beyond Barak's (2005) notion of the adversarial, such as negotiating with Republicans and others in an attempt to effect mutually responsible connections. As stated by a UDA respondent:

> It took me time to realise. When Sinn Fein started to get votes they were getting about a tenth of the Catholic vote. I know it's much higher now. But what I noticed was that if they did something bad like Enniskillen or that their vote went down. That made me wonder about Catholics. Most didn't like the IRA, so I wondered about what I had been told that all Catholics were Provies. They just weren't, so then I wondered why had we been stiffing [killing] people just because they wanted a united Ireland? I wanted to stay in Britain and the majority of Catholics would have been agin [against] shooting me because I felt that way … It was a hard lesson to swallow, when you realised that what you were up to wasn't real, wasn't what them [Catholics] ones really thought. But I never looked down on Catholics like the way Paisley did. I just couldn't cope with the killing of our people. It was a shit world in which you were drawn into the killing because you were angry by what you saw. (UDA respondent, Mid Ulster)

In sum, Loyalist violence was pernicious, destructive and at times whole-heartedly malicious, but the representation of it has failed to understand how the experiential circumstances of violence presented competing routes, recognitions, legitimacies and counter-legitimacies and various agencies and actors. There is as much value in asking why violence stops as opposed to why the adversarial nature of it arises (Boyce 2002). The main lesson that emerges from Loyalist violence is that a narrowly structured and homogenous reading of it does not aid the explanation of its form and the meaning of internal inspection and rereading.

Notes

1   The main periods in which violence emerged from within the Protestant working class was in the 1880s, the years preceding World War I, the early 1920s and the post-1969 period – the periods when British administration in Ireland was challenged.
2   Patterson (1982: 29) also argues 'the original unity of the Unionist movement was based on much more than the sectarianism of the Orange Order'.
3   The Sunningdale Agreement aimed to create a devolved power-sharing executive for Northern Ireland. It also contained a Council of Ireland that would provide influence over Northern Ireland's affairs.
4   In Northern Ireland only.
5   In the same article written in June 1994 Adam's also predicted 'the present intense speculation about the possibility of an IRA cease-fire in this climate is unhelpful and wholly misinformed'. The IRA called a ceasefire four months later. Available at http://cedarlounge.wordpress.com/2010/02/15/left-archive-an-phoblacht-sinn-fein-7-july-1994/ (last accessed 8 November 2011).
6   Rosie Cowan and Owen Bowcott stated in their article entitled 'Freed Ulster killer paid £50,000 salary for being police informer' (*The Guardian*, 16 February 2009) that Torrens was an alleged informer.
7   Torrens Knight was to later join the LVF whilst imprisoned.
8   These include those who at the time of their death were non-combatants, including ex-service persons, alleged informants and unintended targets.
9   Patterson (1982: 28) also notes 'sectarianism will undoubtedly be an element. But it will not have a pre-given significance, its importance will be determined by specific circumstances'. Moreover, 'the material basis of sectarianism is in this sense much more a question of territory ...'.
10 Available at www.wordpress.com/2010/02/15/left-archive-an-phoblacht-sinn-fein-7-july-1994/ (last accessed 15 June 2006).
11 *An Phoblacht/Republican News*, 15 January 1998.
12 Middle Unionists is a UVF term that applies to the political and middle classes.
13 http://en.wikiquote.org/wiki/Ian_Paisley (last accessed 8 November 2011).
14 http://cain.ulst.ac.uk/othelem/organ/docs/tara73.htm (last accessed 8 November 2011).
15 The CLMC issued a ceasefire statement ending 'operational hostilities' from midnight on 13 October 1994. The CLMC represents the UDA, UVF and RHC.
16 Jim Gray was killed in 2005. He has been head of the East Belfast UDA and had been stood down by the Inner Council due to his involvement in drug-dealing. Prior to his death he had been arrested regarding money-laundering. This arrest

and his criminal activities were read as a risk to stability within the UDA and Gray was a liability if he was to inform on others.

17 The killing took place in broad daylight on 28 May 2010 and was the first Loyalist killing in five years.

18 The full UVF and UDA statements of intent can be found on the BBC News website at http://news.bbc.co.uk/1/hi/northern_ireland/6618365.stm and http://cain.ulst.ac.uk/othelem/organ/uda/uda111107.htm (both last accessed 8 November 2011) .

19 For more details on Loyalist decommissioning see Report of the Independent International Commission on Decommissioning, 25 February 2010. Available at http://cain.ulst.ac.uk/events/peace/decommission/iicd250210.pdf (last accessed 8 November 2011).

It always surprises me that Republicans
know so much about our collusion.
They know more than me. For them
killing was politics but for me
now it's just a sad history.
(UVF respondent)

2 Collusion: myth, reality and complete ignorance

Popper (1994) contends that any analysis of those involved in political violence should be cognisant of the reality that violence must be understood as relative and conditional but always with intention. Thus intention was linked to the 'legitimisation' of violence and was carefully constructed between competing versions of propaganda-seeking discourses and variant justifications. With regard to motivation and the capacity to form the 'principles' and reasons for violence those groups that are viewed as 'pro-State' fair less well in terms of explanation and support regarding wider academic analysis (Rummel 1994). Being explained as adjuncts of the State and therefore as collaborators in the maintenance of the status quo and its various instruments of 'terror' means that such groups are rarely considered as having validity on their side. Acts of collusion are understood as additionally problematic given the greater predisposition to be legally and morally able to hold the State as opposed to non-State groups to account for the commitment and promotion of violence. Evidently, a State that was involved in the extra-judicial killing of its citizens, whom it is duty-bound to protect, raises obvious examples of law-breaking but also of deep immorality given the monopoly it has over the regulation of society, law-making and violence. Ironically, extra-judicial State violence is criminal activity by the State 'self'. Without doubt illegal State as opposed to non-State violence must be viewed separately as extra-judicial violence challenges the State as the agent of legal and normative regulation, especially when paramilitary groups are used as a proxy for the exertion of State power.

In the presentation of political violence the search for accountability has increasingly led to assertions that Loyalist violence was attached to collusion with the security forces. Sluka (2000: 129) makes the following assertion concerning the denial of such violence:

> The official position of the British authorities is that there is no State terror in Northern Ireland, and certainly no death squads. When pressed they admit that

there is Loyalist terror against Catholics, but insist that they have nothing to do with it. When pressed with evidence such as the fact that hundreds of members of the security forces have been convicted of involvement with Loyalist paramilitaries, they claim that this collusion is informal – individual acts by rogue soldiers and policemen – and not a reflection of government policy or a military strategy. All of these are political lies.

Within such a perspective the State supplied Loyalists with weaponry, spotted targets and in so doing supplied names and addresses. It is also contended that they removed security instruments such as road blocks prior to Loyalist attacks and did not prosecute known Loyalist offenders. In addition, it is alleged that the security forces not only planned but were in situ when attacks occurred and supplied, covering fire for Loyalist attacks. In addition, the allegations of collusion also include a failure rigorously to investigate Loyalist killings, and a failure to advise those who were being targeted about the details Loyalists held on them. The failure of sections of the security forces to inform each other about the threats of violence and the hindering of investigations by members of the security forces has also been assumed. The utilisation of Public Interest Immunity certificates at trials and inquests in order to withhold information is also presented as a cover for collusion-centred activities. However, Sluka[1] does not provide evidence of any State direction of terror but merely repeats assertions made by others and produces some peculiar data and commentary.

A more sophisticated understanding of State-centred collusion lies within Cohen's (1996, 2001) work and his classification of State denial concerning wrong doing that presents a useful typology regarding extra-judicial State violence. He identifies three forms of denial; literal, interpretive and implicatory. Literal denial is apparent and based upon an absolute promotion that wrong-doing by the State or its representatives never occurred and allegations that it did are either mendacious or false, or 'mutually reinforcing denials that allow no meta-comment' (Cohen 2001: 64). Interpretive denial emerges when State-sponsored transgressive acts are increasingly difficult to hide. This can lead to a form of acceptance that 'something happened', but the allegations made are exaggerated or the event in question is an isolated example, such as 'rogue' members of the security forces acting without State approval but with an obvious failure of senior security personnel to control extra-judicial activity (Brysk and Gershon 2007).

Implicatory denial emerges when evidence pinpoints active State engagement in the terror directed at its own citizens and invokes the 'values' of righteousness, necessity, victim-blaming and the uniqueness of the problem given the burdens placed on the State's legitimacy by terror groups (Morrow 1997). Thus the State relativises some form of deviant behaviour on its part, in that its actions are somehow justified for the moral 'good', given the 'sickening deviancy' of non-State protagonists. Therefore, when collusion is exposed State combatants do not necessarily fully admit to it but intimate that wrong-doing has been centred on an organisational goal, for example during the killing of IRA activists at Loughgall,[2] that was centred upon 'freeing the hands' of State combatants that were 'tied' by laws and human rights norms. Thus wrong-doing is summoned as an act in the common 'interest'. Jamieson and McEvoy (2005: 511) state that there are two broad definitions of collusion:

> At one end of the continuum is so-called 'bad apple' collusion, wherein intelligence information on suspected Republicans has been passed on to Loyalist paramilitaries by individual members of the security forces sympathetic to their cause. At the other is what has been termed 'institutional' collusion, wherein collusion with paramilitary groups has been organised, planned and bureaucratised by elements of the security forces and which have, in some instances, implicated institutions and individuals with the criminal justice system as well as political elites.

Cohen's typology is relevant when discussing Loyalist paramilitary attitudes to collusion with regard to their general acceptance of implicatory denial and their desire to present collusion as a valid reaction to Republican violence. For some Loyalists collusion was a rational, organisational-driven goal in terms of delivering their violence, although they constantly caution that the majority of that violence was not aided by the British State and that many of those who were both members of the security forces as well as Loyalist groups were 'rogue elements'.

The most obvious conclusion reached when discussing links between paramilitaries and State security force elements is that of rogue members who provided some support, especially soldiers who would pass on montages of alleged IRA members on their departure from a tour of duty. There were only a minority of those spoken to who alleged a systematic form of collusion. The following explains the general perspective:

> Frustration and the fact that you had to check under your car every morning to see if there was a bomb. The car that you were putting your kids in to take them to school. The car you had to drive your kids in by different routes. All of that. The burden of that and other things made a few officers pass things on. But the idea that somebody sat in Downing Street and said 'get the UVF to whack so and so' is just nonsense. So I wouldn't call it collusion but what happens in a dirty war. But then I have to state as I always say why if there was collusion did our violence drop in the 1980s. A Republican would tell me that the securocrats told me to stop. Rubbish, I know why it slowed down because we debated the reason why the tactic of widespread killing wasn't working. I was there but Republicans tell me I am wrong. But I was there that's why I know what happened. (UVF respondent, North Belfast)

Other dominant themes include that security forces did not plan attacks but turned a 'blind eye' to some activities and did not prevent some violence in order not to expose their agents. Those Loyalists involved in collusion were informants who generally stymied violence and provided information that led to weapon seizure and arrests. Such persons were planted within organisations – the most notable example being the UVF member Mark Haddock – and therefore were directed not by their respective leaderships but by rogue security agents, a situation that Loyalists would argue is not collusion with them per se but rather links between the security forces with individuals or small bands of such persons. Those persons are assumed to have driven violence post-1990, an allegation that is supported by the data presented in Chapter 1. They are also understood as those who tried to subvert the development of progressive loyalism; in this sense a belief that collusion was as much concerned with undermining loyalism as it was with republicanism. One would expect that if collusion was a State-directed policy that Loyalists would claim it more readily – to do so would bolster their sense of legitimacy as well as deconstruct the notion of them being illegitimate armed groups. It would also challenge the notion of their criminalisation and permit them to state that they had authority on their side. It would seem feasible that claiming collusion as a state policy in which Loyalists acted as agents of terror would embolden their desire to expose the exploitation and future maltreatment of them.

Loyalists also contend that the Republican exposure of collusion is a signal that the IRA and Sinn Fein wish to dominate the issue of victims and control the propaganda of death and commemoration through presenting and locating acts of collusion in order either to disguise the extent of their previous 'wrongdoing' or camouflage that they are now part of the political establishment. As noted:

> They need to pretend that they are anti-British so as somebody doesn't turn round and says 'look at those ones standin' there shaking hands with the Brits'. So if they keep poking at the dirty tricks they think people will go 'look they are still fighting against the Brits'. Mad, isn't it? (UDA respondent, North Belfast)

Jamieson and McEvoy contend that academic analysis of State crime requires 'a move beyond a monolithic conceptualisation of the State and a more subtle grasp of the different modalities of proxy agency' (2005: 504). This a crucial point analytically when weighing up the nature and meaning of State-centred collusion. For the State and security force members there has been a desire to silence the knowledge of deviant acts, whereas for victims groups and Republicans there has been a desire to expose such stillness (Mullin 1998). However, the British State, due largely to international pressure and agreements tied to Sinn Fein including themselves in the governance of Northern Ireland, has sponsored and funded a series of public investigations and inquiries. Manifestly, collusion for Republicans is an 'exact' science within a discursive and ideologically constructed battlefield in which State 'wrongdoing' is incontestable. For many Unionist and Loyalists evidence of collusion does not obviate against their stronger sense of the injustices driven by

Republican violence. Obviously, Unionists and Loyalists – even if they understand collusion or dirty tricks as they would have it as illegal – view it as an embodiment of implicatory denial/reason.

This bifurcation indicates that the interpretation of conflict emanates from divergent ethno-discursive frameworks, experiences and understandings (Shirlow and Murtagh 2006). Yet few have bothered to identify how collusion is understood and opined by Loyalists. Somewhat unsurprisingly, the reductionist idea that all Loyalists were 'knee-deep' in collusion is commonly presented despite some Loyalists identifying collusion as detrimental to them and that they have variant opinions, knowledges and perspectives on it. It has been discursively easier to present collusion via lumping Loyalists together as an unthinking, emotionless cabal, similar to the process of criminalisation more generally. At times it would appear that every act of Loyalist violence was based upon the State as puppeteer and the Loyalist as mere puppet. Even Rolston (2000, 2005, 2006), who has written on the extent of collusion, acknowledges that '… Loyalist paramilitary organisations cannot merely be seen as State-run counter-gangs. Their autonomy from State forces is beyond doubt' (2005: 193).

Part of the reason why groups such as Loyalists, in terms of their interpretations of violence and harm, are under-explored relates to certain academics conveniently lumping Loyalists into an amalgam of pro-State or right-wing militias and the death-squad activists more commonplace in Serbia, Latin America, Asia and Africa. The inadequacy of such a process of simple homogenisation of pro-State terror groups is conceptually lazy and propaganda-driven and tells us nothing about the variant motivations, practices and scale of terror operationalised by such divergent groups (O'Malley 1983). Neither is their sufficiency in viewing the British State in the same manner as the unelected regimes that once prevailed in Chile, Central America and Argentina. This is not to deny that rule-breaking by the British State's security apparatus is not illegitimate as it is plainly erroneous, but to suppose that such violence is not relative with regard to its intensity across variant political systems is nonsensical. Co-joining all State terror into a canon of misdeeds that does not explain the differentiation in the forms of conflict, State construction and modes of violent enactment is intellectually sloppy. If anything a democratically elected government that supports or turns a blind eye to collusion is more culpable than an unelected dictatorship. As Rolston argues it is the very nature and implication of law and human rights obligations that may encourage a State that is meaningfully democratic to turn towards the support of collusive acts. As he notes:

> At the same time, death squads and democracy can coexist; moreover, the transition to democracy and indeed elements of democracy itself – the attempted primacy of the rule of law, humanitarian principles, international benchmarks and scrutiny – can increase the chances of death squads appearing. (2005: 189)

The term 'death squad' is an emotive and not particularly helpful one, akin to the employment of the word 'terrorism'. It invokes such a sheer sense of brutality and viciousness that it merely promotes an alternative reaction to it through which Loyalists invoke the counterbalance of Republican violence. The term has a lineage that is related to violence directed by the State, but for Loyalists it is viewed as a term utilised in a vacuum that denies other realities and emotions of violence. Furthermore, the RUC and the various security forces did aim to protect life and did provide extensive information to those targeted by Loyalists, and also had a higher detection rate for Loyalist violence and seized significant quantities of Loyalist armaments and weaponry. In addition, they ran informants and thus prevented a significant level of Loyalist violence. In sum, to descriptively equate the security forces in Northern Ireland as akin to that which existed in Latin America and other arenas is in terms of scale plainly misguided, as is the denial that sections of the British security forces were not involved in dirty tricks and injudicious behaviour. Given the multiple forms of collusion and the information presented below it is possible to conclude that the 'truth', of collusion lies somewhere between the extensive claims of collusion and the literal denial of it.

Collusion, in whatever form, was an intrinsic part of power-related practice that subverted legality with the aim of undermining the capacity of Republicanism and even transformative loyalism. The extent of it in terms of direction and whether it went as high as Downing Street or as low as rogue officers can only, with certainty, be ascertained at the lower end of that scale. The scope of collusion and whether it functioned as a directed policy or an opportunistic ability remains debated. In essence, the dispute over collusion and the theatre regarding its various meanings, interpretations and structures has failed to garner much in the way of inter-community agreement. That does not mean that Loyalists do not see it as regrettable or even fortunate but the assertion of collusion as experienced by them is particularistic and experience inspired. Loyalists also view the lack of fact-finding and admission around Republican violence as a de-motivator in terms of their acknowledgment of their own violence, and at that point it is not a case of denial, as opined by Sluka, but a desire for balance before disclosure, irrespective of the legal modalities.

State collusion with Loyalists,[3] if it occurred in any form, should never be accepted as a valid reaction to an extraordinary situation even in the face of the provocation of Republican violence. Within its own terms the State must not engage in illegitimate and deviant behaviour, and it is now evident that in so doing the effects of collusion will haunt Northern Irish society for years to come. Even in examining the emotions that drove collusion, that it may have 'shortened' the conflict and that it was reactive to pernicious violence is folly. The long-term effect of collusion is that it led to deaths, undermined the rise of transformative loyalism, provided significant propaganda opportunities for those opposed to the British State and presented that State as illegitimate and contested. Collusion thus 'legitimised' a significant part of Irish Republican discourse. The web of collusion is peculiar, murky and obscure and seems to have within it a complex set of ironies and counter-positions. On one occasion when interviewing a Loyalist the following complex narrative emerged:

> *Respondent*: The Jackal[4] would never work with Billy Wright, he was a tout.
>
> *Author*: But he [the Jackal] was also alleged to have been involved in collusion.
>
> *Respondent*: You miss the point of what I'm saying, Wright was a tout and that's a very different thing. The Jackal worked with rogue elements.

There is a crucial need for Loyalist involvement in collusion to be examined via disparate lenses. Some have no knowledge of it or only imprecise familiarity with certain incidents and thus conclude that much of what is stated about collusion is therefore, via their experience, embroidered and exaggerated. Others were aware of it but purposefully refused to engage in such activities, whilst some have a more extensive knowledge and obviously hold a more developed awareness. Therefore, there is no complete denial of collusion but amongst each of these Loyalist types there is a shared sense that collusion was an exception rather than a norm. In particular, Loyalists, if they admit to collusion, see it as linked to rogue officers and rarely if ever contend that it was an active policy driven by the State. A common assertion is that if collusion was such an active policy 'then why did we kill so few Provies?' (UDA respondent, East Antrim). Furthermore, there are also claims of non-State collusion and examples of information on targets being fed to Loyalists from within the nationalist community, an aspect of collusion that is rarely mentioned, recorded or even recognised.

Collusion: 'the evidence'

Thus far, the debate on collusion has been framed generally by variant positions between those who wish to expose, those who wish to deny and those who wish to claim significant acts of collusion in order to bolster their 'pro-State' credentials. The majority of allegations made against the State's security forces relate to the RUC's Special Branch, the Forces Reconnaissance Unit attached to the 14th Intelligence Company of the British Army and the Mobile Reconnaissance Force, trained by the SAS. The role of these agencies was to gather, usually via informants, intelligence regarding paramilitary organisations, but as argued by Dillon (1990) members operated beyond the conventional codes and practices of their parent organisations. These groups were supposed to be co-joined in terms of ongoing activities via the Joint Irish Section which itself allegedly reported on a weekly basis to the Joint Intelligence Commission chaired by the sitting Prime Minister (O'Halpin

2007). The central allegation, as detailed elsewhere, is that these counter-terrorist groups undertook counter-insurgency tactics following a model of tactics espoused by Brigadier Frank Kitson, who was central to army strategy in the early 1970s. Much of what has been debated and examined as collusion is linked to high-profile deaths, generally those of Pat Finucane, Rosemary Nelson and the victims of the Dublin and Monaghan and McGurk pub bombings.

Bruce (1992, 2000) is more reticent than Republican commentators on the level of collusion and postulates more upon the level of proof, examining the motives of those Loyalists involved in collusion and contending that there is insufficient evidence regarding the extent of collusion as claimed. His general supposition is that political and ideological concerns shaped the understanding of collusion and that both Republicans and Loyalists wish to accept as true the extent of collusion in order to fortify respective legitimacies. In his review of Sean McPhilemy's (1989) book *The Committee*, Bruce challenges most of what is commonly thought through adopting the following broader analysis:

> There are Loyalist paramilitary organisations. There are teams of Loyalists who murder Catholics. There are Unionist politicians. The vast majority are law-abiding; a very small number have had links with terrorists. There are a bewildering array of Loyalist associations and organisations that pursue a Loyalist agenda in a wide variety of sometimes conflicting ways. There have been RUC officers who have committed vigilante murders and there have been officers who have aided the UDA and UVF. There have even been officers plausibly accused of supplying information to the IRA. As I have noted elsewhere … the most plausible accounts of collusion concern the early days of the Troubles and the Ulster Defence Regiment, rather than the RUC. (2000: 79)

With regard to collusion Bruce (1992) challenges a series of allegations regarding State-Loyalist collusion. Although not denying some forms of broad and even participant assistance – as well as encouragement – Bruce provides alternative evidence regarding many of the claims made at that time. Much of what Bruce denotes is linked to his call for circumspection of the extent, form and character of Loyalist collusion. Bruce has also asserted the following:

> Republicans argue that there is no significant difference between the UDA and UVF and the Crown forces; it is all State terror. Nothing in my research leads me to that conclusion. Although they would like to be seen in that light, the UDA and UVF are not branches of the State's security force, as 'the men behind the wire' can testify. (1992: 269)

Bruce's sense that loyalism contained certain autonomy is presented against the imperious idea that Loyalists were merely 'bunglers who cannot assassinate without assistance from the security forces' (1992: 204). He argues that anyone who accepts the argument that loyalism was merely State-inspired produces 'a recipe for belief despite the absence of evidence' (1992: 204). However, some of his points appear to have been superseded by a series of inquires and investigations that have become more commonplace since the onset of the Belfast Agreement and the formation, in particular, of the Office of the Police Ombudsman (2007). As argued by the Republican activist and commentator Jim Gibney:

> The Pat Finucane killing is probably the most public example of this. At least four of the people involved were members of the British security system, all of them. I think that tells you a lot about the British securocrat system including the RUC and Loyalists. To me they were inter-changeable, inter-linked and working broadly speaking to the same objectives. The British Crown forces were the open sharp edge of State oppression against Republicans and nationalists and they covered that up in legalities of the State and got away with it on that basis and then they used the Loyalist paramilitaries to do what is often referred to as their dirty work. Collusion clearly was a central plank of the government's plans to frustrate the Republican efforts. (Interview 2005)

Furthermore, according to Relatives for Justice:

> 'C' Company was at that time the most active unit in the UDA. Active means it was killing a lot of people. Nothing peculiar in that, after all that's what Loyalists do. But 'C' Company was unusual in that a high proportion of its targets were either IRA suspects, Republicans or high profile people whom most Protestants would regard as Republicans. They seemed to be a cut above the average Loyalist gunmen in that they were targeting the Provos more than the general Catholic community. (2008: 3)

The respected journalist Ed Moloney (2000: 1) has also reasoned:

> The reason 'C' Company knew so much about the IRA was because their intelligence chief, one Brian Nelson was an agent working for a special body of British Military intelligence called the Force Research Unit, better known as FRU, which specialised in running agents deep in the murky world of Loyalist and Republican paramiliarism.
>
> Thanks to military documents unearthed by BBC journalist John Ware and revelations by former FRU members and ex-UDA personnel we now know that FRU was working 'C' Company like the accelerator pedal in a deadly armoured car.

There is a question over the extent to which such assertions over C Company knowing 'so much about the IRA' can be measured against available statistical evidence. Most certainly in terms of available date the supposition made by Relatives for Justice that C Company targeted more Republican activists than Catholic civilians is not validated. This is not to deny that C Company was not involved in some form of State entanglement, but data regarding the deaths of Republican combatants and activists linked to the IRA or Sinn Fein points to a less obvious situation. As noted in Chapter 1 Loyalists did not kill significant numbers of Republican combatants and political activists in comparison with all killings committed by them. In sum, thirty-five members of the IRA and Sinn Fein were killed by Loyalists between 1969 and 1994. In the period 1990–1994 the targeting of Sinn Fein activists by the UDA did rise and was of particular note. As it is only possible to measure targeting in the terms of what is explicitly known about victims who have been claimed as IRA combatants or Sinn Fein members any comments made on C Company can only operate with regard to the robustness of available data. It could be contended that C Company and other loyalists did after 1990 target persons linked to Republican combatants and activists, such as acquaintances and family members, but again as arose in virtually every discussion with loyalists was why, if they were 'provided' with so much material on Republican activists, did so few of them get killed, an undoubtedly brutal but statistically valid point.

A key allegation concerning C Company and the collusion nexus that is linked to Brian Nelson is that it led to an upsurge in UDA violence. Obviously Nelson was not active following his arrest in 1990 and therefore, unless material was prepared by him and stored and then utilised post-1990, his role in terms of actual deaths of Republican combatants and activists would appear to be relatively limited. Nelson had been recruited by the FRU in 1985 and between then and his arrest the UDA killed one IRA combatant, Caimhin MacBradaigh, and no Sinn Fein activists. There were attacks conducted in Belfast by the UDA at the homes of Republican activists and combatants and some of these resulted in the death of their relatives and friends, but again the numbers of such deaths is low compared with that of Catholic civilians. The death of Terry McDaid in 1988, whose brother was a Republican activist, and the attack on the first Sinn Fein Lord Mayor of Belfast, Alex Maskey, in 1987 are events of note. Nelson was also linked to the death of Francisco Notarantonio, a Catholic civilian, and Pat Finucane, a prominent lawyer. The former was a set up, according to Loyalist sources, as C Company were after IRA intelligence officer Freddie Scappaticci but were diverted to Notarantonio, a civilian whose Italian last name was used to redirect and convince the UDA that they had 'hit' the correct target. In essence, it is alleged that Nelson prevented Scappaticci's death, as he was directed by his handlers to protect this prominent IRA informant.

In the period 1980 to 1984, prior to Nelson's recruitment to the FRU, the UDA killed twelve civilian Catholics and members of the Republican movement. Between 1985 and 1989 this rose to twenty-two. However, in the 1980 to 1984 period four Republican activists were killed by the UDA whereas between 1985 and 1989 one, as noted above, was killed. It is commonly alleged that the aim of collusion regarding Nelson was to reduce the killing of civilians and to 'up' the killing of Republican activists. If so, such a policy during his period as an UDA intelligence officer was 'unsuccessful'. At the same time the UVF killed four IRA members and a Sinn Fein activist.

Within the same two periods the number of deaths committed in North and West Belfast, the area in which C Company operated, remained the same – at ten in each period. Therefore, the assertions about Nelson are more complex and in fact his period of influencing C Company did not lead to a rise in their ethno-sectarian violence which was dissimilar to the violence engaged in by other sections of the UDA at that time.[5] If anything it was the arrest of Nelson that led to the rise of Adair and the period of acceleration in C Company activity and, as noted by a senior UDA respondent:

> I have been told that Nelson did have a lot of information but people I'm told started to wonder why if he did like, were we not getting at the Provisionals a lot more than we were. That's when the talking began about who he was working for. In a way he was a break on us as he was getting ones scooped [arrested]. The bit that confuses me is that he stopped more killings than he had got done. He set lots of our ones up. Then when he was scooped you really saw a big jump in the violence so the real impact as I see it was that Nelson was managing the violence and keeping it low, real low. Once he went Adair was in charge and then you seen how Nelson had been doing bits and pieces to cover his arse but also stopping things to. The worst thing that happened was Nelson being lifted. Stevens [leader of the Stevens Inquiry] did what was right in terms of the law but he removed an element that were easier to control and in a weird sort of funny, but not funny ha ha way, he got rid of the ones who didn't want to get back into the heavy duty stuff.
>
> Look I think it is very simple. The army had all the names and addresses of Provisionals who had been in prison plus the names of many more who weren't. They had a massive lot of stuff on them people. So why was the killing of them so low? (UDA respondent, East Belfast)

Since 1970 the deaths of Republican/Nationalist activists equated to an average of seven per half decade. Loyalists state that the rise in victims post 1990 was based upon victims being former Republican prisoners who they had encountered in prison, or persons who were more visible to them due to Sinn Fein's increased political visibility. Therefore, we have two perspectives regarding the growth in such violence. First, a Loyalist sense that they were better prepared to plan such attacks with some but not complete assistance. Second, a counter position adopted by Republicans that Loyalists were aided directly to kill such persons via security-force policy. Undoubtedly as emerged in extensive interviewing the issue of collusion for Loyalist's is one of smaller scale collusion than Republicans contend.

In considering the areas in which violence was undertaken against IRA combatants and Sinn Fein activists it is notable that Mid Ulster emerges as the main site (eight persons) for such violence and when conjoined with North and West Belfast these Westminster constituencies account for 57.7% of all such deaths. In Mid Ulster all but one of these killings were conducted by the UVF and again the areas in which Loyalists were most 'successful' in killing combatant or political Republicans were areas in which C Company and Billy

Wright operated. When examined in terms of organisational responsibility[6] after 1970 the UDA claim to have killed ten Sinn Fein activists and seven IRA combatants, whereas the UVF claim to have killed ten IRA combatants and seven Sinn Fein activists. As noted by as Loyalist source:

> We could never get at the Provies despite the nonsense about us getting all this information. But we could get at Shinners [Sinn Fein members] in the 1990s as they were in council chambers and out and about during elections. As far as I know that is how they were targeted. They took up the politics and were more visible to the likes of us. (UVF respondent, South Belfast)

Unlike the killing of Sinn Fein activists the killing of IRA combatants did not rise in the period 1990 to 1994. The two peaks for such violence were 1969–1974 and 1985–1988, but again the numbers killed were low although the impact is significant in terms of allegations of collusion. In the period between 1990 and 1994 Loyalists killed 153 Catholic civilians and claim the deaths of thirteen IRA combatants and Sinn Fein members in Northern Ireland. In sum, 92.1% of these deaths during that period were of Catholic civilians. Despite such evidential fact there remains among some loyalists a sense that their actions were more targeted than the data suggests. As the following quote explains, the passing of information, according to a senior Loyalist source, concurs with Republican contentions concerning collusion, but again the statement concerning more selective targeting is not validated by the data in terms of the share of Loyalist victims who were Republican combatants or Sinn Fein members:

> After the 80s the UVF and RHC tried to be more selective in attacking Republicanism. We had seen the strategy going not in the way we had hoped and the people didn't turn against the IRA but it was the only way we had to turn the war against the Republican movement. In the 80s and 90s the strategy changed. The difficulty in the early days in identifying targets, and I have to tell you that we were getting information from the security forces but it was very hard to tie these people down and I think the intelligence units within the UVF and RHC combined forces. And make no bones about it that we got information from the security forces simply because their hands were tied. That shows the difference in strategy from the 70s to the 80s and 90s. (RHC respondent, West Belfast)

Therefore, if collusion was a force behind Loyalist violence then in statistical terms the vast majority of victims remained as Catholic civilians. Before proceeding to the evidence that has emerged from official sources, it is important to note that the issue of collusion and the validity therein has been obscured by high degrees of assertion and contention; the key point is that unofficial sources have presented such a blanket notion of loyalists driven by the security forces that it is near impossible to separate propaganda from fiction and fact. A central problem is that in the noise of assertion and self-assuredness that collusion was a State policy there has been less space for open and informed dialogue. As the following quote powerfully illustrates, it would support Republican analysis but among Loyalists it would raise questions regarding the source and the names of the persons killed. More than anything it leaves open, due to not listing exact information, the interpretation over whether the source is an embittered or status-seeking former combatant or a person who wishes to present a form of remorsefulness. Within ethno-sectarian discourses the quote may either be interpreted as proof-positive of State wrong-doing or be understood as plain gibberish. It may well be accurate, but it is not robust in terms of the information supplied:

> There's no doubt about this. My unit was guilty of conspiring in the murder of civilians in Northern Ireland, on about 14 occasions. My unit conspired in the murder of civilians in Ireland. (McKay 2000a: 1)

The Stevens Enquiry (2003) found that the killings of Pat Finucane and Brian Lambert, a Protestant student mistakenly identified as a Catholic, could have been prevented and arrests made earlier given the knowledge held by security personnel. Stevens noted collusion in both deaths relating to a willful intent to not record evidence, an absence of security force accountability, a purposeful holding back of evidence and the mishandling of agents. As stated:

> The failure to keep records or the existence of contradictory accounts can often be perceived as evidence of concealment or malpractice. It limits the opportunity to rebut serious allegations. The absence of accountability allows the acts or omissions of individuals to go undetected. The withholding of information impedes the prevention of crime and the arrest of suspects. The unlawful involvement of agents in murder implies that the security forces sanction killings. (Stevens 2003: 16)

Stevens' extensive report, although largely unpublished, indicated how security agents were involved with certain persons and provided them with intelligence to undertake violent acts. One such person was William Stobie, who had been involved in the killing of Pat Finucane. As the very able journalist David McKittrick (2001: 1) noted:

> After his acquittal, Stobie himself called for a public inquiry, saying that he and Mr Mulholland had been 'pawns in a bigger game, caught up in a tangled web spun by very powerful people'. The Nelson and Stobie cases established that the UDA unit involved in the Finucane shooting had been thoroughly penetrated by the security forces.
>
> Nelson, who was working for military intelligence, had supplied information on the target while Stobie,[7] who was working for Special Branch, had supplied the weapons. These uncontested links with the intelligence world mean that even observers sceptical about conspiracy theories concluded that in this instance foul play has taken place.
>
> The accusation against the intelligence authorities is therefore that some

elements in that murky world may have conspired in the killing of a lawyer who was regarded as a thorn in the side of the security forces.

The release by the Public Records Office in 2004 of a military intelligence file entitled 'Subversion in the UDR' which was perhaps presented to the Joint Intelligence Committee highlighted concerns that the UDR was infiltrated by members of groups described as Protestant extremists and, as noted:

> Some members of the UDR, who also belong to subversive groups, undoubtedly lead 'double lives', and even with the aid of intelligence it is occasionally difficult to persuade a CO (*Commanding Officer*) that one of his men is a risk. Indicative, but not typical, is the case of a member of 1 UDR, apparently a good citizen (the Deputy Chairman of a District Council) who had the following traces:
>
> a. Subject was OC (*Officer Commanding*) of Ballymena UDA
> b. Subject had obtained ammunition for the UDA
> c. Subject was suspected of illegal arms dealings, and of acquiring an SLR and an SMG in Scotland, and of selling them to the UDA. (2004: 1)

The same document highlighted that in the previous year the UDR had lost or had stolen some from them some 190 weapons compared with the British Army, who had lost sixteen weapons. It concluded:

> … in every case there is considerable suspicion, which in some instances is strong enough to lead to a judgment that an element of collusion was present. (2004:2)

It was also alleged that:

> It seems likely that a significant proportion (perhaps five per cent – in some areas as high as 15 per cent) of UDR soldiers will also be members of the UDA, Vanguard service corps, Orange Volunteers or UVF. Subversion will not occur in every case but there will be a passing on of information and training methods in many cases and a few subversives may conspire to 'leak' arms and ammunition to Protestant extremist groups. (2004: 4)

Although, it was also stated that:

> In the last three months however, 29 of the 99 rejected applicants for the UDR were turned down because of the existence of subversive traces on them. (2004: 5)

Retired Canadian judge Peter Cory's (2004) report on a number of notorious killings also suggested evidence of State complicity and called for a public inquiry. Further evidence emerged concerning the 1992 death of five Catholic civilians by the UDA in a bookmakers shop in South Belfast and the conclusion of the Historical Enquiries Team (HET) was that a Browning pistol used in these killings had been given back to the Loyalists after being secured previously by the RUC. With regard the Loughinisland killings,[8] an eyewitness has alleged that her witness statement was lost and on her own volition she found one of the getaway cars at an RUC officers home hidden under a tarpaulin. The Stevens and Cory reports add to knowledge of other forms of collusion regarding the failure to rigorously investigate Loyalist killings, and a failure to advise victims that they were being targeted and that details on them were held by Loyalists. In May 2010 the report into the death of Rosemary Nelson, a lawyer in Lurgan killed by the RHD in 1999, concluded that there was no direct involvement by the police in her murder but that they had failed to protect her with regard to known threats against her.

When the Police Ombudsman for Northern Ireland (2007) published her report on collusion between the police and the Mount Vernon UVF she reported that Special Branch officers knew that their informant, Mark Haddock[9] (noted as Informant 1), and his gang were involved in over a dozen murders. She also concluded that Informant 1 was recruited through his '*long-standing friendship*' with a police officer and had been a Special Branch informant since 1991 to 2003. The report had come forth in part due to the killing of Raymond McCord, a UVF member killed by the Mount Vernon UVF in 1997. Prior to and since this report his father, also called Raymond McCord, has run a campaign against Loyalist organisations and nefarious activities therein.

Informant 1, it was alleged, had provided over 400 pieces of relevant intelligence, which was significantly less that the information that was received upon him and his illegal activities. During his time as an agent he was allegedly involved in the murder of ten individuals and the attempted murder of ten others and was purportedly involved in other serious crime including targeting individuals, a bomb attack in the Republic of Ireland in 1997 and a host of informal social control punishment attacks, dealing in drugs and perverting the course of justice. The report also noted that Informant 1 did not enjoy 'informant status' and that he had never been fully investigated for the majority of the crimes he had committed. He was noted by a police officer as:

> a particularly difficult source to handle who tells only a fraction of what he knows and for this reason would require strong, careful and fully controlled and co-ordinate handling. (Police Ombudsman for Northern Ireland 2007: 28)

Officers who were interviewed for the report had concluded that this informant was a 'protected species', with further allegations that he was paid in excess of £79,000 during the twelve-year period from 1991 to 2003. In addition it was alleged that ten killings conducted by the Mount Vernon UVF could have been prevented or were known about without prosecution or investigation. UVF respondents state that Haddock was already an informant prior to his joining the UVF and if that had been known he would have been immediately expelled. He is often depicted as a bully and also as something of a Robin Hood character who would dispense money to local residents. Irrespective of the minutiae of who Haddock was and how he operated, it is evident, as noted by McKittrick, that 'none the less, although this is in one sense merely the latest in a line of revelations, it is one of the worst cases of police misbehaviour and one that yesterday produced widespread shock' (2007: 1).

Loyalist interpretations of collusion

Some Loyalists have no qualms about accepting there were some examples of broad and participation assistance. However, they constantly echo Bruce's proposition that the RUC in particular aimed to undermine their violence and that collusion seriously affected their capacity due to the information supplied to the security forces by Loyalist informants. For Loyalists collusion is understood as an issue of scale, in that it was less common than Republicans contend and that:

> for every five or ten men in cahoots with the Special Branch or some other spook there were 200 or 300 in the Crum or Long Kesh locked up because they had stepped outside the law and was being punished. Them lads weren't up to their knackers in collusion. The facts are plain and simple enough, your average RUC man hated us and wanted us locked up just like they did the Provisionals. (UDA respondent, West Belfast)

If anything, 'your average RUC man' was highly successful and as Bruce (1992: 274–275) notes with regard to prosecutions:

> between 1981 and 1987 Republicans were responsible for 386 deaths and 148 were charged imprisoned ... Loyalists killed 69 of which 130 were charged ... in early 1982 the RUC's conviction rate for Republican murders was between 50 and 60 per cent while that for Loyalist murders was between 90 and 100 per cent.

Finding it easier to imprison Loyalists was generally due to the running of informants, the lack of Loyalist discipline compared with Republican organisations, and that sections of the Protestant community were prepared to inform the security forces about Loyalist activity given that they viewed the RUC as the legitimate voice for their concerns.

Most of the Loyalists interviewed did not view much of what is stated about collusion as a direct State-Loyalist relationship but instead invoked the idea of infiltration and argued that access to training and weaponry was a tactic that was employed especially with regard to the easier-to-join UDR, and that being close to 'rogue' members of the security forces led to an upgrading of their information base. Essentially they viewed their members who joined the UDR and to a lesser extent the RUC as those who were there to gain information, learn how to use weaponry and also seize and steal munitions. Such infiltration was rarely understood, during extensive interviewing, as guided by securocrats or based upon any direct policy by the State, although they admit that in some instances 'a blind eye was turned by some who were a bit ah you know sympathetic' (UVF respondent, Mid Ulster). Instead the nature of such infiltration was viewed as opportunistic and it was seen that many 'rogue' members of the UDR, in particular, were either removed or caught and imprisoned. In certain cases it was also contended that UDR members involved in sectarian violence had come to join paramilitary organisations due to extreme 'provocation':

> Some had had enough. One fella I was inside with couldn't cope after a fella in his town was killed by the IRA. He knew who killed that man and he always says that the killer would laugh at checkpoints and say things like 'thon man we whacked was an easy target and no one will go to Long Kesh for it'. He always said that he just snapped and went over to our side … that's not collusion but somebody who just snapped. (UVF respondent, Upper Bann)

Among Loyalist respondents there was a constant sense of members of the security forces who had suffered mental breadown and reacted violently due to intense pressure and possible symptoms of post-traumatic stress disorder. A contention made regarding weapons being 'stolen' from Palace Barracks in Holywood was linked to a serving officer whose:

> head had gone. The man's head had gone and from what I know he just turned up at the UDA headquarters and handed the weapons over. When he turned up the ones in the office were, what's the word? Like shocked and thought it was a stitch up when he just turned up outta the blue like. I think they even thought it was a set up, but I heard he was so messed up in the head they just thought he had gone mad and his story made sense. He just drove out of the barracks and up the road as his head was turned. (UDA respondent, East Belfast)

Some argued that there were security force members who would 'lend a hand', provide information and even weaponry, but the same persons also cautioned that many more of the forces were repulsed by Loyalist violence and were frustrated by colleagues who were not. A further point made by Loyalists is that if the State had wanted them to direct killings they would have supplied 'clean weapons' rather than have them undertake the acts with 'dirty weapons' used previously that could be traced across any landscape of killing. With regard to the specifics of Brian Nelson, a Loyalist source stated that Nelson did source weaponry in South Africa but argued that they had, because of suspicions regarding him, misinformed him about the trimming of the shipment of those weapons:

> Look Nelson never knew when the shipment was going out. He had been found out by then. He was one of a few UDA men who had information about UVF weapons and the next day them guns was found. The top people knew he was a tout, so they made sure he didn't know about when the weapons were coming to us. So the people who said he did were or are just wrong. The security people only knew we had them when we had them safe. By the time Nelson knew the weapons

had been shipped [from South Africa] they were on the way to Belfast. He had been sent off to get other weapons in South Africa when they was loading them on the boat. Sent on purpose like so as he wouldn't know. So he was used to get the weapons but never told when they were sent, how and when they would get here all of that. (UDA respondent, North Belfast)

There are undoubtedly variant voices within loyalism regarding the extent, nature and meaning of collusion. Much of that is framed, as would be expected, by the extent of knowledge, length of involvement and place within the Loyalist hierarchy. There is never a complete denial that collusion, understood largely as rogue State elements, occurred, but there is a complex narrative regarding the allegations made. Although it is not always articulated in precise terms, Loyalists have a sense of the entanglements of discourse and action that emerges between combatants in their varied attempts to present legitimate versus illegitimate value systems. For those who accept that collusion occurred such acts are viewed as generally justified and natural given their perception that the State's hands were 'tied' by law, codes and human rights agendas and that the response to threat was hindered. This, in turn, constantly stimulates the commentary, widely held within unionism that Republicans only seek human rights for those who died at the hands of Loyalists and the British State. Obviously Republicans did not have human rights to offer as they were not a State formation. What is particularly irksome to Loyalists is when human rights are sought for members of Republican combatant groups. Loyalists think of warfare as a conventionalist undertaking in which they would deny the invocation of their own human rights, and even accept their own criminalisation, if they had been a victim of collusion:

> Loughgall is ah the best example. You go out to kill, you're set up, and may I say by your own people who are working for British intelligence or who want you off the scene, and you get ambushed. Then your people demand we should all think about your human rights. If Loyalists went out and some Loyalist tout set them up and the SAS whacked them then you would have to say 'well they knew what would happen if they stepped outside the law'. Yeah, the State shouldn't ambush people and the law says that, but you aren't reading law books when you go out to kill!
>
> I understand what Republicans say about Loughgall and I understand how that can be seen as wrong, but I think sometimes Republicans are a bit confused. They paint murals of their ones who murdered people and who died at the hands of what they call British State and Loyalist collusion. But they don't write at the bottom of the mural, 'This lad above, never respected the human rights of his victims'. (UVF respondent, Newry and Armagh)

This is paralleled by the constant statements such as 'when they shot a Protestant businessman for selling goods to the RUC, there were no human rights then', or 'when they shot a police officer they didn't shout a warning' or 'when planting a no warning bomb they didn't account for innocent peoples' human rights'. This is an ongoing concern for Loyalists who see the constant inspection of their violence and evidence of their collusion as a primary but unbalanced because of what they see as a purposeful lack of inspection into Republican violence. Loyalists at times even appear stupefied by the lack of fascination, beyond unionism, of 'the malicious nastiness of Republican violence' (UDA respondent, North Down). This drives a further sense of alienation among Loyalists about the lack of concern with regard to their community's experiences of what they value as unmentioned loss and suffering. In addition, the activities of the HET, tasked with resolving killings in which there were no prosecution, is seen as one-sided given that the majority of cases reviewed thus far have been linked to Loyalist violence. Of course the HET's report on the Kingsmills massacre is a sufficient example of investigation into Republican activity. Kingsmills in many ways is seen by Loyalists as symbolically equal to Bloody Sunday given that eleven Protestant workmen were gunned down by the IRA – ten died – while their Catholic colleague was permitted to escape. The gunmen enquired as to whom was the Catholic member of the group and some of the Protestant workmen made gestures for him not to step forward as they believed their assailants were Loyalists. As with many incidents no one was prosecuted and the HET have stated that the weapons used were employed in other IRA acts – a finding that challenged IRA denials of their involvement. Undoubtedly, the rolling out of further HET reports has the capacity to destabilise the process of peace-building.

Collusion as propaganda

There was an agreed acknowledgement among many Loyalist respondents that Republicans invest energy into pushing for investigations of collusion for several reasons. First, it is viewed as being centred upon shaping public perceptions via widening the propaganda value attached to the negative labelling of Loyalists and therefore producing a sense that the victims of Loyalist violence are part of the mutually oppressive nexus of British-Unionist identity and action. Second, Republicans, it is claimed, push for investigations of collusion in order to deny any motive for Loyalist violence and in so doing render them as not reacting to Republican violence but as mere pawns of the British State. Third, exposing collusion is based upon a process of shaming and invoking the idea that somehow such disclosure will undermine unionists and provoke a recognition that maintaining the constitutional link with the United Kingdom is invalid due to the British State's manipulation of Loyalists into violence. As presented by a former Loyalist prisoner:

> I was at a meeting with IRA ones. They banged on about collusion and how we had been led by the nose, how they [British State] had put the gun, put it in our hands, how we had been fooled by the British when we pulled the trigger. It never seemed to matter to them what they had done to the Prods [Protestants]. I said

'look you have all the smart people on your side and you will dig and dig and keep digging and you'll prove this and that and whatever and whatever you lot find will not change how those against you think about, about you lot. It won't make us ones think any different about who we are and what we are and if you think it will your on a hiding to nothing.

Then I said to them ones 'you didn't win your war so you are trying to win the way people think about it. There's other facts about the Troubles and you won't be able to hide that. You're like a big child playing hide and seek. You are seeking this and hiding that.' Did they think if they go collusion, collusion, collusion every minute they open their bakes [mouths] that people are going to say 'them ones is right and we was wrong?' I'm not about hiding anything, what happened was a crock ah shit and a lot of people are dead who shouldn't have been murdered. I want to move on and I don't see what banging on about the past will get anyone. I'll accept what the Provos did to my community and move on, but it's them ones who seem to be stuck in the past. We will keep moving on and they can waste time on the collusion thing. I sees the past as a crock ah shit and not a game of scoring points agin' each other. (UDA respondent, West Belfast)

Fourth, Republicans, it is contended, are concerned at exposing collusion as they 'need' to hide the concessions that they made during the Belfast Agreement. Finally, and most importantly for Loyalists, evoking and 'proving' collusion is based upon Republicans directing and controlling the public memory of violence. Loyalists contend that the examination of collusion is merely about the exploitation of the dead that suits Republican agenda-seeking or, as one respondent explained:

Do you think Sinn Fein and the Provisionals really care about those people? If they cared so much why were they killing all around them? They killed and we hit back. If they cared so much about the past why aren't they owning up to their own murders? Why are they only interested in the big cases that will get the media involved like Finucane, Nelson and their own members? What about the Disappeared? What about their own people they killed? I know the difference between what's right and wrong, I know what they did to people. But the way this all works is the people on the street don't have any importance to them people, unless they were killed by us and the security forces were egging us on. It's a disgrace.

Yes, let's get the, the truth about all that back then, but at the minute it is all about the truth the IRA want, not the truth about the IRA. (UDA respondent, South Belfast)

A similar perspective is centred on the loss of civilian Protestant lives and the contention of a desire to camouflage Republican violence:

If you want to talk about cover ups the greatest cover-up is the Provos trying to pretend they are the only ones who know the truth of the matter … they want plenty of smoke but not the screen on which you write La Mon,[10] Kingsmills, the Disappeared, Teebane,[11] Bloody Friday, whacking the Officials whatever else you can think of. Claudy,[12] Protestant people forced out of Londonderry all that, the way 20,000 Prods were forced out of Londonderry, tying a man to a lorry[13] and using him as a human bomb. Aye and shooting a wee young girl because she was handing out Census forms.[14] Do you want me to go on? (UDA respondent, Foyle)

The issue of scale

In discussing the topic of collusion Loyalists generally contend that it is more complex than presented by Republicans. Many claim no direct knowledge of collusion and in some cases respondents spoke of actually being fearful of becoming involved in it. As explained:

> This fella said he had a lot of info and would share it with us. I said no, we weren't doing it that way. The reason was simple. If we had used that info it would have meant that the one who gave it to us was a tout. Sure as anything that was what he was. I and a few others never wanted nothin' to do with it. It just meant too many risks and there were plenty in the Crum and Long Kesh who were there as they had been in with someone too close to the Branch men or something like that. (UVF respondent, West Belfast)

For some the idea that there was collusion came much later in the conflict and was tied to regrouping and the intention to put pressure on the IRA to enter into a negotiated peace:

> I think that sortta of thing came a lot later, if it did at all. The idea that in the 70s that we were being looked after and all that is complete shit, complete shit, that's all it is. Maybe later there was something going on and from what I know the plan was to get at them [Sinn Fein] and use killing to pressure them into peace. Maybe then dirty tricks were played but not before I went into Long Kesh in the late 70s. If there were dirty tricks it was the odd peeler or something but not what you are saying some sort of governments policy.
>
> Let's just say a lot of it was lads sitting round drinking and then someone would say 'let's stiff a Taig'. So someone would go off and get a weapon and that was that. It wasn't high powered operational stuff but a mix of alcohol, and too much of it and anger. (UVF respondent, West Belfast)

In some instances Loyalist spoke of having no intelligence from the security forces but pondered on what may have been upon them in psychological terms if they had. As noted by a former prisoner:

> If there were things going on I would have been there. Let me put it to you this way. If I had the information to get a Provo I would have used it. No ifs or buts about that. Do you think I wanted to go out and kill some Catholic who was probably hard working and decent and had a family and was killed because he was simply walking into a Catholic area? If I had the right intelligence I would have done a Provisional and maybe then I would be able to sleep better at night and not be so upset about the one I did time for. (UVF respondent, North Belfast)

Linked to such a narrative is the notion that in contradiction to the postulation those Loyalists were aided by the security forces the opposite was a more common reality:

> I can't see it at all to be honest and upfront about it. From what I see the security forces were out to get us and that was their job. People told me that the UDR waved the likes of us through checkpoints. That's just a fantasy, a big lie. It's a real laugh when you get into thinking about it. I wish they had waved me through and maybe I wouldn't have ended up inside. (UDA respondent, North Belfast)

In some cases Loyalists have viewed the evidence on collusion and provide counter-arguments regarding what has been presented. In particular, it would appear that some Loyalists have acquainted themselves with the Relatives for Justice website and in particular their report entitled *Collusion 1990–1994, Loyalist Paramilitary Murders in North of Ireland* (Relatives for Justice 1995). That report questions why the RUC and British Army were incapable of using their surveillance techniques and technology to detect Loyalist activity, especially near police stations and army barracks, when Catholics living nearby were killed. In relation to this a respondent asserted:

> You see that stuff on that website about Catholics killed near police stations and how could that be. How could it be that the IRA could blow up a police station, like when they wanted? So people says there is collusion because Catholics were killed by us near a police station and the peelers sat inside and watched it. Is that what they are saying? Did they sit and watch as the IRA planted a bomb outside. It's just effing stupid nonsense.
>
> Look lets be straight about this. Some people I think got intelligence from a few cops and soldiers here and there. But it was pretty useless, from what I hear, as there were no addresses and the likes of that. Also you have to put this into your mind. The fact of the matter was that if someone got something from a sympathetic source fine and well, but then they had to do something with that intelligence. The main problem was plain as the nose on your face. If three or four people gave someone information on a target you could be sure that 500 or 800 others were trying to lock them up, catch them in the act, put them inside. There was no secret codes or nods and winks in the way people say. (UVF respondent, North Belfast)

Another respondent viewing the same source concluded the following:

> That Relatives for Justice lot have a page on collusion. When I read it I was struck by the fact that they listed so many people, like piles ah Catholics, that the RUC went to and told them they were about to be hit. That's a funny sort of collusion isn't it? Republicans always say that Northern Ireland was like Latin America or some mad like dictatorship. Ah, just like General Pinochet that. I'm sure he sent his cops around to people's houses and says to them, 'don't be in tomorrow at teatime as we are coming to get you' … I'm not denying things happened but not the way that is said and definitely nothing like some banana republic in which

some dictator killed all around him. The end point is this. If there was collusion it didn't involve that many IRA men being put six feet under. (UVF respondent, North Antrim)

The most common assertion concerning the information received concerns the numbers of individuals killed and the argument that collusion was less commonplace given the status of victims and the randomness of Loyalist violence:

> You see if we had all that information and intelligence that you asked about then why are there so few IRA ones or Shinners lying in their graves? The way people talk you think we were set up to get at them, a lot of shite, a complete lot of shite. You didn't need any help to get at a Catholic. You just went past a peace wall and picked a house, as you were pretty sure you'd get one. Doing that could even mean you would get a Prod who was living with a Catholic, and that tells you a lot about not having the right stuff to get at the IRA. So if we had all the help you think we had then why are there so few IRA men lying in their graves? (UDA respondent, West Belfast)

In challenging the discourse of collusion some respondents clearly understand the issue as one of scale and counter the suggestions made by Sinn Fein and victims' groups through asserting that they lacked information regarding Republican targets. However, the related issues among respondents was never one of complete denial but of scale, security force ability to apprehend and impede Loyalist violence and a sense that collusion was linked in particular to elements within the security forces and groups of Loyalists such as C Company and the Mid-Ulster UVF, who most argue were probably those most implicit in collusive activity.

Information from 'other' sources

In countering or exploring the issue of collusion Loyalists contend that information and intelligence material also came from a variety of sources and in many instances from beyond the security forces and from within the Catholic community. In many instances this was noted as information that came from those disgruntled with the IRA or who had friends or families intimidated by them. In some instance Loyalists allege that precise information on specific targets and the layout of buildings came from friends and family members of Republicans and in some cases from former Republican prisoners. In another instance it was asserted that information was sold and distributed both to Loyalists and Republicans via the same source:

> A police officer was selling information to us and [IRA member name redacted and now deceased] in North Belfast. When we found that out he was selling to [name redacted] we stopped buying the stuff he had … Yeah he had a drink problem, dead now that fellah, his head was done in, a big drink problem was why he was doing it. (UDA respondent, East Belfast)

The extent and validity of such allegations is difficult to gauge with regard to accuracy but it does appear from the following that a peculiar terrain of information gathering came from 'abnormal' but free-flowing sources:

> Catholic people who knew someone like a UDA man's brother or something would ask to speak to someone and would then ask us to get so and so. Usually there was a beating or some abuse of a friend or them or something. I remember hearing about a woman said she'd been raped. Businessmen who were fed up paying money to the IRA and who had been threatened by them would also supply intelligence … Yeah, there were people who was Catholics who told us things. Well that's what I heard anyways. (UDA respondent, Lagan Valley)

In speculating that such interactions may have taken place it is interesting that what could be identified as 'other' community collusion has not been spotlighted as prominently as other forms of it. If such evidence led to attacks or deaths then the issue must be raised regarding why such actions are virtually unknown within public discourse. Therefore, they are either untrue, are only now emerging or there has been an active sense of such information being submerged. Several Loyalist respondents argued that Republicans were aware of such 'treachery,' but had refused to recognise it as it failed to fit into the discursive notion of what collusion is within the Republican narrative.

Collusion as control

A less common theme related to the notion that the supply of too much information aimed to destabilise Loyalist intent and activity via a sense of diversion and using an oversupply of intelligence to, somewhat ironically, slow Loyalist attacks:

> You see the montages they were used to stop us. The soldiers provided that information to us but after a time people was in a way of thinking that they gave us so much that we couldn't get our act together. People had say fifty names and so they looked into the first one and went 'nah that's too hard'. So you went to the next one and the same thing 'nah too hard'. If they had had one or two names they would have gone for them never minding how hard they were to get. So the montages were not as useful as people say, or so I'm told, as they made people spend so much time looking into them. (UDA respondent, East Belfast)

In addition to this there is a conspiratorial notion that information was supplied so that the security forces could determine who Loyalists were and in doing so track the receiver of information. Some Loyalists propose that arrests were affected by the handing out of information and that the persons identified as having received that information were tracked and prosecutions followed. Loyalists also point to the 'dirty tricks' played against them by the security forces in basically two forms. First, certain persons involved in collusion halted, impeded and undermined Loyalist violence and were also prominent in providing the evidence that led to significantly higher than Republican rates of imprisonment. As Bruce (1992: 264) argues:

> Nelson was a UDA man helping the security forces rather than the other way round. His information allowed large number of UDA plans to be subverted while the UDA gained nothing in return.

Second, Loyalists who were involved in steering the organisation away from violence contended that the 'hawks', especially those linked to C Company and the LVF were permitted to engage in nefarious activities such as drugs, prostitution and other forms of illegality and indeed killings. The retired CID detective Johnston Brown, who was to eventually bring Johnny Adair to account by taping him talking about his violent activity has publicly wondered on several occasion 'why the authorities sat on that information for so long'.[15]

Republicans: 'take heed'

Loyalists, when considering collusion, make counter claims against Republicans through asserting that sections within Republican ranks who have not yet been exposed were working for the security forces. Thus they assume that Republicans are invoking an inspection into collusive activity and in so doing may open up a series of accusations and facts concerning their own collaborative activity. In some cases it was alleged that a handful of intended IRA combatant targets were not killed by Loyalists who had observed them in the company of Special Branch or FRU. As explained:

> If I was them I would shut up about all of this. There are more people in their organisation who were touting other than Donaldson, Adam's driver and the Steaknife. I think they are starting to realise they're on a tightrope about this. I don't think they want to push all this stuff as much as the victims groups. I've even heard that said. It's funny when you think they have started something that may bring some of them down. They should take heed of that. (UDA respondent, North Belfast)

A much more serious accusation is that some members of the IRA organised non-aggression pacts with Loyalists once they knew that the latter held precise information about them. This was not a commonplace assertion but the following form of contention was made on several occasions, although the accuracy of it remains open:

> It was like this. I'll give you an example, a case and it's this. The [*group name redacted*] got the intelligence on Republicans and went on to get a good few of them. The [*group name redacted*] in the same area did nothing and they had the same intelligence. You know why they didn't do nothing, it's because the Provisionals approached them, and us too, and said 'if you don't use that informa-tion against us we won't get at you'. We said 'no', the [*group name redacted*] agreed

with them. So there's collusion for you, that's a reality for you. The Provisionals in this area knew what we had and struck a deal to protect themselves with the [*group name redacted*]. (Respondant's details redacted).

Again as with many assertions and propositions it is difficult to prove or corroborate such allegations. However, they are known and stated by Loyalists and utilised to link the IRA into a form of collusion through the notion that they reached agreements with, in certain places, Loyalist leaders in order to insulate themselves from an intensified threat. A more obvious form of inter-organisational collusion relates to Jim Craig, a prominent UDA member known for his criminality and extortion. It is alleged that Craig developed a relationship with both the Irish National Liberation Army (INLA) and with at least two members of the IRA and engineered the deaths of Lennie Murphy, the notorious leader of the Shankill Butchers gang, and a UDA rival in order to overtake his criminal enterprises. It is also contended that he had the firebrand Belfast councillor George Seawright killed with Republican assistance. As stated by the Ed Moloney (2000: 1):

> Craig's fate was sealed when UDA leader John McMichael was killed by an IRA booby trap bomb in his car at Christmas 1987 just before he planned to assassinate the IRA's intelligence chief in Belfast. His death set off a major internal investigation by UDA bosses and the finger was pointed at Craig. He was duly gunned down in an East Belfast pub some months later.
>   The evidence that clinched Craig's assassination was a video tape of Craig meeting his Provisional IRA contact, a man who can now often be seen in Gerry Adams' company[16] up at Stormont. The tape was made by the RUC Special Branch's surveillance unit E4A, two of whose members handed it over to the UDA. Once they saw it the UDA leadership sentenced Craig to death.

If such contentions are true then they have a significant propaganda value for those Loyalists who did not commit to non-aggressive pacts. If untrue they still assert and maintain a significant misinformation value for Loyalists against Republican analysis. Ultimately and at each point the link between sections of loyalism and informants within republicanism points to the part-control linked to Loyalist/security force relationships.

Conclusion

There is no doubt that at some scale certain Loyalists were more fully pro-State activists than others, which brought them into the part-service of State-sponsored violence. Collusion was undoubtedly relative and was practiced more by some and not at all by the majority of others. There was no blanket leadership of Loyalists by the security forces and where collusion did occur it was linked to certain individuals and an understanding that intelligence leaks and direction was accepted as 'necessary' in terms of undermining what they viewed as Republican-based violent cajoling. If collusion was a reality it was directed most at civilian Catholics; again the exact numbers are unknown, but most certainly the minority according to Loyalists.

It is also the case that linkages and signs of collusion made some Loyalists analyse the invocation, practice and maintenance of the social order that they intended to serve. As with their sense of betrayal by unionism, the impact of conflict produced the twin outcomes of imprisonment and rejection. The initial shock of conflict undermined the ability to determine a more feasible identity that understood the complexities of society, political domination (from within) and class consciousness. The shift from being used for 'your muscle' (or, for most, watching others who were) to becoming self-cognitively awoken to the extent that the unity of such purpose was itself questioned is an important conclusion on how transformation pertained. It was in realising that their fetishisation of the State was more imagined than complete and that Unionist unity was less real that the idealised relationship between the State-security pinnacle and the Loyalist base that shared interests began to disentangle. Missing in much of what has been proven or asserted about collusion is that transformative Loyalists were adapting their knowledge and capacity in a more positive manner as they questioned any direction of loyalism by elements external to them. In some instances it was the realisation of some, even if limited, structure of collusion as a form of control that pointed to a different direction.

> I knew we were being sold a pup. That is why I pushed for transformation. We were, and I mean a handful of people, being used. I didn't like that one bit. Me understanding is that it didn't make me less of a Loyalist. It just made me think that the whole situation, in a way of speaking, was a mess. We could only move on if we were independent from outside voices and forces. Most weren't but those who were linked in with the security forces were trouble makers at the end of the day. So I don't think there was that much collusion but among those who were in on it you got the big egos. So that's how you know there wasn't that much of it, as most of the lads weren't strutting about like the handful who were in on the, that collusion thing. (UVF respondent, Lagan Valley)

Notes

1 Sluka states that the New Lodge was the worst place for conflict-related killings. In terms of electoral wards Ardoyne endured more deaths. There were roughly 83 conflict-related deaths in New Lodge and around 109 in Ardoyne. He also adds the killing of Protestants by Loyalists onto the list of Catholic civilian casualties. This is a bizarre construction and omits the fact that the killing of Protestants by Loyalists was more nuanced than assumed. He does not provide any commentary on Protestant civilians who were killed.

2 An event in 1987 when eight IRA members were killed/ambushed during an attempted attack by them upon a police station. There are several theories

regarding this event and the allegation that some of those killed were against the IRA's move towards peace-building and that such persons had been exposed by agents within the Republican movement. The majority of analysis is based upon the actions of the SAS and questions regarding why the eight individuals were not arrested.

3   In 2003 the UVF released a statement on collusion regarding the Dublin and Monaghan bombings in 1974. Part of that statement stated 'throughout the many years of controversy as to who was responsible for the 1974 bombings of Dublin and Monaghan, the UVF continually stated that it planned and executed the operations'. Allegations of collusion were noted as 'sheer fantasy'. Copy of statement held by author.

4   Robin Jackson, a brigadier in the UVF who died in 1998.

5   It could be postulated that Nelson's influence was beyond C Company but that is rarely asserted. It was also commonplace during interviews for Loyalists to assert that Nelson is not dead but living in Canada.

6   Between 1969 and 1994 Loyalists were responsible for the deaths of ten other Republican combatants. This included two from the IPLO, 4 from the INLA and four members of the Official IRA. Of these five were killed in the 1970s, three in the 1980s and two in 1990s. In sum, three were killed by the UDA, six by the UVF and one by an unknown Loyalist.

7   Not long after making these comments Stobie was to die in suspicious circumstances.

8   In 1994 during a televised World Cup game in 1994 between the Republic of Ireland and Italy six civilian Catholics were gunned down by the UVF.

9   Mark Haddock is depicted within UVF circles as a person driven by ego and personal status. He was expelled from the UVF and denied the right to serve on the Loyalist wings whilst imprisoned, a sign of being an outcast. It is also alleged that he was driven by elements intent on encouraging Loyalists back into conflict.

10   In 1978 an IRA incendiary in the La Mon Hotel led to the death of twelve civilians. The IRA claimed that they had tried to make warning calls but had been unable to do so due to a vandalised phone.

11   In 1992 eight Protestant workmen were killed in an IRA bomb attack. They had been targeted as they were construction workers at a nearby security base.

12   In 1972 nine civilians, both Catholic and Protestant, were killed in a series of explosions. The IRA denied involvement but the Police Ombudsman's Office stated in 2010 the attacks had been conducted by a local priest and IRA quartermaster. They also alleged that the police investigation had been undermined in order to non-identify the priest's involvement as it would have spawned a more vehement Loyalist backlash.

13   In 1990 Patsy Gillespie was forced by the IRA to drive a bomb into an army checkpoint. He and five soldiers were killed. A Catholic, he had worked in a canteen in an army base and had been described by the IRA as part of the 'British war machine'.

14   In 1981 census worker Joanne Mathers was killed in Derry. The IRA had demanded the non-completion of census forms. Mrs Mathers was a mother aged twenty-nine.

15   http://cpgb.org.uk/article.php?article_id=379 (last accessed 8 November 2011).

16   The person is probably Denis Donaldson who was exposed as a State informant and killed in 2006.

*When I read the Belfast Agreement I
went howl [hold] on a wee minute. We
wrote the likes of that in the 70s. I laughed
and thought it took twenty odd years for
everyone to become a Loyalist.
(RHC respondent)*

3 Idea-building and the beginning of Loyalist transformation

With regard to identity shifts that would be required to sustain conflict transformation Bruce (2004: 502) advanced the idea that when Loyalists moved out of violence, 'they gave up far more of the identity that had sustained them for 25 years than did Republicans'. The implication and meaning of this interpretation is a crucial starting point in realising that transition is more problematic for groups such as Loyalists, when their beliefs and ideas have been linked to a wider supposition, however imagined, that they existed in order to aid wider hegemonic group interests and in so doing undermined their capacity to locate an independent and socially radical voice. The issue was not that Loyalists did not have discourses for peace and transformation, but that these had been submerged by the rise in Loyalist violence in the early 1990s and various internal and external obstacles that operated against radical cognition within.

The juxtaposition with regard to Irish Republican achievements is illustrative of the problems that Loyalists have encountered. In crude psychological terms Irish Republicanism was centred on and gained certain achievements. IRA violence led to the collapse of the Stormont regime and the Hunger Strikes led to international odium being directed at the British State (Bew et al. 1979; Bew at al. 1995). The British State's strategy of normalisation and the eventual delivery of fair employment legislation were paralleled by social mobility among significant sections of the nationalist community and the evolution of Sinn Fein as the dominant political representatives of Irish nationalism in Northern Ireland. On the other hand, working-class Protestant communities witnessed the removal of 'their' State and the ascendant direction politically, culturally and socially of the nationalist community. The relative certainties of labour market access have been torn asunder by de-industrialisation and the emergence of a flexible economy has provided limited access to those who are 'under-educated'.

In territorial terms there has been a shrinkage of 'Protestant' space in certain places, due to demographic flight and the creation of communities in which the remaining populations are increasingly residualised and structured by aging, welfare dependence and low socially mobility. This has occurred in some areas to such an extent that the reproduction of some communities in terms of demography and facilities is increasingly difficult. In evaluating such change there is a dichotomy between understanding, via an ethno-sectarian frame, the idea that turmoil, crisis and collapse is centred upon 'pefidious' Albion and its concessions to Republicans and the alternative understanding that such processes are linked to the realities of globalisation, technological change and outward migration due to standard forms of social mobility in the 1960s and 1970s. This is not to deny that violence did not promote out-migration and that urban policies undermined neighbourhoods (Kingsley 1989), but as a senior UVF member noted:

> The role of a Loyalist is to say what is true and not like the DUP to say things that people want to hear, like it's the fault of the IRA. There are many reasons why our communities are in decline, and as a Loyalist it is my place to say why I think so. That can mean me saying 'it's the fault of Unionists who look down their noses at us, it's our fault as we never challenged our betters'. It's as much our fault because we don't do enough for ourselves, it's because of wider social, society like changes. If I was to say it was the fault of Sinn Fein, what people here want to hear, then I wouldn't be a Loyalist, I wouldn't be telling the truth. (UVF respondent, Strangford)

Such commentary promotes a discourse of being 'duped' by the State and political unionism and that Loyalists erroneously served the interest of 'the people' who generally rejected (in public at least) their violence. It is also evident that positive and progressive loyalists have rejected the discourses of sectarianism and fortified notions of homogenously defined unionism. This shift was based upon an appreciation of the complexities of societal shifts and that reductionist ideas, especially when they were tied to ethno-sectarian narratives and readings, did not permit or indeed promote intra-community connection. If we accept that the Protestant community's sense of Britishness is grounded in emotion and sentiment (Southern 2005, 2007) and not simply in the production of considerations that merely amount to supremacism[1] then progressive Loyalist discourse must be understood via an alternative set of connotations and construction. Part of that shift was required to stretch beyond the following nexus:

> The 'constitutional issue' – the supposed threat to the very existence of the State – was therefore crucial not simply in terms of mobilising the population against the IRA but as a means by which the Unionist bourgeoisie waged the class struggle against its own proletariat. Throughout the history of the State the Unionist Party would use the threat of the constitution as an ever-present reason why Protestant workers should put loyalism before class interests.[2] (Patterson 1982: 29)

Given the severity of criminalisation set against Loyalists there is a general rejection that loyalism constitutes a valid and constructive vocabulary or set of ideas. If there is an acceptance of a positive Loyalist vocabulary it tends to refer to the period around the ceasefires of 1994 and the presentation of some Loyalists as peacemakers. Neither perspective suffices as they fail not only to recognise the nature of Loyalist discursive construction but also the longevity of Loyalist ideas. It must also be remembered:

> At the same time, conflicts can also be the source of creative thinking and of the development of new ideas, new technologies, or new forms of social interaction ... (Barak 2005: 140)

There is an intricate relationship within loyalism linked to moving onward and the signs and practices of internally and externally rendered rejection. As noted by Billy Mitchell:

> We have people who don't want to move on. These people relish the rejection by outsiders of progressive loyalism. The thinkers within loyalism are rejected by elements within their own organisations and by virtually everybody else. We are rejected because of our past, because we challenge middle unionism, because we demand change for all of the people. All of this rejection aims keeps us out of civil society. It is a case that progressive Loyalists simply and always swim against the tide. (Billy Mitchell, former UVF prisoner)

Within academic deliberation there is a more solid recognition of the potential for progressive Loyalist thinking and action:

> Obviously it cannot be known at present how this process will turn out and what political form new loyalism will ultimately take. But in its organisational work as well as its class-based ideology, new loyalism fundamentally challenges the legitimacy of the Unionist ruling elites. Ideologically and organisationally these community activists seek to promote a class consciousness, and in so doing aim to alter the current power relationships in the Unionist community. (Cassidy 2008: 412)

The rationality of progressive loyalism has been in its attempts to articulate and practice non-exclusive discourses that aim to evolve former combatants into what Habermas (1992) termed 'responsible participants'. The creation of such persons is reliant upon a political and community formation that rejects mono-cultural declaration and purpose and instead seeks truth in determining the cause of asperity, poverty and social exclusion. In that sense that requires no longer relying upon blaming Irish Republicans for Loyalist ills. Therefore, progressive Loyalist validity claims must rely upon factual bases as opposed to ethno-sectarian conjecture. As Habermas (1992: 314) contended, those persons who aim to transform their dialectical intent must locate an 'obligatory moment of accepted validity' and when doing so become the 'carriers of a context-bound everyday practice'. Within that context Loyalists would be required to work on a base of reasoned and evidenced-centred 'social-pragmatic transformation'.

Early ideas

As early as 12 July 1977 Gusty Spence's speech as the UVF's OC in Long Kesh articulated a sophisticated series of ideas concerning the futility of violence and overt ethno-sectarianism and the promotion of political power-sharing. Spence's verbalisation of a progressive and thoughtful loyalism was contingent upon the expression that persecution in whatever form merely furthered and conditioned the sources and resonances of sectarian disputation and that the concept of freedom was erroneous if it was pursued at the expense of the 'other' community. For Spence it was fear and mutual misunderstanding between communities that drove sectarian violence and asperity. Part of the reasoning that has remained within progressive loyalism is the nature of critical intro-spection and the labelling of negative discourses and practices within; a feature that is somewhat unique to it within the Northern Ireland context. As Spence asserted:

> Even yet we still have men nonsensically counselling that victory is just around the corner. Victory over whom – the IRA? Or do they mean victory over the Roman Catholic community? … The fears of Roman Catholics will not go away because bigoted Unionist politicians say so.[3]

Spence divided loyalism into those who understood the vagaries of conflict and a loyalism 'plagued with super-Loyalists', the latter denying the rationale of peacemaking and accommodation and choosing to label those who aimed to effect ideas of transformation as either 'taig-lovers' or 'communists'. The charge of 'reds under the beds' was utilised by mainstream Unionists to undermine progressive thinking. In July 1987 *Combat* (1987), a magazine produced by the UVF, presented an article entitled 'Booked any Good Reds Lately' which focused upon an article by the Rev. Martin Smyth, then MP and Orange Order Grand Master, that had appeared in that year's 'Twelfth' Booklet. Smyth had condemned an article in the *Morning Star* (Whitfield1987) in which the PUP had stated 'if peace was to break out tomorrow, the biggest enemies of the Loyalist working class would be Paisley and Molyneaux'.[4] In response to this the PUP asserted the following:

> Historically the Unionist working class were always used and abused by the Unionist Tories and capitalists and contemptuously discarded and ignored when they served their purpose of putting an 'X' at the appropriate Unionist candidate and when difficult to cuckold were branded as communists! … this is not the first time this person has adopted innuendo to smear people who have at long last, realised that socialism and loyalism are not incompatible …(*Combat* 1987).

Within the progressive Loyalist context it was determined that the political leadership that came from the DUP and UUP had abused and misused loyalism in a concert of ethno-sectarian positioning. Transformative Loyalists, in the 1970s, issued a firmament of Loyalist consciousness which aimed to expose the hierarchical and caustic nature of Unionist leadership, challenging Unionist orthodoxy. No longer being used as pawns to uphold ethno-sectarian unionism was an avowed direction that Spence wished Loyalists to follow. Ahead of other politicised groups at that time, Spence encouraged and predicted that:

> Eventually Loyalist and Republican must sit down together for the good of our country. Dialogue will have to come about sometime, so why not now? There is no victory in Ulster, not for the IRA, or the UVF, the police or the army. There is only victory for humanity and common sense.[5]

Such commentary and vision may seem counterintuitive but it had enough currency to lead to a significant reduction, up to the Anglo-Irish Agreement, in Loyalist violence. That does not deny that ethno-sectarian violence did not continue or that 'super-Loyalists' did not remain. However, what this and the work of the UDA around *Beyond the Religious Divide?*[6] (New Ulster Political Research Group 1979) and *Common Sense* (Ulster Democratic Party (UDP) 1987) achieved was a novel sense of disputed loyalty that was not simply linked to the idea that the State was insufficient with regard to undermining Republican violence. These Loyalists aimed to challenge their powerlessness in class terms, develop an alternative Unionist discourse and reject elements that urged an upholding of an ethno-sectarian agenda. Part of that consciousness-raising was linked to Loyalists feeling abandoned when imprisoned by those 'who had egged us on and never went to prison' (UVF respondent, North Belfast), the realisation that pan-unionism was a myth in class terms and an appreciation of the suffering in social, cultural and violent terms that was also endured by the Catholic working class – thus, the Catholic community deserved equal rights and Loyalists should assert the requirement of power-sharing. Such Loyalists placed themselves at odds with Republicans who rejected such overtones as merely concerning the 'reform' of an irreformable State as well as Unionist leaders who preferred majority rule.

Peculiarly, and despite the possession of an extensive ethno-sectarian baggage, progressive Loyalists fashioned an image of the Belfast Agreement. Somewhat ironically the Loyalist notion of a rehabilitated State was rejected by all those political actors and agents who now govern and administer Northern Ireland, via a similar architecture of governance. This is not to romanticise transformative Loyalist discourse, but what the opinions and documents produced by progressive Loyalists highlighted was that the pathol-ogisation of loyalism was limited and that rejection of such ideas by the electorate, republicanism and unionism possibly undermined the potential for an earlier peace process. As Billy Mitchell contended:

We called for peace in a negotiated manner. The Provisionals just rejected us and the rest called us deluded. The rejection by the Provisionals of us was sectarian. It was simply a united Ireland or nothing. They didn't see Unionists as equals and didn't accept our constitutional rights. It was them who could have jumped into the peace-building. If the IRA had taken us seriously a lot of people wouldn't have died. They just couldn't see that we were talking about equality and working-class unity. They just couldn't see strength in that unity. I know it was all complicated but at that time some of us were in advance of them in terms of ideas. At the time I used to wonder if they had any ideas at all. At times I just wondered if anybody had any ideas at all except for us.

These Loyalist thinkers were:

given space to try the political thing but it just failed. That space was the big reduction in the killing. But once Thatcher brought in the Anglo-Irish Agreement you may have just torn all of that up. (Senior UDA respondent, South Belfast)

Positive and inclusive Loyalist discourse was to ebb and flow in terms of influence but it was to become the chosen route to explain and sustain the Loyalist ceasefire and the subsequent input into the Belfast Agreement and succeeding conflict transformation initiatives and instruments.

Transformative Loyalist discourse

In broad terms the positive Loyalist thinking and identity formation that emerged in the 1970s was loosely tied to the concept that Loyalist violence was legitimate, in terms of the threat of Irish unification, but had at times served the erroneous leadership of vocal Unionist leaders. This was coupled with a requirement to expose the nature of social dislocation and challenge a unionism disinterested in the plight of the socially excluded. As Patterson explains:

The UDA, although clearly having its origins as a unification of vigilante groups in working class districts of Belfast, was very early articulating the traditional populist message that the Protestant masses had been betrayed by the 'fur-coat brigade'. (1982: 31)

Therefore, challenging insufficient and worsening socio-economic conditions was no longer disloyal and did not serve Republican agendas as the attainment of any accommodation with Republicanism had to maintain the constitutional position of Northern Ireland. As noted by David Ervine:

Gusty Spence and others started what was to become the peace process. It was the way he spelt out how we had been manipulated that was key for me and learning new ideas. That came back to me when I was in talks that led to the Belfast Agreement and a certain person was doing that usual rejectionist thing and I pointed out to him that we needed a peace process as we were the ones who were harmed and intimidated and beleaguered. It was OK for them sitting up in a leafy suburb or wherever and being in a world so far away from the one we lived in. It took me back to the learning we did in prison. It was the same old rejectionism from the fur coat and 'I never get harmed' brigade, who wanted us to carry the can and live in poverty. It was the aul 'dupes no more' that came to my mind. (Interview 2005)

By the time of the peace negotiations that led to the Belfast Agreement, thinking Loyalists had determined the need to locate a space for their own version of loyalism and one within which Unionist leaders could no longer encourage violence in private and deny such utterances in public. As Andy Tyrie noted when interviewed:

> Part of me being a Loyalist was about challenging unionism. You have to remember that we not only wanted to stop Republicans but a lot of us weren't happy with how unionism operated. The way you got the best jobs if you were in the Orange or the Masons or something like that. We knew that we were treated by our own people in ways we didn't like. It was a hard one as we wanted an end to discrimination to, but the priority was to fight Republicanism first. So we had all sorts in with us and hundreds of opinions and ideas and ways of thinking and ideas about what we should do.

What Tyrie indicates is that loyalism was a collective that stretched discursively from the labourite, even socialist, to the right-wing ethno-sectarian. Loyalism was thus in its initial stages a paramilitary campaign that invoked the constitutional threat as the *modus operandi*. In defending the union there was a central discursive frame that rallied an eclectic group. therefore ideas that upheld transformation and power-sharing were undermined by internal and external friction. In terms of designing a non-sectarian and pluralist discourse loyalism was unlike Republicanism. There were similarities in that both movements contained peaceniks and militarists, but they were dissimilar in that Irish nationalism, more broadly defined, wanted and demanded Republican transformation, whereas certain Unionist leaders viewed progressive forms of loyalism as communistic, ecumenist-driven and centred upon concession-making and thus betrayal. In effect, thoughtful and enquiring Loyalists were cut adrift from supportive external agencies and pan-Unionist acceptance. Nearly forgotten is that Loyalists were at the forefront of demanding a written constitution and have continued to challenge the antagonism of mainstream Unionists to human rights and equality-driven legislation. Such persons understood that preserving the union had to be centred upon Northern Ireland becoming an equality-driven and thus attractive – in comparison with the Republic of Ireland – society in which to live. For progressives the experience of conflict threw up a milieu of questioning and the non-acceptance of belligerent and hostile unionism.

The emergence of positive Loyalist discourses should not be considered as a shift from a Protestant fundamentalist rhetoric toward an appreciation of pluralist ideas given that many of its originators came from trade union, labourist and even inter-community backgrounds. A main current within initial progressive Loyalist ideas was that the conflict was predominantly centred upon a civil war that was being reproduced by deluded rabble rousers (Garland 2001). Such a discourse also acknowledged that identities were multiply constructed. As Finlayson (1999) demonstrates, such persons were devoted to a re-evaluation of history which included a discourse of fidelity that had been met with alienation and in which those opposed were not only Republicans but also the Unionist elite or those Unionists, such the DUP, who sought to undermine peace initiatives that were centred upon the realisation of social equality for the working classes. That narrative was set to subvert previous readings of devotion, belonging and fealty to the British/Unionist bourgeois establishment (Coulter 1994, 1999a, 1999b). Somewhat ironically some of the people involved in brutal sectarian acts were now accepting that such acts were, as noted by one UVF member:

> No longer necessary, if they ever were. By the late 70s for me the war was over, as it should have been a long time before that. There was no need to return to it as we had been directed by people whose interests weren't ours anymore. I just felt abandoned by it, to it all. The Republicans didn't want to negotiate and the bigots wanted to fight on. These people were fernenst (against) moving on in a different way. Me and others just felt squeezed by it all. All I wanted was to live in Northern Ireland and to share it with my Catholic neighbours. But no one listened and that's why I went enough no more. (UVF respondent, Fermanagh and South Tyrone)

The class-consciousness that arose within sections of loyalism was certainly detectable in the early 1970s, and its emergence was important in that it emerged out of ethno-sectarian construction, but as Finlayson contends:

> it is necessary to leave behind the *a priori* assumption that class should have been the organising principle of popular political movements in Ulster. (Finlayson 1999: 48)

As a motivating principle for political action, class had generally been subservient to the politics of ethno-sectarian asperity. Not surprisingly the somewhat socialist line promoted by the PUP, with its obvious inter-community overtones, has been responsible for their electoral limitations (Bruce 2001). Again, the reason for the stifling of progressive Loyalist discourse can be understood within the context of wider developments and Unionist fears. As noted by a UDA member from Foyle:

> You are thinking about class and the way we was controlled by big house unionism and Paisley's anger. You knew what class you were and that the people above you wanted you there. But here in the city the Prods were fleeing the cityside in droves. So you weren't going t' say 'we must understand our class position'. Were you?

Mines [my] opinion, is that just would ah been have been daft. Wans [people] around here weren't wanting to hear that. It was all about the Provies and the fear and the intimidation. There was no space for saying what you thought.

The Ulster Workers' Council (UWC) strike in 1974 typified the heterogeneity of Loyalist agency. Those involved included William Craig, leader of the Ulster Vanguard movement that typified a right-wing challenge to reform, Ian Paisley with his evangelical populist bandwagon, and Glenn Barr who adopted a variant class position to both and who supported power-sharing. All three were merely united by a desire to undermine the Council of Ireland. As Barr noted at a conference on 19 November 2010 at Queen's University Belfast:

> Some were for power-sharing and others not. But we were all against the Council of Ireland. That meant you had all types of opinions within the UWC strike.

The experience, for example, of operationalising such an ideologically defective trinity of leadership encouraged some Loyalists to begin to explore their own experiences of the conflict and their role in the reproduction of it. Such self-introspection also began along an axis of wonderment regarding why loyalty to the status quo had led to criminalisation and Unionist abandonment. As noted by a UVF member from Upper Bann:

> The first night that I was locked up I was praised by the prison officers for what I had done. My first thought is that they were more sectarian than me, the second was I was less sectarian than them and they were the ones locking me away.

Such corroboration for Loyalist activity by those 'locking you away' testified to a conundrum in which the meaning of the term Loyalist had obvious and inherent contradictions. Loyalty, for progressive Loyalist thinkers, led to obvious confusion in that stepping outside of the law was punishable whereas making speeches that arose ethno-sectarian animosity was not. Therefore, the sense that defending Northern Ireland's constitutional position was merely legitimate if asserted by the State and mainstream Unionists broke for some the whole body politic of Unionist synchronisation. The testing of the allegory of Unionist solidarity and subsequent imprisonment was a manifest consideration regarding to whom loyalty was owed. For progressives it was increasing owed to themselves and there was no longer a co-joining between them and the mainstream Unionist leadership. As noted by a former UDA prisoner:

> I thought I was protecting the Protestant people as the people wanted. Then I was locked up and told the people didn't want that and we was just plain criminals. So I had to ask myself 'why did I do that?' I thought it was for the greater good and I was told it was and that's what I thought Paisley was saying. Then I started to think if Paisley wanted that to happen then he should put his sons into the paramilitaries and let them go to prison … We were just cannon fodder to these people, that's what they wanted us to be. In our place doing their biddin' when they sat at home with their families. (UDA respondent, Lagan Valley)

Emerging documents and statement made by sections of the main Loyalist paramilitary groups in the late 1970s reflected upon the causality of violence, the potential for inter-community dialogue and the requirement to challenge sterile ethno-sectarian politics. Loyalists advanced novel ideas concerning a Bill of Rights, a written constitution and a far-reaching form of electoral proportionality to a devolved assembly, as solutions to the problem of majority rule in a contested society. Despite the earlier rejection of the Council of Ireland Loyalists also furthered the idea of meaningful cross-border relationships with the Republic of Ireland on mutually agreed terms. Furthermore, Loyalists felt aggrieved that when meeting with the Official and Provisional IRA they had been capable of brokering a short-term ceasefire in 1975. The collapse of that ceasefire, by Republicans, was according to senior Loyalists a further undermining of their efforts to shift the conflict into non-violent confrontation. Again this led to a sense among progressive elements that only they were viewing peace-building as a serious strategy. It is difficult to think of any other group of thinkers within Northern Ireland who have been so constrained, over such a sustained period, by both internal and external factors and commentary. While Loyalist thinkers thought of controlling their own destiny via organic intellectualism and designed more suitable narratives that would lead to peace, others remained active and awaited the 'defeat' of the IRA, something that transitional Loyalists appreciated was not going to come about.

The UDA also tinkered with the idea of an independent Ulster as an alternative within which 'Ulster Catholics' and 'Ulster Protestants' would evolve a power-sharing administration based upon the uniqueness of Ulster (although in fact the boundaries of Northern Ireland) culture, identity and custom. For the UDA members who pursued such an idea trust was no longer 'there in English secretaries of State who lied to us over and over again' (Andy Tyrie, interview). Concerns over perfidious Albion may have been a factor in the construction of a discourse of independence, but the central logic of what was being advanced was a recognition of some willingness and more importantly requirement to secure the confidence of the minority community in a shared and agreed political settlement. The rejection of such a plan by Republicans was centred upon their requirement for Irish self-determination but it was recognition on the part of Loyalists that not all were opposed to power-sharing both conceptually and in practice. However, as Andy Tyrie noted when interviewed:

> Some of the younger DUP and Ulster Unionists were impressed at our thinking, but the older ones saw it is a compromise and simply as a threat. They were dead set against us and made sure others were to.

Admittedly not all Loyalists subscribed to such ideas, but the suppression and rejection of a developed consciousness that was beyond the usual script of ethno-sectarian meta-narrative and quasi-intellectual drivel indicated the fear that such cognition induced, especially among clueless and unthinking Unionists. There was a narrow space into which progressive Loyalist ideas could emerge and that was ultimately further narrowed by criminality and growing racketeering, extortion and as the conflict drew on, drug dealing and prostitution (McAuley 2004; Silke 1998b, 2000). As Jackie McDonald surmised when interviewed;

> When I got out of prison I went to the Taughmonagh Club and the music came on. I looked around and all these young people were dancing and bobbing up and down. They were on drugs. What had happened to loyalism? There was a cancer inside that had to be rooted out.

A more developed argument that has been pursued by Graham Spencer (2004, 2008) is that the military strategy was always the primary focus of paramilitary loyalism. However, as noted previously, Loyalist violence dipped significantly in the 1980s although there was at times an uneasy relationship between the militarists and progressive elements. As Edwards (2009: 153) suggests, the 'truth is that the political instrument has always played a secondary role in the UVF's strategy'. However, the notion of the UVF's 'Kitchen Cabinet' constantly working on ideas and approaches is more symptomatic of Loyalist evolution, and for some the politicisation of those with influence within the UVF was not as leadership constrained as the undermining by 'the rednecks who simply wanted to get at Catholics' (UVF respondent, West Belfast).

The identification of positive and progressive strains within Loyalist thinking as far back as the 1970s raises an interesting question: to what extent can we speak of a 'new' loyalism (Cassidy 2008; McAuley 2002, 2004, 2005; McAuley and Hislop 2000; Mitchell 2003)? If the concept of 'new' is to be measured at the level of progressive ideas circulating within paramilitary organisations about what contributions they might be able to make toward resolving the Northern Ireland conflict then, arguably, there is not much that was novel post-1994. To present the more public face of progressive loyalism as somehow 'new' (although this is not exactly the point McAuley made) after 1994 undermines the character and complexity of loyalism and renders such newness as somehow artificial and without a distinct lineage. The reality that progressive spokespersons were equipped, despite many limitations, to come to the fore after the IRA ceasefire of August 1994 presents a case of long-term preparedness, probably even hope. When the CLMC declared its ceasefire in October of the same year, a far from minimised form of progressive loyalism appeared and permitted Sinnerton (2002: 7) to conclude that what emerged was not 'new' despite the appearances:

> In the wake of the Loyalist ceasefire of October 1994, many were surprised, and some astonished, by the appearance as if from nowhere of a new personable breed of spokesmen, open-minded, down-to-earth and capable of expressing their

unionism free of the banalities and grating clichés which merely encouraged audiences to turn away.

Accepting change

There is no quantifiable evidence regarding how previous ideas and present approaches to conflict transformation are either greeted or received within the Loyalist body politic. What is known is that the practices of conflict transformation are being outplayed, that those who are in charge of the main paramilitary groups support peace-building and negotiation and that their intention is to undermine a return to violence. Without doubt the ideas presented by Loyalists over some thirty years were the backbone of a peace strategy that was evidenced during peace discussions after 1994. As early as 1975 the UVF were arguing for a 'declaration of intent to forsake the gun (at least for a spell) in favour of dialogue' (*Combat* 1975). The desire for dialogue was not simply based upon negotiation between combatants but evidently was linked to a strong and, what was to become, endurable sense that loyalism was being manipulated by:

> … emotionally unstable and bigoted element within Loyalist circles. As a political leadership they are a sick joke – a mixture of inane [sic] hacks and power hungry clerics who would not recognise the truth if it kicked them in the face. These are the men who have cunningly and purposefully fused religion with politics and festered fear amongst the Loyalist community for their own designs and to regain power. (*Combat* 1995)

Again the depth of the hostility towards the DUP was not, as McAuley (2004: 528) explains via the commentary of Cusack and McDonald (1997), an 'already harbored mistrust about parties like the DUP' that 'after 1985 were transformed into deep hostility'. Both the leadership of the UDA, especially after the UWC strike, and the UVF had held such antipathies to the DUP more than a decade before and had operationalised them in their attack against Loyalist dupery. In his Remembrance Day speech in 1977 Gusty Spence delivered a further reconciliatory and anti-sectarian call that acknowledged the requirement for compromise and recognition of the futility of violence. He detected, long before mainstream Unionists were to acknowledge it, that the Union had been secured and that the IRA had failed. As stated:

> The war situation in Northern Ireland has changed dramatically and requires serious and radical re-appreciation on the part of the para-militaries. Further violence is useless and counter-productive since the aim of the Loyalists of self-determination has been achieved. There is a need now for reconciliation with our neighbours whose aspirations differ from ours. Negotiation and dialogue can fill the vacuum of violence. It will take courage of course and will mean give-and-take

on both sides, but I am confident that with honesty and good will a breakthrough can be achieved in our present polarisation log jam. We must have more resolution in the pursuit of peace than we have in the pursuit of violence. (*Combat* 1977: 4).

In parallel with such developments the UDA developed a series of ideas concerning an agreed settlement. *Beyond the Religious Divide*, published in 1979, promoted Ulster independence and a constitutional arrangement centred upon the main communities accepting the commonality of an Ulster identity and the removal of British and Irish forms of constitutional sovereignty. As pleaded:

> We need to create a system of government, an identity and a nationality to which both sections of the community can aspire. We must look for the common denominator. The only common denominator that the Ulster people have, whether they be Catholic or Protestant, is that they are Ulstermen. And that is the basis from which we should build the new life for the Ulster people, a new identity for them. Awaken them to their own identity. That they are different. That they're not second-class Englishmen but first-class Ulstermen. And that's where my loyalty is. (New Ulster Political Research Group 1979: 2)

Bruce (2001: 33) commented upon the document's structural proposals for government:

> The proposed constitution was modelled on that of the United States. ably of academic and professional people rather than of professional politicians. The cabinet would be answerable to committees drawn from an elected legislature. There would be a detailed bill of rights and a judiciary responsible for safeguarding civil liberties.

The UDA's next venture into conflict resolution came in 1987 in the form of *Common Sense*[7] (Ulster Democratic Party 1987). This document was a reaction to the Anglo-Irish Agreement of 1985 and the onset of Unionist angst and a growth in Loyalist violence, due to fears regarding the removal of Northern Ireland's constitutional position. The preface to *Common Sense* points to the problems caused by the Anglo-Irish Agreement:

> At the time of writing we are suffering yet another Ulster constitutional crisis, this time provoked by the Anglo-Irish Agreement. Violence, intercommunity strife, polarisation and uncertainty are all at a higher level than at any time for almost a decade. The 'accord' will not bring peace, stability nor reconciliation to Northern Ireland because it is a contract between two governments and not an agreement between those in the cockpit of the conflict — Ulster Protestants and Ulster Catholics. (Ulster Democratic Party 1987: 1)

A key component in both *Common Sense* and UVF statements of that time echoed John Paul Lederach's (1997) contention that a sustainable peace requires grassroots involvement as a crucial accompaniment to the efforts of political elites and leading figures in civil society (Racioppi and O'Sullivan See 2007). In what has the appearance of a document committed to interpreting the complex ethno-sectarian matrix *Common Sense* upheld the notion that the UDA's role was not sectarian in a religious sense but assembled around the fears of Irish unification:

> Ulster 'Protestants' do not fear nor mistrust Ulster 'Catholics' because they are Catholics but because they believe them to be Irish Nationalists — fifth columnists — uncommitted citizens, intent on the destruction of Northern Ireland in pursuit of a united CATHOLIC-GAELIC-IRISH NATIONALIST-REPUBLIC. (Ulster Democratic Party 1987: 1)

Therefore, the outcome of such thinking was that:

> Ulster Loyalists live in a State of eternal siege; a people instinctively driven by the overpowering need to defend the frontiers against the enemy without, and to suppress the enemy within. (Ulster Democratic Party 1987: 1)

In turn, Catholics are thought to misinterpret Protestant concerns and anxieties and lamentably consider them to be desirous of Unionist hegemony and political control:

> Ulster 'Catholics' generally believe that Ulster 'Protestants' wish to preserve an ascendancy society; a religious and political hierarchy from which they are excluded, or 'alienated', for no apparent reason other than that they are Catholics (the symptoms of mistrust and uncertainty are mistaken for bigotry and intransigence). A situation which 'Catholics' resent bitterly, and have increasingly demonstrated that resentment. (Ulster Democratic Party 1987: 1)

Thus the UDA presented the notion that ethno-sectarianism was an ever-repeating cycle of Protestant defensiveness and Catholic disaffection that could only be resolved by removing the constitutional claim over Northern Ireland, creating the conditions of a Republican ceasefire, safeguarding power-sharing and endorsing equality centred legislation – what Jackie McDonald calls 'the Belfast Agreement for slow learners' (interview with author). In sum, *Common Sense* called for a:

> Devolved legislative government for Northern Ireland and a written constitution. A set of constitutional laws, agreed by Ulster Catholics and Protestants together which would lay the foundations on which to build a new progressive democracy. An agreement instituted by Ulster people at referendum which can only be changed by Ulster people at referendum. (Ulster Democratic Party 1987: 4)

Common Sense was no sooner published than, not unexpectedly, it was subjected to criticism. Mark Langhammer and David Young (1987: 14) were soon to argue that it:

would be easy to make too much of this apparent shift in UDA attitudes, not least because the UDA is not primarily an organisation geared toward the development of new forms of political thought.

There is a utopian slant which underlines Langhammer and Young's cautioning against the UDA proposals because it was insufficient to cause people to be represented as 'socialists, liberals, conservatives or communists' (1987: 14). But *Common Sense* was a document emerging during conflict and was challenging the orthodoxy of violence and the reproduction of ethno-sectarian relations. It may, like the Belfast Agreement, have institutionalised ethno-sectarian politics but it was an attempt to direct conflict into a transformative phase. Critics of *Common Sense* did not go unchallenged. Leading UDA member, John McMichael, stressed that 'Common Sense is an attempt to face up to the situation, identify the fundamental issues and address them pragmatically' (1987: 12). The main thrust of the document was to create a settlement capable of tackling the problem of Protestant anxiety about the constitutional position of Northern Ireland and Catholic disaffection regarding a State that was felt to offer them little. But given such criticisms as Langhammer and Young's and their concern about the fossilisation of ethnic politics in Northern Ireland, McMichael referred to the relative success of the Northern Ireland Labour Party before the onset of conflict.[8] The *Common Sense* authors' argument was that its recommendations would create an opportunity for class politics to gain a foothold with the possibility of a remodelling of the voting preferences of Protestant and Catholic alike. Previously, and ahead of most Unionists, McMichael also noted that 'it's essential that we work closely with the South [Republic of Ireland] especially in agriculture and tourism, as things which would be of economic benefit to us both' (Rowthorn 1981: 28).

The importance of these two documents most probably lies in a complex matrix of underpinning later initiatives after 1994. However, significance also lay in its rejection and the failure of it to further the UDA's political ambitions. The vacuum created by the rejection of this political venture and the removal of its architects led to a sustained level of violence. The rejection of *Common Sense* still provokes a sense of a lost opportunity:

> The Provies just rejected our thinking again. We were exposing ourselves as afraid and even sectarian. We wanted the Troubles to stop. We felt that we were wearing our heart on our sleeves. We were prepared to question ourselves and it did us little good. Republicans could never do what we did, they could never question themselves. They were more like Paisley in that way of thinking. The ones who won the peace were the ones who never questioned themselves and that's why the way things has turned out. They didn't change they just grabbed the opportunities. You just have two big blocs who really don't want to share this place with each other. No, not one bit. So you asked about a lesson. What I learnt was that if you were genuine and asked yourself difficult questions it just made you into a person

who would never get elected. If you hid behind lies and said 'I am perfect' then the voters liked that. So the war was won by the liars. (UDA respondent, East Belfast)

In 1981, a year that witnessed Republicanism making its first serious political advances in Northern Ireland for several decades, the PUP made a presentation to Northern Ireland Secretary of State, Jim Prior, which discussed the party's desire for a devolved administration. The plan was fourfold: paramilitary organisations should call a ceasefire; troops should be withdrawn to barracks; the RUC should be accepted as a legitimate police force by all people in Northern Ireland; and subject to the previous three conditions being met, an all-party conference should commence which was inclusive of those political parties that were established before 6 October 1981. The PUP suggested, some seventeen years before the Belfast Agreement, that cross-border cooperation was acceptable in relation to tourism, fisheries, energy and agriculture. In addition, the PUP argued for a shared democracy that would allow 'military organisations the opportunity to pursue their aims through political persuasion and not through force of arms' (1981: 2). This in the same year that Ian Paisley was promoting the idea of a 'Third Force' to tackle Republicanism and arranged an unsuccessful day of action to undermine the governance of Northern Ireland. As Paisley was so doing the PUP accepted that the British government was not able to defeat the IRA militarily – an acknowledgement which when voiced eight years later by Secretary of State, Peter Brooke, ignited Unionist anger – furthering the reality that Loyalists were more cognisant of certain undeniable realities. As the PUP had argued:

> The Provisionals cannot win and attain their main objective. The British Government can never achieve a 100 per cent military defeat of the Provisional IRA and their support groups ... they are in a stalemate situation. (1981: 2)

In 1984 representatives of the PUP met the then Secretary of State Douglas Hurd and presented a Bill of Rights for Northern Ireland which was rejected because the proposal would affect government policy for all of the UK. The PUP's advocacy of a political instead of military approach to deal with the Northern Ireland problem is interesting in terms of strategic approaches to countering violence and the acceptance of Sinn Fein as a legitimate – if IRA violence was to stop – political party. As with the UDA, the PUP remained

> totally opposed to the undemocratic formation of a new unitary Irish State without a referendum of the people of Northern Ireland. (PUP 1985a: 1)

The peacemaking and reconciliatory component of the PUP's 1985 manifesto was also evident and was articulated as follows:

> We have maintained for many years now, that it is possible to obtain peace and reconciliation in our community. But it must commence IN THE COMMUNITY amongst the representatives of ALL on a totally non-sectarian basis. This offer of

'agreeing to differ' on the constitutional issue has already brought a system of cross-chamber voting within City Councils, certainly it was witnessed in Belfast City Hall in the past with Loyalists and Nationalists agreeing on matters common to their respective communities and setting the divisive border issue aside. (1985a: 1)

The 'bottom-up', grassroots, approach to conflict transformation is clear and is captured in the phrase that reconciliation 'must commence IN THE COMMUNITY' and 'among the representatives of ALL' and on a basis that is untarnished by ethno-sectarianism. Instead of the context of local politics being regarded as a relatively insignificant sphere for peace-building it was identified as an important example of inter-community interactionism. In agreeing to work with Sinn Fein the PUP was endorsing, with regard to mainstream unionism its independence of thought and action. The PUP's document 'Sharing Responsibility' (1985b) up fronted the mutual legitimacy of the Unionist and nationalist traditions, strongly advanced power-sharing, and denoted the importance of other material and cognitive aspirations:

> Freedom from fear and violence, social deprivation in all areas, negations of basic human rights and many other issues have not received the public emotional attention that they so richly deserve. The result has been catastrophic. (PUP 1985: 2)

Such Loyalist discourse presented a strand of thinking that transcended the over-bearing influence of constitutionally designed politics. Although not set in an argument that was open to any form of Ulster independence, 'Sharing Responsibility' nevertheless reflected the position adopted by the UDA in *Beyond the Religious Divide* and in *Common Sense* that the 'people' are central to the transformation of the problems of Northern Ireland. As asserted in 'Sharing Responsibility':

> Now we have to move away from the negative entrenched positions; accept that the answers lie within the province among ourselves. (1985b: 2)

As Bruce (2001: 30) explains, the nature of the PUP's discourse in 'Sharing Responsibility' was one that:

> ensured minority influence by mechanisms similar to those put in place 15 years later by the Good Friday Agreement.

In 2002, following the collation of a number of documents, the UVF/ PUP presented its *Principles of Loyalism*. This document reflected the thoughts of one of the keenest thinkers within loyalism *per se*, the late Billy Mitchell. As Edwards and Bloomer (2004: 14) explained:

> The *Principles of Loyalism*, an internal UVF-RHC- PUP discussion paper, penned by Billy Mitchell in 2002, is the first document to seriously reflect upon Loyalism

as a political creed. It is a work grounded in the principles of the Solemn League and Covenant, considered by many historians to be the birth certificate of modern Ulster. Although the *Principles* are largely theory-driven they do make a connection with community-level practitioners. And rather than being a monochrome work of historical curiosity, then, the *Principles* seek to marry theory and practice, and to imbibe a genuine sense of historical and cultural legitimacy into the Protestant working class identity, all at a time when cultural yearning in sections of Loyalism and Unionism has been undermined by the somewhat unwelcome trend towards manufactured language and culture.

The Principles of Loyalism amounts to a comprehensive and deeply insightful account of the Loyalist tradition and its location within the wider Unionist community. Noteworthy is the understanding of the meaning of the Union based upon citizenship and the removal of ethnic chauvinism and exclusivity. This point is made accordingly within *The Principles of Loyalism*:

> Citizenship for the British subject is not about a national identity or cultural exclusiveness. It is about sharing a political identity that transcends religion, culture, language and ethnicity. In short, it is about living in a multi-cultural and multi-ethnic pluralist society rather than in a society where citizenship is based on national identity, religion and cultural exclusiveness. (2002: 23)

The *Principles* also contains an important section on conflict resolution which falls within the document's discussion of the UVF's attempts to respond to the conflict by means of political resistance and not only violent resistance. In this context the document uses the subtitle *The Long Kesh Experience* to account for the germination of the movement's political ideas. Simply put, the experience of incarceration presented UVF prisoners with the opportunity to reflect carefully upon the Northern Ireland conflict and the factors that resulted in their imprisonment. Under the direction of Gusty Spence, who Sinnerton (2002: 74–90) refers to as the creator of 'Spence University', the exploration of the political dimensions to the conflict eventually generated positive ideas regarding how to transform it. *The Principles of Loyalism* represents an important comment about this equally significant aspect of loyalism and helps commentators make greater sense of the factors that enabled the CLMC to proclaim a ceasefire in 1994.

   If one is to view the copy of the Belfast Agreement signed by those who contributed to it there is an interesting array of signatures from Loyalist representatives that is disproportionate in terms of their respective numbers and share of the popular vote. In sum, it presents an interesting symbolic depiction of the role Loyalists had played. The contribution of Gusty Spence, Billy Hutchinson, David Ervine, Dawn Purvis, Davy Adams and Gary McMichael among others had been set against a violent and difficult terrain in which to build such a pluralist outcome. The Combined Loyalists Political Alliance (CLPA) and CLMC had in January 1994 held a conference in response to the

Downing Street Declaration. In the run up to the IRA ceasefire on 31 August Loyalists killed thirty-five people. In addition, the INLA killed three members of the UVF and Raymond Smallwood, a key figure in Loyalist transition, was killed by the IRA. During that period and despite such violence and provocation the CLPA and CLMC met with the interlocutor, the Reverend Chris Hudson, to seek a meeting with the then Irish Foreign Minister Dick Spring and continued ongoing discussions between the Irish and British governments were held with assistance from the Reverend Roy Magee. Some six weeks after the IRA ceasefire the CLMC announced the Loyalist ceasefire. On 15 October, two days after the ceasefire call, the PUP met with then Taoiseach Albert Reynolds and a week later attended with the UDP events in Washington DC hosted by the National Committee on Foreign Policy. In November talks were held with the new Taoiseach, John Bruton, which was succeeded by exploratory talks with the Northern Ireland Office. During that time Noel Lyness, a Catholic and mature student, was beaten to death in the Village area in Belfast by Loyalists.

The publication of the *Frameworks for the Future* document by the British and Irish governments led to a series of further meetings with a joint UDP/PUP delegation meeting the Secretary of State Patrick Mayhew in September 1995. At that time William Elliott, a member of the RHC, was killed by his own organisation and Norman Hanley, a civilian Catholic, was beaten to death. In the period between November and December 1995 Ervine and others held two secret meetings with representatives from the IRA, which then led to meetings with the SDLP. On 6 February 1996 the PUP travelled to Iveagh House (home of the Irish Department of Foreign Affairs) for what became a robust meeting with Dick Spring, then Foreign Secretary. It is alleged that the Irish officials did not during the meeting mention their Dayton-style proximity talks proposal. When that proposal was released the next day to the media the PUP appeared somewhat undermined in the eyes of the UVF given the Irish officials' silence on the matter. Two days later the IRA bombed Canary Wharf and graffiti painted by a prominent UVF member on the Shankill Road read 'Who does Ervine speak for? He doesn't speak for the men on the ground'. Despite this and the killing of Thomas Sheppard by the UVF the PUP remained constant in their determination to seek a political accommodation, much of which was guided with extensive consultation with the UVF/RHC. In April 2006 the PUP presented a scenario document to the CLMC arguing for a commitment to the democratic process. This was followed by the Forum elections and relative electoral success for the UDP and PUP. As multi-party talks began in June without Sinn Fein the Forum for Political Dialogue was opened. Within weeks the Drumcee protest erupted, the larger Unionist parties walked away from the talks and the Mid-Ulster UVF killed Michael McGoldrick. The SDLP then removed themselves from the Forum. Billy Wright and Alex Kerr, who were each aiming to undermine Loyalist transition, were expelled and 'sentenced to death' by the CLMC. On 7 October the PUP visited prisoners in Long Kesh in order to gain support for the peace process – whilst so doing the IRA fired a missile into Thiepval Army Barracks. Near the end of 1996 the PUP and UDP met John Major at Downing Street and forewarned of instability if talks were held up due to the impasse over decommissioning.

During the impasse Loyalist violence began to rise. In May 1997 talks delegates travelled to South Africa to meet political parties and study the political transition out of apartheid. Soon after, multi-party talks resumed and the British and Irish government presented proposals for decommissioning. The election of a Labour government injected more substance and flexibility into the peace process with the government's report on parallel decommissioning. Loyalist violence remained, and in July 1997 the UK Unionist Party quit all talks and the Forum and the DUP removed themselves from the talks but not the Forum. When Mo Mowlam, then Secretary of State, appeared to waver on the 'principle of consent', the PUP sought and received a written assurance from her regarding this crucially important variable for Unionists. This permitted the PUP and the Ulster Unionist Party (UUP) to make a case for entry into the substantive negotiations. In December 1997 the Irish government released nine IRA prisoners and Loyalist prisoners rioted in Long Kesh in reaction to what they viewed as a one-sided political process. The PUP had been unaware that the releases were to have been granted and again were interpreted, especially among elements within the UVF, as lacking influence or status regarding the decisions made by the Irish state. As LVF violence increased and two Loyalists were killed in 1998 by Republicans, the Loyalist political representatives remain focused and substantial participants in the peace process and the creation of the Belfast Agreement on 10 April 1998. Evidently the complex and emotive terrain in which such perseverance was to become evident, and the support given to David Trimble in order to sustain a faltering UUP approach, was indicative not only of the capacity but more so of the desire to sustain and build conflict transformation.

Conclusion: somewhat failure and success

Investigation of progressive loyalism encourages fresh consideration of the phenomenon. By identifying its political dimensions it can be concluded that there was more to loyalism than naked sectarian violence. Perhaps understandably, popular comprehension of loyalism has been shaped by paramilitary violence to the extent that such violence has severely overshadowed the political side of loyalism. Accordingly, we find that what Loyalists had to say about a future settlement in terms of inter-community support for new political arrangements, sharing power as well as responsibility for the new political order considerably *predates* the Belfast Agreement. In this sense Loyalists can be considered to have been ahead of mainstream unionism and even at times republicanism. However, without an established political powerbase from which to proclaim their ideas to the Unionist electorate and the marginalisation of Loyalists vis-à-vis the wider Unionist community generally, it is unsurprising that the progressive elements of Loyalist thought were either relatively unobserved or disguised from memory.

As Bruce (1995a, 1995b) has pointed out, the essential problematic for Loyalist thinkers was that many Loyalists desired revenge as opposed to 'more abstract goals' (1995a: 188). Revenge and the sharp psychology of defending Loyalist place remained predominant given the desire to maintain the ethnosectarian 'integrity' of a particular geographical area (Southern 2008). The territorial dimension of Loyalist militancy embedded, for some, strong senses of presence and the assertion of a need to reconceptualise identity appeared unnecessary. Whereas Sinn Fein could garner support concerning the immediacy of State violence and connect that to Catholic socio-economic disadvantage, progressive Loyalists had to contend with the reality that their radical assertion for socio-economic justice was simply read by some as 'Provie-speak'. Therefore, in the complex morass of conflicting Unionist loyalties, subservience to hierarchical unionism and the threat of ongoing Republican violence, progressive and class-centred Loyalists could only find a somewhat persuasive edge within their respective parent organisations.

For Loyalists, as long as Republicans were engaged in violence they were presented with little opportunity but to behave in a similar fashion. The violence which plagued Northern Ireland did not offer much by way of an opportunity to explore the political option for Loyalists but it did for Republicans. However, when the opportunity arose to transform the conflict through politics, loyalism was capable of making a significant and important contribution in peace negotiations, significantly reducing ethno-sectarian violence, establishing conflict-led initiatives and ultimately evolving and developing those who were to become 'responsible participants' which embraced challenging ethno-sectarian discourse and asserting the perniciousness of conflict (Alway 1995).

The Loyalist contribution to conflict transformation can be observed on a number of fronts: first, in calling and maintaining, despite a tortuous path, a ceasefire; second, participating in the multi-party talks process; and third, defending the Belfast Agreement when it was under considerable attack from powerful anti-Agreement Unionist elements both during the talks and after the settlement. Before 1994 Loyalists were not given the opportunity to allow their political ideas to surface – at least not to a significant extent – and that was partly due as noted above as the wider recognition of elements within the Unionist electorate who were concerned by Loyalist criminality or who viewed such progressive idea as too advanced, although individuals such as David Ervine, Billy Hutchinson and Dawn Purvis were to both gain an inter-community vote. These persons were also key to the design of the Belfast Agreement and also in terms of their links to the Labour Party were able to 'shift the Labour Party away from a nationalist agenda and reduce the influence of those within that party who supported a united Ireland' (Billy Hutchinson, interview).

Further, when the British government signed up to the constitutional conditions of the Belfast Agreement, confirming that any change to the current constitutional status of Northern Ireland could only come via the 'consent principle', Loyalists experienced less anxiety about the intentions of their 'own' government. What is obvious in the documents analysed above was a preparedness to reach a compromise with the nationalist community in a manner which was not reflective or absorbed by majority rule. Those documents also challenge the readings of loyalism that aim for homogenisation.

The Belfast Agreement held out significant positives for transformational loyalism, although the process has been uneven and challenging. It secured the Union in terms of removing armed threat which allowed them to legitimise the notion that their violence had brought the IRA to the negotiation table, and as a much-needed resource that could be utilised to undermine the 'rednecks', it promoted rights and inclusion and for some was the conclusion of a discursive process of identity renegotiation and the assertion of a long and difficult process of Loyalist ownership of their ideas and concerns. In political terms that strategy has been electorally less influential but in terms of developing the peace process and sustaining conflict transformation it has borne some fruit, some of which has yet to ripen.

It should be noted that although occurring during the height of Loyalist violent activity in the early 1990s, the UVF and UDA did maintain a ceasefire, not reciprocated upon by Republicans, for ten weeks in 1991 in conjunction with the inter-party talks which British Secretary of State, Peter Brooke, had arranged. Fundamentally, Republican ideas and their morphology could be attached to a political programme that was primarily linked to the burdens endured by the Catholic population, whereas similar Loyalist ideas that invoked class issues were met by a generally conservative Unionist people for whom the threat of the IRA to Northern Ireland's constitutional position remained as a key discursive motivator. However, there is now a dissimilar class position for Loyalist thinkers in that some, unlike their forefathers and mothers, no longer feel obliged to offer unrequited fealty to the Unionist body politic. Therefore, as Cassidy has surmised transitional loyalism 'is perhaps best understood as an incipient or aspirational form of the class movement' (2008: 411).

Notes

1 In *Combat*, a call by the UVF to oppose the Anglo-Irish Agreement notes 'To the Roman Catholic population we say: our actions will be taken, not against you or your community, in no spirit of ascendancy over you' (1985).

2 As Patterson (1982) states, the Northern Ireland Labour Party was essentially a pro-union party but gained an inter-community vote and because of this was also viewed as a threat to the future of the Unionist State given its leftist credentials and idealism.

3 Copy held by author.

4 The then leader of the Ulster Unionist Party.

5 This point is reiterated in several editions of Loyalist newspaper. In 1982, for example, a *Combat* editorial asserted 'Politicians on all sides of the spectrum must realise it is their duty to build a just and stable government'. Undated and untitled copy held by author.

6 In a *Marxism Today* interview, Danny Morrison, the then publicity director of Sinn Fein, stated that with regard to *Beyond the Religious Divide?* nationalists would never 'accept power-sharing, they won't accept power-sharing even under optimum conditions of a continued Union with Britain (Rowthorn 1981: 31). Moreover, Loyalism as a philosophy, it was stated 'will always reach a dead end or it will turn back on itself and produce vicious sectarian violence' (Rowthorn 1981:31). Somewhat peculiarly Morrison also noted that talks between the IRA and the British government was for Loyalists 'hearsay and anathema' (Rowthorn1981:31) despite Loyalists calling for such negotiated talks several times before 1981.

7 In an interview in *Marxism Today* in 1981 John McMichael noted that 'the important thing must not be to set up either to institutionalise sectarianism as it did in 1974 or to create an artificial parliament … (Rowthorn 1981: 30). McMichael also stated, in the same interview 'that makes us a democratic party. Unlike the Provisional Sinn Fein, which refuses to put candidates before the electors and refuses to work towards a united Ireland through democratic means' (Rowthorn 1981:28).

8 McMichael also noted in *Marxism Today* that *Beyond the Religious Divide?* aimed to create a situation in which 'the decisiveness of sectarianism within our society would gradually disappear' (Rowthorn 1981: 28).

*When someone asks 'what's a
Loyalist?' I always want to say
'not that eegit Johnny Adair'!
(UDA respondent, South Belfast)*

4 A Mad Dog and a Regal Rodent: interpreting the wreckers and spoilers

Stedman (1997) has focused on those who aim to spoil peace processes that
they perceive as threatening their interests and concerns. Although his
analysis is related to political parties it is obvious that his typology of intent,
leadership and the refusal to adapt can also be translated to those who aim to
undermine the path of conflict transformation within non-State combatant
groups. One of Stedman's (1997: 6) conclusions is that peace negotiators
should 'choose an effective strategy for managing the spoiler'. However, there
are significant and at times developed reasons why those who aim to spoil or
even wreck peace processes do so and in many instances they place themselves
beyond the elite-level nature of conflict resolution. There are those who are
conflict profiteers and who have amassed and sustained corpulent and
consumption-driven lifestyles. Some are mesmerised by the status achieved
and are so psychologically attached to past violence that the surrendering of
status is unacceptable to them. At times determining who is for or against
peace is confusing as some offer a public face for peace-building but privately
continue to re-arm, kill and maintain extortion and other forms of racketeering. There are also those who assert serious concerns about peace-building
and react to what they see as betrayal by their political/paramilitary leaders
(Newman and Richmond 2005, 2006; Østergaard-Neilsen 2006; Richmond
2006; Smooha 2002). For some Loyalists the concept of consocialisation and
power-sharing was pure anathema. Such persons are more grounded than
others in ethno-sectarian discourses. Stedman (2000) posits three modes of
interaction regarding spoilers that include

> 'giving the spoiler what it wants', socialisation is 'changing the behaviour of the
> spoiler to adhere to a set of established norms' and coercion is 'punishing spoiler
> behaviour or reducing the capacity of the spoiler to destroy the peace process.
> (Stedman 2000: 182–183)

One of the limitations of Stedman's typology is that the capacity to adapt and aid the spoiler into peace is more variant than assumed given that those who aim to undermine peace can present to themselves a logic for undermining what appears to them as wholly unsavoury and objectionable (O'Kane 2010). A further alleged problem noted by Loyalist respondents was that those engaged in aiming to wreck the peace process received security force and political assistance.

The divisions that were exposed in the period after the 1994 ceasefire among Loyalists illustrated a deep fracturing within loyalism between those who wished to transform and those who wished to maintain violent conflict and criminality. A crucial factor in the recognition of inter-Loyalist conflict is the acknowledgment that Loyalist groups undertook performances and modes of agency that were neither static, even or at times logical. The onset of peace-making did not create a linear and agreed path, but instead the vagaries of Loyalist composition emerged. For those committed to peace there was an obvious logic which reasoned that a cessation of violence would lead to a growth in Loyalist politics and that former combatants would undertaken the role of activists dedicated to community renewal. For other Loyalists the rolling out of the peace process was viewed as mere concession-giving to Republicans and the loss of 'status'. This can be viewed against a context when figures within the two largest paramilitary groups were investing hundreds of hours in discussing and briefing combatants about the benefits of peace, securing arms to reduce the potential of violence and underlining the benefits of a cessation of violence whilst others were undermining such activity in a purposeful and direct manner, through open hostility and increasing criminality.

Johnny Adair and Billy Wright (known respectively as Mad Dog and King Rat)[1] in particular engaged in a series of activities that greatly undermined transitional loyalism. Both were driven by ego and due to the upsurge in violence after the Anglo-Irish Agreement had gained a paramilitary status that they would not yield. Adair's motivations appear confusing as he was initially dedicated to the peace process although he was, via C Company, to become embroiled in significant violence and a series of attempted internal UDA coups. Wright was more motivated by what he constructed as a traditional form of uncompromising loyalism and his view that the peace process was an act of betrayal. Not only did the groups they led remain engaged in violence but, it is contended, also embroiled both in criminality and security force collusion. A fundamental problem for those who wished to advance Loyalist transformation was the evident problem of how to manage Loyalist dissent. As noted by a UDA member:

> Why did the Shoukirs, Adair's lot and Billy Wright get away with what they were up to? Why did the police turn a blind eye to these people and what they was up to? Why weren't they taken off the streets? The people who were left to sort them

ones out was the leaders of the UVF and UDA. No one helped, no one came to us and said we will put them ones behind bars. So we had to sort the problem out again and again and that meant a lot of violence and that meant that we were doing what we didn't want to do, that is getting back into, up to our necks, the violence thing. So take it from me, if they had locked them ones up then there would have been no feud. You have to think this. Who is pulling the strings here? (UDA respondent, North Belfast)

After 1994 a series of new Loyalist groups emerged that maintained violent action and activity. The largest, the LVF, was led by Billy Wright. The other new group, the Red Hand Defenders (RHD), was a composite of members from the LVF, C Company, the UDA and the Orange Volunteers. Both of these new groups were generally viewed by established groups as fanatical bigots. As Gillespie recognised:

The emergence of new Loyalist paramilitary groups such as the Red Hand Defenders and Orange Volunteers, their attacks on Catholic homes and businesses and their relationship with groups supposedly on ceasefire also posed questions about the 'modernisation' of loyalism. (2001: 268)

Groups such as the LVF, who wished to continue the conflict, understood that they were countering the hegemony of a Loyalist leadership who they deemed as embroiled in the betrayal of traditional Loyalist discourse and practice. Thus they invoked the idea of being engaged in acts of resistance against what they determined as attempts to undermine Loyalist cause and meaning. Too much has been made of feuding as merely concerning inter-thug warfare and there has been an imprecise analysis of the discursive factors that conditioned inter-Loyalist violence. This has led to a situation in which conflicting discourses of loyalism have generally been left unexamined. The anger and overt ethno-sectarianism of the LVF, for example, is often reduced to a simple fracture within loyalism as opposed to a more accurate reading that the LVF embodied a particular strand of loyalism that other Loyalists had rejected. The general omission of a more coherent analysis of Loyalist feuding undermines a valid analysis of the divisions between reactive forms of Loyalist resistance and a political settlement seeking loyalism. As presented by David Ervine when interviewed:

I think that what we saw being enacted within loyalism was almost a carbon imprint of what was going on within the Unionist community. Yes and no that interesting debate of yes and no was eventually played out among paramilitarists. There is an element of paramilitarism that felt well we know, excuse my language, but we know the Provos are lying, conniving, cheating bastards so we'll say we are pro-agreement but meanwhile back at the ranch we will do things that are underhand and unreasonable and things like that and that created amazing conflict within the Loyalist community because other elements did not do that and the conflict obviously exploded in our faces.

For Ervine, ego, status seeking and ethno-sectarianism influenced the likes of Adair and Wright. However, others were, according to Ervine, Janus-faced and in public were pro-settlement but in private anti-Agreement – a form of game-keeper by day and poacher by night:

> There is always a deal that there is a penchant for some politicians to be King of Ulster, similarly there has always been a penchant for some paramilitarists to be king of loyalism and the vehicle of yes/no became quite an interesting battle. I clarify that by saying there have been many cases where I have been dubious about people's commitment to peace.

In the case of groups such as C Company and the LVF there has been an insufficient interpretation of the multiplicity of power relationships that they became embroiled within. The conspicuous exclusion, via academic analysis, of those Loyalists who publicly asserted a desire after 1994 to maintain identities based upon moralistic, religious, right-wing or inflexible fascistic philosophies undermines the meaning and significance of the contrary position of Loyalists who had a deep commitment to the peace process. The process of cabalisation, through which loyalism is purposefully divorced from the reality of possessing alternative and internally divisive vocabularies and intentions, undermines the actuality that the wreckers and spoilers were not merely continuing and asserting Loyalist violence but understood that in so doing that they were challenging a voice that promoted an oppositional political, social and cultural path. For them the peace process was discursively and culturally dangerous. In sum, the feuds were not simply about warring drug barons fighting over the spoils of Loyalist territory.

Loyalist splits

The LVF and C Company aimed to secure Loyalist places not only to promote their criminal empires but to also present identifiable spatially centred strategies of resistance (Gallaher and Shirlow 2006). In particular, their reaction to the peace process was tied to reactive ideological forms that were primarily concerned with defining the 'requirement' for Loyalist violence and a defensive reaction to transformative loyalism. With regard to the peace process both groups undertook forms of hermetical sealing and ideological corralling and aimed to undermine the fluidity of Loyalist transition. Wrapped up in these divisions within loyalism was the immediacy of the cult of personality:

> Obsessed by media Adair was fast becoming a caricature of the terrorist godfather, a cult figure whose face was rarely out of the newspapers. It was only a matter of time, it seemed, before his thirst for power and celebrity drove him into open confrontation with his fellow Loyalists. (Lister and Jordan 2003: 1)

Such persons were driven by ego but there was significantly more to their desire to control and assert a non-settlement-driven loyalism. The divisions between progressive and regressive modes of loyalism were driven by alternative senses of symbolic mediation and channelled via variant frameworks of elected and restricted representations (Bjorgo 1995; Juergensmeyer 1997). With regard to the motto 'we are the people', which constitutes the very nature of Loyalist devotion, the LVF and C Company claimed ownership over the broad Loyalist mass. Such contested claims of possession became a key site of conflict. As C Company and the LVF extended their recruitment and preached conflict they ran up against the grain of transformative Loyalists aiming to demobilise and counter the use of violence. As the journalist Henry McDonald noted:

> One organisation, the UVF looked for a political way forward reaching out for compromise with Republicans and nationalists. The other sought to gain hegemony within the Protestant community by becoming more sectarian and belligerent and by painting the UVF as crypto-communists and 'Fenian' lovers. (2000: 1)

An innermost characteristic of the division between progressive and regressive loyalism concerned the manner in which identity was constituted and predisposed by layers of social meaning and the interpretation of conflict. Pursuing peace required remodelling an alternative interpretation of Loyalist meaning. For rejectionists the same wearied narrative of Republican threat and Protestant annihilation was invoked. Billy Wright, in particular, maintained an extreme form of fundamentalist loyalism tied to an immovable and passionate understanding of identity, resistance and belief. Such groups presented loyalism as:

> permeated with the notion of 'sacred history' and heroic mythology ... embedded within the symbolic matrix of ... 'sacred centres'. (Azaryahu and Kellerman 1999: 109)

Steve Bruce's work on Loyalist feuding pinpoints a reality that 'like any competing organisations, the UDA and UVF have rarely been on good terms' (1992: 124). Bruce points to a series of disputes, prior to 1994, most of which were based around drunken brawling, attempts to use feuding in order to take command of either organisation and somewhat ironically in a desire to stop the sectarian murder of Catholics. Bruce illustrates how progressive loyalism was constantly hindered by 'strong pressure from less thoughtful members to retaliate' especially among those for whom there was an 'absence of status as a social or political force' (1992: 133). Therefore, those who promoted Loyalist transition were not confronted in the post-1994 period by feuds due to brawling and the mere performance of masculinity (Messerschmidt 2000; Zarkov 2001) but were undermined by, as they saw it, militarists and external political agents who feared the development of political consciousness-raising among Loyalist paramilitaries. As Billy Mitchell asserted when interviewed:

> The period after the ceasefires has been the worst ever in a way for progressive Loyalists. They are being assaulted at every turn. There are middle Unionists egging on the likes of Billy Wright, there are people in the security forces turning a blind eye to the likes of Adair … Doing nothing about Loyalist drug dealers is based upon presenting Loyalists in a way that undermines Loyalist transformation. There is a strategy against Loyalist transformation.

Divisions within loyalism became centred upon illicit and licit discursive moralities, which were conditioned via offensive and violent exclusionary practices. What appeared within the Loyalist landscape was a division between those who were the 'true' and 'honest' defenders of Ulster Loyalism. The peacemakers saw a new vision that heralded a removal of violence as the best opportunity for the Protestant working class to invest energy into community renewal. The rejectionists viewed non-aggressive loyalism as a treacherous, devious and malign force, which aimed to destroy the body politic of Loyalist identity. For the progressives their 'legitimacy' was formed around the notion that they unlike 'other' Loyalists were involved in providing a positive and honourable leadership to working-class Protestants. For regressive Loyalists such transformation-influenced loyalism was antithetical and viewed as threatening, hostile and belligerent; the progressive Loyalist 'other' became increasingly denoted by rejectionists as 'lundys' (a Northern Irish version of Quisling) and 'touts' (police informants). In condemning each other the most serious allegation performed against the 'other' Loyalist paramilitary group was that they were a pariah, on the one hand, upon the Protestant community due to their engagement in drug dealing, pimping and other anti-social behaviour, or on the other 'capitulators' who were signing up to a pan-nationalist constructed and driven peace process. Obviously, such discursive divisions undermined the idea that loyalism is merely thoughtless and asocial. As the feuds evidenced it was constructed around complex narratives and contested counter-narratives.

Thus divisions within loyalism attempted to confirm people into oppositional communities and lay before them the bare preferences of 'good' or 'bad'. The construction of atavism between reformist and regressive elements was at times obsessed with establishing relations of equivalence in which the subjects were locked into what were perceived as legitimate moral and illegitimate immoral definitions of intent. Evidently, membership of a particular paramilitary group was tied to a subject position within which the subject must promote the purity and sanctity of that organisation. Renditions against the 'other' were attached to denouncing such groups for failing to accept the 'true' notion of Loyalist identity. The possessive expression of allegiance to either progressive or regressive Loyalists created a sense of personal allegiance and belonging which led to a collective defiance to the 'other' group. Loyalty was so important that, within such a context of division, it lead to violence against those who shared similar but not the same beliefs. Both wished for the maintenance of Northern Ireland's constitutional position but one side recognised that that had been achieved whilst the other viewed peace talks as the unravelling of constitutional status. In simple terms both saw the other as treacherous swindlers.

Shove your doves and the Shankill feud

The most significant feud was centred on the Shankill Road area between C Company, led by Johnny Adair, and the UVF. The press and other opinion formers represented the hostility between these groups as territorial clashes caused by the competition over drug and associated criminal empires. There is no denying Loyalist paramilitaries were associated with extensive patterns of criminal activity but there were other factors that motivated Loyalists other than criminality and financial greed.

For C Company there had been a distinct form of 'status' acquired during conflict and the logic of peace-building and conflict transformation provided few if any avenues for such status to be reproduced. C Company read the peacemakers as ultimately weak and emasculated and viewed peace negotiations as providing a vacuum in Loyalist authority. C Company, as with other UDA companies in North Belfast, aimed to spread their sphere of influence into areas dominated by other Loyalist groups. This generally concerned recruiting young males, a move that obviously undermined Loyalist authority. In symbolic terms the positioning of C Company into maintaining violence led to turning the Lower Shankill into the 'true' centre of Loyalist belief and endurance as evidenced by the ethno-sectarian nature of wall muraling in the post-1994 period (See Chapter 6).

C Company was a major player in the reproduction of violence before and after the paramilitary ceasefires. When examining the activities of C Company the press has dedicated most of their analysis to the personality of Johnny Adair. This is not surprising given Adair's self-representation as the most prominent member of contemporary loyalism, and his constant desire to appear on television.[2] Adair represents himself as the Loyalist who 'took the war' to the IRA in the late 1980s and early 1990s and performed a series of savage violent acts in a period when paramilitarianism was beginning to be influenced by wider political negotiations. A key event that led to a growth in Loyalist violence was the Anglo-Irish Agreement which permitted the Irish State to have a say in the internal administration of Northern Ireland. These events were met with a new wave of 'better' trained recruits into loyalism and a growth in Loyalist violence. As noted by a Loyalist respondent:

Most of us had drifted away, we just knew the war was basically over. Even the Hunger Strikes or the Anglo-Irish Agreement didn't really stir us up. I suppose we just thought things had calmed down a lot and the thing would fizzle out. But we we was wrong as along came a rough sort ah lads who were into the violence thing. I was never into the violence thing but these lads were. When they arrived and I wondered if the word defence in UDA meant anything to this lot. It was like a pack of attacks dogs. (UDA respondent, West Belfast)

This new generation, known as the Young Turks, came not only to command a significant part of UDA violence but were a different type of high risk-taking combatants. As a member of C Company noted:

The UDA were sleeping and we knew it was time to up the ante. It was time to make sure once and for all there wouldn't be a united Ireland.

The unfolding of the Anglo-Irish Agreement and wider frustrations concerning inactivity led to a series of coups within the UDA as the Young Turks came to the fore. This came at a time when the parent organisation was attempting to enter democratic politics based upon pluralism and power-sharing and more conscientious members, such as Jackie McDonald were imprisoned. Within C Company the onset of a new leadership led to the deaths of around twenty-five individuals mostly within North and West Belfast. The press has constantly fetishised Adair's fearsome reputation as he himself has promoted the idea that he ruled C Company with ferocious power and authority. His reputation was furthered by his distinctive shaven head and his constantly exposed muscular torso and his 'legend' and bravado was spread by talk of him often walking through Republican areas looking for targets whilst wearing a Glasgow Celtic jersey. However, the praising of Adair was not universal within the UDA, as Jackie McDonald observed when interviewed:

These people had brought a cancer into loyalism. The drugs and the crime and the seriousness of that and the desire to fight and kill and keep on doin' it. I knew early on that Adair and his likes would be a problem for a very long time to come.

Undoubtedly Adair's desire to spread his authority after 1994 was important, but that does not in itself explain the Shankill feud. While his personality intensified divisions between C Company and the UVF there were other motivational factors of equal and greater importance. The most observable factor was the emergence of violent feuds between the UVF and the LVF in the late 1990s. Wider allegations also concerned Adair being represented as an agent of Special Branch and as a barrier to political progress. His supporters identified him as Mad Dog, a nickname that was linked to the notion of his capacity for violence. For the UVF he was identified as Daft Dog, especially after he incriminated himself to a local police officer who had tape recorded conversations with him that led to his imprisonment.

C Company also acted as a force opposed to wider political morphology.

An early sign that C Company was opposed to the 'peace process' was evident in the mid-1990s when several walls in the Shankill Road had the motif 'Shove Your Doves – J Adair' painted on them (Gallaher and Shirlow 2006). Despite the paramilitary ceasefires of 1994, C Company continued to promote discourses of ethnic purity and racial/religious superiority. Resistance to the 'creeping and destroying of the Protestant people by the ones betraying loyalism' (C Company respondent) was understood as being based upon preserving a way of life hostile to a post-conflict settlement that did not uphold 'a Prod victory over the Provies and all them ones who want a United Ireland' (C Company member). C Company members perceived the peace process as eroding the values of Protestant cultural heritage and were firmly opposed to those who promoted a pluralistic doctrine. C Company espoused an ideology within which Catholics were not viewed as an ideological group but as representatives of, as one C Company respondent noted, 'papists' evil', a notion of Catholicism that was during interviews constantly cross-referenced with the 'triumph' of Protestantism within Ireland during the Williamite Wars. In a significant statement of intent in 1997 a C Company respondent stated:

> That battlefield has not been won. Loyalists can win that battle against the IRA. It is too soon to have peace. When we say – we are 'simply the best' that means we can fight on. We will fight on and not sign up to the betrayal of the Loyalist war. C Company are not weary and we will get others to fight on. Figthin' on is the right thing to say and do. It always was. You can only defeat Republicans by fighting on. They are too smart to negotiate and talk to. Fight them 'til they lose!

And:

> Loyalism is about fighting on, it is about preventing a doomsday. When Johnny Adair gets back he won't be talking to Sinn Fein, he will be waiting to get back at them ... They [other loyalists] are the ones negotiatin' with Taigs. The people we should be repellin' themins [those ones] who want to triumph all over us. (C Company respondent)

A key allegation against C Company is that they attacked Protestant communities whilst disguised as Republicans in an attempt to stoke ethno-sectarian violence. As noted by a prominent UDA respondent from South Belfast:

> He was all for the peace process and then he was going against it. He started to try and kick start the whole thing. There was an attack near here and his people came into, near Linfield Street wearing Celtic tops. The car had tape over the registration plate and I saw the footage on a CCTV tape. They jumped out and threw a few pipe bombs and people told me they were shouting 'Up the IRA' and that sort of thing. They did that all over the place in an attempt to pretend that Catholics were attacking Prods.

According to prominent UDA members, C Company and the others Adair initially influenced, such as the Shoukris, began to assert the need to retain and promote ethnically supremacist and ultra-nationalist modes of political practice. These sources contend that for such persons devotion was tied to the protection of what they construed as purity, Loyalist affiliation and a self-reflexive interpretative framing of power (Bairner and Shirlow 1998). Ideological confrontation, for C Company, remained insufficient if it did not operationalise the medium of ethno-sectarian discourse. These reactive forms of cultural opposition were also tied to notions of cultural dissipation, besiegement and disintegration. As a UDA respondent from Lagan Valley argued:

> Adair is not a Loyalist, he is against the Loyalist people and their decision to move on. He is the opposite of what loyalism is about. He is into bogeyman loyalism, as he wants to scare and intimidate people. His loyalism is about hatred and being anti-Catholic. He is exactly what the DUP want. A Loyalist who cannot accept sharing and accommodation … His war is not over as he is about a loyalism that people like me have tried to remove for many years. It is not just about his ego it is about taking the conflict on and on and doing so because he supports the anti-Agreement camp, he doesn't want Catholics about the place.

There was ample evidence given via interviews with UDA members that C Company and others operating in North Belfast aimed to undermine the peace process through violence and in particular via the Holy Cross[3] dispute. That conflict was against the advice of senior UDA leaders and fused around the loss of Protestant territory and the use of violence to provoke what was to become the disgusting intimidation of children. The roots of Holy Cross lay in the expulsion of C Company members from the Lower Shankill by the UVF (Ashe 2006). Once settled into the Protestant Upper Ardoyne area they, with others, sought to expand their influence through undertaking the mass intimidation of Catholic children walking to their school located within the area. As late as 2003 C Company was blamed for attaching a bomb to the Holy Cross girls' gate. Such activities did not happen without internal criticism:

> It was a disgrace. You had so much bedded down and then the Holy Cross thing. I was sick to my stomach by it, but knew that it was an attempt to provoke a Republican reaction. The ones behind it thinking that people would come and support them. We put a stop to that. I told the ones under me that C Company and the Shoukris had about fifteen hard men to their name and the rest were wee lads filled with drugs. I told them that they would be expelled and dealt with if they signed up to any more of this. I told them that even though the peace process was hard that we were keeping our ceasefire. I told them that the war was over and that these people only wanted to manipulate them for their own ends. (UDA respondent, South Belfast)

The events that led up to the Shankill feud were tied to a series of factors including alternative political practices, personality clashes and overt representations of organisational strength. The LVF was formed in Portadown in

1996 after the UVF disbanded their Mid-Ulster group. This occurred due to a section of the UVF in Portadown engaging in the murder of Catholics and a continual refusal to accept the UVF's ceasefire of 1994. The then leader of the UVF in Mid-Ulster, Billy Wright, was placed under threat of execution by the UVF if he did not leave Northern Ireland after midnight on the 1 September 1996. Wright refused to do so and formed the LVF, which was generally based within the Portadown area. His refusal to leave Northern Ireland was publicly supported by DUP MP Willie McCrea. The LVF was a beacon for those Loyalists who were opposed to peace negotiations. Billy Wright (who was later shot dead in the Long Kesh in 1997 by the INLA) developed strong links between his organisation and C Company. C Company's leader, Johnny Adair, who had a framed photograph of Wright on his mantelpiece, identified Wright as a figure who, like him, was prepared to challenge the appearance of peace consultations with Irish Republicans and nationalists.

In 1995 Wright had been 'interviewed' by the UVF regarding the arrest of Lindsay Robb who had been caught in Scotland in 2005 trying to acquire weapons, probably for the Mid-Ulster UVF. The fact that Robb, who was to be killed several years later after his imprisonment, was a member of the PUP caused obvious friction during the peace process. Robb was to support the LVF when he joined them in Long Kesh and was the first LVF prisoner released in 1999. The Robb case illustrated that members of the LVF aimed to re-arm and were working against the wishes of the UVF leadership. Adair and Wright also supported the Orange Order protests at Drumcree through visibly being in attendance in 2000. At that time Adair appeared with around thirty muscular compatriots wearing T-shirts with the UFF motif and the words 'Simply the Best, Their Only Crime Loyalty' emblazoned upon them – including one sported by Adair's dog, Rebel. This show of strength indicated how transitional loyalism operated at that time within the UVF. Local UVF members who had remained loyal to the leadership had wanted, in response to Adair, to provide their own 'show of strength' at Drumcree but had been persuaded not to by the leadership in Belfast, a situation that Billy Hutchinson wryly commented upon when interviewed:

> You really had to wonder who was pulling the strings. Who wanted a shaven-headed muscleman with a dog in a T shirt to be the symbol of loyalism? There were so many people against progressive loyalism you just started to see all of this as a concerted campaign.

Around the same time shots were fired at the police from the Lower Shankill area in an attempt to create the impression that Republicans had broken their ceasefire. The situation was only to worsen. Adair, although he did not publicly state it, supported the formation of the LVF and after Wright's death in prison he created even closer close ties with the LVF who hosted a large party for him when he was released from prison after the Shankill feud. That type of linkage with the LVF would have broken paramilitary 'ethics' as it indicated disloyalty to the parent group However, the odium that was poured upon Adair for forming such links was to be exacerbated by the LVF killing in 2000 of Richard Jamieson, a prominent UVF member in Portadown. Jamieson, who constantly referred to the LVF as the DVF (Drug Volunteer Force), had been killed as he was developing a dossier on the organisations drug-based activity. As stated by Bruce (2004: 516):

> Adair's siding with the LVF broke a fundamental principle of paramilitary relations. Thus when Adair cultivated the LVF he was deliberately infringing two important principles. He was claiming that the UDA had a right to interfere in the internal affairs of the UVF (which had expelled the LVF) and he was showing a lack of fidelity to his own organisation.

Therefore, when Adair invited the LVF to attend a 'Cultural Parade Festival' he organised in August 2000 he was publicly flaunting his 'prowess' and 'capacity'. This 'festival' was centred upon the dedication of thirteen new murals painted in Hopewell Crescent and Shankill Parade in the Lower Shankill area, and it is estimated that around 8,000–10,000 people attended the event. The UVF and its supporters were not invited, nor did they attend.

During this event C Company and their affiliated marching bands paraded out from the Lower Shankill area and up the main Shankill Road. There is no doubt that the aim of the parade was to openly insult members of the PUP and UVF. As the parade stopped outside the Rex Bar, a place recognised as a UVF bar, an LVF insignia was unfurled. This act was seen as discourteous and as an attempt to challenge the influence and command of the UVF in particular. As a series of fights began C Company members opened fire upon those inside the bar. Later that night members and associates of the PUP and UVF who lived in the Lower Shankill area were intimidated from their homes; this included attacks upon the home of Gusty Spence. The intimidation of Spence in particular was denoted as equivalent to 'throwing Santa out of his grotto and not a good idea' (UVF respondent, West Belfast). The media coverage of the feud depicted it as a turf war between criminal empires, with the ejection of some thirty families from the Lower Shankill depicted as a desire by C Company to remove 'other' competing criminal elements. In fact those excluded included persons related to UVF members or those who had rejected and stood against C Company's illicit activities. As Billy Mitchell noted in a statement read to the author:

> What about the thirty odd families that were violently expelled from the turf of the Lower Shankill? Were these men, woman and children all expelled from their homes because they were competing for a slice of criminal action? If the turf war was over drugs, prostitution and rackets the media needs to tell us how many prostitutes the elderly disabled pensioner whom we saw on television last Monday was pimping for? They need to identify how many businesses were paying

protection money to the young lady who had her wedding plans wrecked when her home was looted and her savings pilfered. They need to provide evidence that people like Gusty Spence were expelled from their homes because they controlled rival drug empires to those of their attackers.

Soon after these expulsions Jackie Coulter and Bobby Mahood were shot by the UVF. Over the next three months five other men who were associated with the UVF/PUP and C Company were killed and the offices of the UDP and a former UDA prisoner group on the mid-Shankill were destroyed in an obvious attempt to drive their presence out of that area. As noted the press has generally, and incorrectly, represented the feuding on the Shankill as a dispute over drug-dealing empires and the control of criminal realms. In reality the feud was linked to wider processes of political fragmentation and a contestation between militants and more politically advanced elements. However, the feud produced among UVF members a strong and enduring sense that Adair was being protected and that the violence he directed was purposefully sponsored by shadowy figures within the security forces:

> [He used] it to his own advantage and when the UVF did respond the security forces put a cordon around him so we would see him as a puppet of the security services and the feud was manufactured by them. Also during the time of the CLMC when loyalism was united and we were of the one purpose, the actions of probably one man and those around him brought the downfall of the vast majority of that. That against the backdrop of a process that was being driven by the government to demonise loyalism to divide and criminalise loyalism. Though it may not be tangible, many people within the UVF and loyalism at large would have felt that many of the actions that could be attributed to division and criminalisation within loyalism can be attributed to people who were directly controlled by the security services and Johnny Adair and the people around him would have been instrumental in that. (UVF respondent West Belfast, cited in Shirlow and Monaghan 2006: 3)

Furthermore,

> The feud with the UDA, again, thought up by other people who walk the halls of Whitehall with bowler hats and a carnation in their lapel, it's MI5 I am talking about. I believe the feud of August 2000 was mainly engineered by Johnny Adair … The purpose was to destabilise loyalism completely. Again there were two individuals who were security services driven, Billy Wright, who would have been the so-called leader of the scum who masquerade as Loyalist, were expelled members of the UVF despite what he put, he was expelled for his heavy involvement in the drugs network. We don't like using the word feud; this was the UVF cleaning up internal matters. It can't be separated that some people profited by the distraction of violence and those who did profited because the security forces were looking elsewhere when they have been conducting illicit business. (RHC respondent, West Belfast)

The following provides a more detailed summary of wider UVF interpretations of the LVF and C Company:

> In many ways that would have been the reason for the anti-ceasefire approach of those, many of which you are talking about. The very fact that a link existed between the Johnny Adair faction and the Billy Wright disciples of the past … another common denominator and that was purely drugs, and that again as a threat to the Loyalist community brought the confrontation to the door of the UVF. The continuing stuff in North and East [Belfast] is to an extent from the expulsion of Billy Wright and others who basically for their own cover attempted to use the guise of loyalism, again as a distraction to pursue their own interests but also made unholy alliances to cover themselves in some small regard. Tried to build up networks serving as business networks as opposed to organisational networks and the individuals involved in that were driven by a need for cocaine and money. Those who were the driving forces behind that had been involved in mainstream Loyalist paramilitarism and had been expelled for a variety of reasons, many under a shadow that there was security force involvement in their activities and therefore the fact that they were expelled, during a ceasefire period, and those people therefore came back and were a sore on the side of mainstream organisations since their expulsion and while they were members also. They kept coming back because of their involvement with the security services. (UVF respondent, West Belfast)

Shortly after the Shankill feud the then Secretary of State Peter Mandelson sent Adair back to prison to serve the rest of his sentence. In his absence the UVF, UDA and RHC leaders negotiated a truce. On his release from prison in 2002 Adair asserted:

> Them people [the UVF] started the feud. We defended our people. We need to get it into our heads that we weren't wrong, and we need to get out of this wee square [the Lower Shankill] and get out onto that Shankill Road where we belong. (Cited in Shirlow and Monaghan 2006: 4)

In overall terms the feud, as far as the PUP was concerned, was not linked to a simple turf war between rival criminal groups. As noted by Billy Mitchell:

> If there has been a 'turf war' for the past year it has been a war to exclude the voice of radical progressive politics from the Loyalist turf. It has been primarily a one-sided war and it has been waged, not just by paramilitaries, but by so called constitutional politicians and religious fundamentalists as well. The object of the campaign is to demonise, marginalise and eliminate the voice of radical democratic politics within loyalism. (Statement read to author)

Senior Loyalists conclude that elements linked to the LVF and C Company formed the group known as the RHD. Their first victim was the RUC constable Frankie O'Reilly, who was killed after being hit by a shrapnel blast bomb thrown at him during a pro-Orange Order 'Drumcree' protest march in Portadown. Attacks by Loyalists upon the RUC were rare and it has been surmised that this particular attack was aimed at O'Reilly because he was a Catholic. In November, 1998 the group shot its second victim, thirty-five-year-old Brian Service, in North Belfast as he was walking home from a predominantly Catholic social club. This type of murder, singling out a lone individual simply because of their religion, was more characteristic of Loyalist activity. The third murder, that of the prominent solicitor Rosemary Nelson in Lurgan in March 1999, indicated a particularly public display of power by the RHD. Rosemary Nelson had been active in high-profile cases and represented the Garvaghy Road residents who were opposed to the Drumcree Orange parade. Her murder was clearly linked to the policy of targeting a high-profile representative whose death, it was hoped, would pressurise Republicans into retaliatory activity. Moreover, the ability to murder an individual with such a high public profile was also aimed at providing the RHD with both status and proven ability.

Both the RHD and LVF had supporters in Belfast, however a concerted campaign by the UVF and UDA to suppress their support base in the city was well-publicised by the killings of John Mahood and Frankie Curry, both of whom were disaffected member of the UVF and RHC who, it is alleged, were trying to establish a support base for the anti-cessation Loyalist groups in West Belfast. Bruce (2004: 518) illustrated the links between C Company and the LVF:

> Gary Smith, a close Adair associate, was convicted in March 2002 of making a hoax bomb phone call in the name of the RHD. During 2002 divisions within the UDA were apparent in conflicting public statements about the RHD. In January of that year the UDA ordered the RHD to 'disband' but in April the RHD was still claiming incidents. Despite having supported the official UDA warning, the North Belfast UDA also used the RHD name to claim the murder of Gerard Lawlor in July 2002.

By 2002 Adair's activities with the LVF and his attempts to overtake the UDA led to his expulsion from the UDA. His return to prison in 2003 rendered him as weakened but the death in February 2003 of UDA divisional leader John Gregg and his friend Rob Carson was 'the final straw'. The UDA blamed Adair, although imprisoned, for the killing and viewed Gregg's death as a result of him endorsing Adair's expulsion. Less than a week after Gregg's death the remnants of Adair's C Company, some fifteen individuals, were physically removed by around a hundred UDA members. In a symbolic act of defiance all murals and depictions of Adair were defaced within twenty-four hours, the legend 'Mad Dog' was replaced by 'Sad Dog', and in an act of emasculation the sexuality of Adair was challenged by the motif, painted across the city, of 'Adair Woof Woof He's a Poof'. As a long time member of the UDA in West Belfast surmised:

There was no place for the likes of Adair anymore. He did fight and he fought well and he fought with brains. But times move on and he didn't. He was beyond hope at the end. He thought he could get the war started again. Nobody much wanted that anymore, we had learned the lesson of fighting. You just got whacked, went to prison or watched as the place got filled with more poverty. Adair is gone, so good, there'll be no more Macbeth with the tattoos.

King Rat and the LVF

The LVF publicly condemned the PUP as 'atheistic communists' who aimed to impose a 'socialist ideology over a conservative people' (interview with Billy Wright). Moreover, the LVF aimed to challenge those forms of loyalism that did not espouse and promote visions of Protestant triumphalism. Unlike the PUP in particular, who supported inter-community peace-building, the LVF sensed Irish nationalism, ecumenism, Republicanism and Catholicism as 'dark and satanic forces' ranged against them. Within this representation the anti-Agreement Loyalists sought to represent the persecuted innocent as the Protestant people who were now being victimised by both Republicanism and transformative loyalism.

Where the PUP articulated the argument that religion was merely a boundary marker that linked rival nationalisms, the LVF contended that Protestantism and its historical conflict with Catholicism remained central to the construction of their identity. Their violence was not simply about repelling Irish Republicanism but was also concerned with a devotion to Protestant fundamentalism. The LVF, in particular, provided a fundamentalist epistemology from which derived the most acicular sense of Protestant militancy. Where transformative Loyalists aimed to convert place via social justice, the LVF sought to enclose Protestant territory, within a desire to exclude dissenting narratives. For anti-Agreement Loyalists defending Protestant place was based upon a form of moral righteousness in which the preservation of what was perceived as a 'God-given territory' was intrinsic, inherent and conscientiously correct (White 1995).

For Billy Wright the territorial renegotiation of conflict, as outlined in the Belfast Agreement, which aimed to create cross-border institutions, power-sharing and the enshrinement of nationalist right in the constitution of Northern Ireland, were inadmissible. Wright positioned himself around the supposition that Northern Ireland is a British/Protestant territory which should be intolerant to any form of consensus-building or cross-community linkage. As Wright noted when interviewed:

> The answer to that question is simple. We are guided by the plight of the Protestant people. The PUP and others have betrayed and not represented that plight. Republicans either as the IRA or Sinn Fein are a threat to the Protestant people. That is the guide to any actions we take.

Resistance, for the LVF, was based upon pursuing ideological purity and resisting all discourses and/or modes of consensus-building, such as the peace process, which fell outside their particularistic interpretation of habituation and political representation. A fundamentalism also linked to the LVF being embroiled in significant drug-dealing. Therefore, reproducing violence was based upon resisting via the principle of subjugating compromise. However, the LVF's resistance was also directed against any person or community involved in intra-community work, cross-border trade or inter-party talks and negotiations. As stated:

> The LVF recognises that key Protestant leaders in the church, politics, industry and commerce, and last, but not least, in the paramilitary world have succumbed to this blackmail and are presently colluding in a peace/surrender process designed to break the Union and establish the dynamic for Irish unity, within an all-Ireland Roman Catholic, Gaelic, Celtic State. (Statement read to the author)

For the LVF the exclusion of the 'other' was linked to their belief that the Protestant community is an elect people who must stand against any ideas or actions that are not constructed around their abstract reading of the past – an article assembled of categories of events in which aggression and faith were mutually inclusive. The overall *modus operandi* for the LVF was inherent and viewed by them as a natural cause of action. A position that echoes Jarman's proposition that:

> This past has not ended, but rather continues to structure the feelings, expectations and fears of those acting in the present … (1997: 168).

In interviewing members of the LVF there was no doubt that they saw loyalism as being divided between secularised and fundamentalist modes of expression and viewed conflict between the two as necessary. There is also no doubt that those opposed to the LVF killed and intimidated those who supported them, expelled others and constantly monitored those who may have been supportive. In one instance thirty UVF members from North Belfast attacked LVF members in a bar in Portadown. The LVF were effectively choked of support in Belfast where in an attempt to stimulate support for anti-Agreement Loyalists they had tried to burn down a Protestant church and Orange Halls in an attempt to provoke a backlash against Catholic communities. The LVF were able to mobilise support and sympathy in towns such as Lurgan and Portadown where the traditional rhetoric of fundamentalist Protestantism held more sway, especially given the numerical decline of the Protestant population in Upper Bann and County Armagh and the contestation over the Drumcree parade.

Given this struggle over the control and legitimacy of Loyalist groups within certain areas it has become clear that what were deemed to be the 'true' Loyalist communities became a point of immense contestation. As Billy Wright noted:

> There are new and true Loyalist places, like Portadown. There is no atheistic communism in Portadown, like you get on the Shankill Road. No talking to those with the blood of Protestants on their hands, such as PIRA. No cross-community work. Just the Red, White and 'True' Blue of Ulster.

Furthermore:

> The betrayers of the people on the Shankill Road have lost the plot. They are involved in Ulster being betrayed!

The latter comment may seem somewhat churlish but it does indicate the belief of fundamentalist Loyalists that 'evil' and 'apostate' Loyalist communities had been created due to the machinations of the peace process, inter-community dialogue and the pursuit of radical Loyalist politics. The emergence of these novel topographical constructs and the repositioning of Loyalist identity indicated a distinct ideologicisation of Loyalist places and related theoretical codes. The articulation of secularism, the promotion of ecumenism and the adoption of nationalist-Republican rights by Loyalists were seen, by the LVF, as contradicting the rationale of religious and political conviction. As a LVF respondent noted:

> Ecumenism is a serious breach of Protestant solidarity. It's depraved you can't reject the word of God on these matters. (LVF respondent, Upper Bann)

In such a reductionist climate of cognition, that was undoubtedly influenced by Paisleyite rhetoric.[4] It is clear that politics, for the LVF, was not an arena within which socio-cultural antagonism could be resolved through normalised patterns of democratic practice and alternative forms of political governance. In uncomplicated terms, as Billy Wright stated when interviewed:

> There is no solution beyond the defeat of the pan-nationalist front, and nonsense it upholds. The DUP are the only politicians not prepared to compromise and we accept and support that fully.

Clearly, any attempt to go beyond theological division through inter-community contact and constitutionally based 'power-sharing' was seen as flagitious and unwarranted. In particular, the astringency of LVF discourse was, in relation to the Protestant community, directed mostly at the PUP via a relatively sophisticated website. The PUP's activities were dismissed by the LVF as a process of duping the Protestant people and of covert Republicanism. In return the PUP was vocal in their denunciation of fundamentalist Protestantism as their agenda, as noted by David Ervine, former PUP MLA, had been 'to free the Loyalist community from the grip of sectarian and fundamentalist politics'.

Given that the LVF and the DUP both rejected the Belfast Agreement and the progressive loyalism of the PUP and the UDP, it is not surprising that such antagonism led to intense hostility between these progressive and anti-Agreement elements. For David Ervine, identity-building at that time was centred upon:

> Freeing ourselves from containment, through promoting a form of politics which takes us beyond traditional sectarian practice. Politics, which takes us out of our community via engagement. Politics which aims to bring working-class Catholics and Protestants together around real issues …
>
> You have to ask why Willie McCrea stood in support of Wright? You then have to ask why Billy Wright sounded like a Paisleyite? My greatest fear about the LVF is that they see themselves as the armed wing of the DUP. (Interview 1999)

Moreover, the desire to articulate a non-sectarian mode of Unionist politics was also based upon other forms of material cognition. As noted by Billy Hutchinson:

> Therefore, breaking out of containment actually means talking about the other realities that exist in Loyalist and even Republican communities. For example, we need to focus on economic and social deprivation, talk about women's rights and think genuinely about tolerant community politics. Breaking out means not simply accepting what we are told is tradition. (Interview 1999)

Hutchinson and Ervine's renegotiation of loyalism clearly indicated the aspiration to reconstruct communities via less traditionalist sectarian discourses. In terms of discharging the spatial containment of the Loyalist 'sanctuary' the ideological goal of reconstruction was to develop what Sack (1998) would acknowledge as 'porous spaces'. However, it is also clear that such a reconstruction process also aimed to ensure that the interaction between the Protestant and Catholic sanctuaries did not dilute the desire to remain within the United Kingdom and to express what were seen as the values of a non-sectarian Protestant culture. Evidently, as noted by Hutchinson when interviewed:

> There is nothing wrong in being a Loyalist and to love one's country. But there is something wrong in articulating a type of politics which is made blind by sectarianism.

Such progressive political ideas were soundly rejected and denounced by the LVF as signs of betrayal of Protestant doctrine. As an LVF respondent in Upper Bann stated:

> The PUP are wicked. They promote the rights of fruits [gays] and fenians [Catholics]. Fruits should be stoned to death not supported.

For the LVF the notion of breaking out of containment and adopting a mode of radical politics which challenges class, gender and sexual relationships of power is problematic to the extent of being unacceptable. In terms of communal devotion and identity the LVF argued that Loyalist places should be constructed around intolerance of what are perceived as non-traditional cultures. In effect the Loyalist 'sanctuary' should be based upon a form of resistance not only to Irish nationalism but also toward secularisation and sexuality equality. The LVF imagined a resistance that implied reproducing and defending the cabalistically sublime stewardship of Loyalist places against all 'others' which are deemed as ethnically or spiritually flawed. Clearly, the protection and reproduction of Loyalist community demanded a devotion and commitment to the antecedents of biblical scripture, although hypocritical in terms of criminal activity engaged within. In sum, the division, which was contested within the context of controlling Loyalist communities, between upholding fundamentalism and the meta-narrative of 'election' is set against an articulate, secular and non-fundamentalist Loyalist culture. As Billy Wright noted, when interviewed, in relation to the secularism of the PUP:

> Billy Hutchinson actually admitted that he was an agnostic. These people have damned themselves and they must be stopped from damning others.

What remained for the LVF was the need to control communities and to ensure their impermeability in the face of socio-cultural and political change and what is construed as secular contamination. As an LVF member (North Antrim) surmised in what appears as fundamentalist rhetoric:

> We have a God-given duty. We are ambassadors for decency and tradition. We take our stand against Loyalist betrayal, cross-community building and Romanism. Loyalism can only tolerate the defeat of the Sinn Fein/IRA machine. There are many fine Loyalists who will maintain that cause. (Statement read to author)

As such, territory was to be eulogised as pure, uncontaminated and contingent upon the reproduction of ethnic election. Resistance for the UVF was not merely about reproducing a particular identity, but was also concerned with defending morally prescribed borders against traitordom. As Wright stated:

> I will not be leaving Ulster. Ulster will not be leaving me. Why did fellow Loyalists turn their guns on me? They are serving an anti-Loyalist agenda, they are serving forces that want to put the people out of Ulster who want to fight on. The fellow Loyalists against me will give succour to the scum of the Sinn Fein/IRA. (Statement read to author)

Policing your own

At the point of opportunity for transitional Loyalists to expand and spread their influence after the cessation of IRA violence the main paramilitary groups were increasingly diverted from such a cause by those involved in unacceptable 'Loyalist' activities. The desire to control those who dissented against the peace process provided a new dimension in the control and legitimation of territory within Northern Ireland. It was this struggle between variant forms of loyalism over the control of ideology and community devotion, which more than anything else indicated that loyalism was endorsing political change and alteration, although the impact of policing such divisions was extremely destabiling. For those who dissented against peacebuilding, the desire to create 'new' resistance-based communities was a key strategy.

> It goes back to the CLMC and again, there was promises made by the three mainstream organisations, the UDA, the UVF and the Red Hand, that no fourth grouping would be allowed to emerge. This didn't materialise. The UVF and Red Hand stuck to what they had agreed to but unfortunately the UDA didn't and this fourth grouping was allowed to emerge and it was an awful thing because it created another vehicle that people could jump onto. In other words, if you were having to discipline someone within your own organisation, tactics became different because where you once would have expelled someone, you had to be conscious of what you were doing because them people would have run and jumped onto this other vehicle, so that vehicle had to be destroyed once and for all because the LVF, and there is proof beyond a shadow of a doubt, started five feuds and the last feud, people were adamant and determined, that this would be the feud to end all feuds.[5] (RHC respondent, North Belfast)

The removal of the LVF, via feud violence, was summarised as follows:

> It has allowed people to refocus and look at the direction of where we are going. It used to be seven days a week you would be talking about the so-called LVF but now basically they are not mentioned and you don't hear it coming from others lips and that that allows us to focus on our transformation. (UVF respondent, West Belfast)

Loyalists contend that the use of violence was an outcome of ineffective policing and that groups such as the LVF were manipulated by shadowy State groups. However, it is also obvious from the following quote that the assault upon authority was a major factor in the re-introduction of violence after 1994:

> The LVF are viewed as nothing more than a drugs cartel. The latest feud was created by people from Ballysillan Avenue area of North Belfast who believed that they could taunt and humiliate UVF personnel on the basis that 'here we had an old and tired leadership who', first of all they believed we were politically handcuffed, and secondly and more importantly, they believed were too old to want to fight. Again they were wrong, they miscalculated. (UVF respondent, North Belfast)

Moreover, there appears to have been a point at which it was decided that such groups were undermining the peace process and ultimately there was a need to remove organisations that could adopt disaffected elements within the UVF:

Reluctantly, because no one gets involved in a feud because they want to, reluctantly you have to do something about it. There is a consultation process going on within the UVF and they want to get from 'A' to 'Z' and there are a lot of letters in between so they have to go through them. Going around those area meetings, it's sometimes up to 3 or 400 people at them. The one re-occurring question was 'but what are we going to do about the LVF', 'how can we go away', 'how can we put our guns away if these people are going to come looking for us or come up our garden path or whatever' … It was patently obvious that these people were just not going to leave us alone and we had to show them in no uncertain fashion that we were not taking this, were not taking this, we want peace, we don't want to use guns, we want to go away but we are not having you [the LVF] standing in the road, it's too important. (UVF respondent, East Belfast)

Again the focus is upon the divisions in discursive morality between progressive and regressive loyalisms.

I think that has been a build up of the different things that's happened within the feuding aspect of loyalism where you had people trying to take over whole swathes of areas and plying their trade and people, good people, within those areas were saying 'no, enough is enough and we are not going to take it'. If we were willing to fight Republicanism to look after our communities then we are not going to let gangsters try to destroy it. (UVF respondent, West Belfast)

Another significant problem for those wishing to transform loyalism was the on-going problem of criminality, the killing of drug-dealers, hostility towards the leadership who were insufficient in the punishing those involved in drug-dealing, and a Loyalist landscape in which some Loyalist areas were significant sites of criminality and others were not. As noted by a UVF respondent in North Down:

This fella came to me and says that so and so would pay me £400 per week if I allowed him to peddle drugs. He was out of the organisation the next day. I and the ones I lead have spent nearly every hour of everyday stopping drugs being dealt by our people. It's simple you deal drugs and you're out. You will be getting a knock on the door. I am fed up with it, it's the PSNI's job not mine. But they just don't do it, so muggins here does it. I'm the one will get a gun stuck in my face and get up the next day and read in the papers that Loyalists are all scum drug dealers.

The Northern Ireland Affairs Committee at Westminster (2002) estimated that paramilitaries were making up to £18 million per year through smuggling, extortion, drugs, illegal fuel-laundering and armed robbery. Among loyalists it was suggested that the LVF, the smallest Loyalist group, was making the most at around to £2 million per annum, the UVF £1.5 million and the UDA up to £1 million. As indicated the vast majority of criminality was linked to Republican groups (Silke 1998a). Despite the obvious conclusion that drug-dealing and extortion causes social harm and is illegal the amounts involved are not as extensive as suggested in the press, and indeed are relatively small when it is considered that organised crime in the UK is estimated at £40 billion annually (Greenwood 2010). In the Republic of Ireland it is estimated that £3million per week is made by organised gangs importing cigarettes. Interestingly Hugh Orde, former PSNI Chief Constable, mooted changes in paramilitary activity regarding illegal drugs:

> cannabis, it is still the most widely seized drug and is still the domain largely of the paramilitaries in terms of fund raising and other activities, but we are seeing some early signs of an attempt to try on behalf of some of the paramilitary groups to distance themselves from that type of activity. (Northern Ireland Affairs Committee 2006: 26)

During the same Committee meeting Orde made the point that determining what is paramilitary crime is complex as it was divided between organisational demand and personal gain through the use of a paramilitary structure. This point was not dissimilar to that made by many Loyalists who contended that much illegal activity was centred upon the exploitation of organisational structures for personal gain. As Orde observed:

> It is very hard to judge what is paramilitary crime and, in the current debate, what is ordinary crime being committed by paramilitaries for their own gain rather than the organisation's gain … (Northern Ireland Affairs Committee 2006: 19)

According to a retired senior police officer Loyalists were less capable than their Republican counterparts:

> a different type of criminality, one that was much more obvious to see. It is fair comment to say that Loyalist criminality is quite ostentatious, it involves senior UDA people walking into Chinese restaurants and not paying for it; it involves people who are what I call 'hand-to-mouth feeders', they got £3000 for extortion and three days later they went to Tenerife. The criminality that was involved in Republicans involved major scams involving oil smuggling, involving lots of other things like that, which was very well put away, quite sophisticated in being put away … the Loyalists never took £26 million from the Northern Bank… (Interview with author)

As David Ervine surmised when interviewed:

> Dealing drugs, involvement in criminality, they are problems that loyalism has to try and cope with; some would argue it doesn't cope very well. I would say in some respects it copes far better than people believe because I am convinced of the degree of manipulation and control among the cardboard cut out characters by the security services. That has made it extremely difficult for loyalism to lead, it's been almost impossible at times where loyalism were controlled never mind lead and there is a fundamental difference between controlling and leading. There is serious, serious manipulation by the security services. Proving it is one thing but laying enough circumstantial evidence to place in great doubt your belief of launderette status of government, I think I can do that.

The issue that constantly arose among Loyalists respondents concerned why the police had not arrested drug dealers an issues also explored in the media (BBC 2007).

Conclusion

The challenge to mainstream Loyalist authority was met with violence. The unravelling of loyalism after 1994 undoubtedly drew those who supported peace into a violent conflict with those opposed to their cultural and political path. This produced a series of deaths with violence being used to undermine any threat to Loyalist leadership and/or authority. The use of violence as a means to resolve issues evidently removed threat and the potential for future violence but again threw up the contradiction between political and paramilitary loyalism. As Edwards and Boomer noted:

> Perhaps the least analysed ramifications of this violence are the detrimental effects militarist actions have had on attempts by politicos to transform the conflict onto a more creative and positive interface. (2004: 20)

As explained by a UDA respondent in West Belfast:

> A few mafia types with their drugs who were obsessed with the glitz and the big cars and the big drug money upset the whole applecart. You had done all this lifting for the peace process and the next thing was being put back at square one, by a pack of self-serving eegits and scum. It put political loyalism back ten years. Some just packed it in and went enough's, enough. A sort of way of dealing with it. However, you looked at it the drug barons hit political loyalism below the watermark. But you have to stuggle on, because no one cares about people here. If we don't struggle on we will go nowhere. I don't mean nowhere fast I just mean nowhere. You look at the Lower Shankill now, it's a better place. Who made it a better place, who made it a better place to live? It was us and nobody else. So as you know you get no recognition for that, but to me the recognition is that the Lower Shankill is a safer place. There is no normality in these places so you can't judge people by the normal rules, this is a very damaged community, and no one cares. But it is now a bit of a better place and we turned it round.

Notes

1　There was a constant reference in interviews with Loyalists that they had provided information to the police about such persons but to no avail in terms of prosecutions.

2　Adair has on several occasions stated that he received assistance from the British army (Adair 2007).

3　A shameful series of events in 2001 when members of the Upper Ardoyne community used violence and intimidation to intimidate Catholic school girls aged five to eleven from entering the neighbourhood in which Holy Cross School was located.

4 Whilst the author was undertaking talks with the LVF in Long Kesh in 1998 and 1999 members alleged that only Free Presbyterian ministers were permitted to provide religious guidance. All members stated that the DUP were to be respected due to their opposition to the Belfast Agreement. Moreover, several members stated that persons involved with the DUP supported their stand. The validity of such suppositions is unknown but was echoed by those opposed to the LVF. In *Combat* (1998: 9) in a article entitled 'Pantomime in Portadown' the following was stated: 'this link between the DUP and LVF was strengthened a short time later with the introduction of the LVF's Policy Document and subsequent interview in which they stated that they were 100% behind the political misdirection of the DUP'.

5 This refers to an episode in 2005 when, via non-violence, UVF members picketed the homes of alleged LVF members in Garnerville, a small Protestant estate in East Belfast. It is alleged that the breaking point came when a young male was asked to hold weapons for the LVF and his refusal to do so led to public confrontations with residents.

Transformation is about asking 'who am I
and why am I driven by fear?' Then when you
get through that you go 'that's where I'm heddin'
[heading] and I want others to go with me
(UVF respondent)

5 Loyalist conflict transformation: beyond idiocy

Fintan O'Toole's notion of loyalism as an idiocy within a fragmented culture (cited in Howe 2005: 4) ignored the nature of Loyalist conflict transformation and its successes when it has aimed for collective and constitutive relationships through which Loyalists can explore the various contexts of conflict and conflict recovery. Personal goals and trajectories are important, but without organisational commitment the peace process may have stalled and there would have been no authority in place to guide and develop wider commitments. A key variable in conflict transformation is the medium and direction of learning that is linked to Lederach's (2005) questions on how to guide the knowledge required in shifting out of conflict, dealing with the impediments to transformation and setting key definitional goals. A fundamental issue linked to such developments is that groups such as Loyalists do not need to abandon their ideological goals and commitments but that they can instead learn how these can be assembled into reasonable, sustainable and developmental aims and objectives (Shirlow et al. 2005).

Loyalist-centred conflict transformation has been tied to what Habermas (1984, 1987) would contend are problem-solving as opposed to problem-seeking discourses. Part of the *raison d'être* of conflict transformation is to recognise that, following Habermas's (1984) life-worlds perspective, the accumulation of 'unreservedly' held customs and traditions are assumptions implanted in each individual's everyday life and are of crucial importance (Cohen and Arato 1992). In a society such as Northern Ireland life-worlds are as shared (fear, poverty and social exclusion), as they are disparate (identity, imagined history, segregation and cultural disposition). The key solution for those involved in conflict transformation is to seek and pursue inter-community communication and dialogue with the 'other' in order to undermine conflict, but at the same time assert ideological difference in order to maintain solidarity and therefore capacity and authority. A significant problem for former combatants is encountered if they move ahead of their constituencies, which is a reason why Loyalist decommissioning was slow and at times the process of change uneven and contested. Evidently, it is in the material sphere of similarity between deprived communities and their experience of injustice, social exclusion and inequality that common interests and values can be asserted. As Mezirow (1989, 1995) implies, conflict transformation should be centred upon the acts that aim for 'effective discourse' and in turn be centred upon participation that is:

> free from coercion; have equal opportunity to assume the various roles of discourse (to advance beliefs, challenge, defend, explain, assess evidence, and judge arguments); become critically reflective of assumptions; are empathic and open to other perspectives; are willing to listen and to search for common ground or a synthesis of different points of view; and can make a tentative best judgment to guide action. (1995: 42)

Ultimately, as Lederach (2005) argues, such a context requires validation via effective participation and long-term goal setting. The spatial boundaries between Loyalist and Republican communities are not as rigidified when we consider socio-economic issues such as crime, educational disadvantage and the impact of conflict in socio-psychological terms. Therefore, working on such issues within an inter-community framework is linked to shared life-worlds. These sites of similarity provide the medium through which conflict transformation becomes 'a process of engaging with and the transformation of relationships, interests, discourses ...' (Miall 2004: 3) because, as Väyrynen (1991: 163) has suggested, conflict transformation creates 'actor transformation'.

Those Loyalists involved in conflict transformation are aware that political settlement does not remove all aspects of confrontation. Evidently, interface violence, militaristic wall murals, parading, disputed territoriality and other forms of disagreement require deliberation and inspection in order to enhance and stabilise a non-violent and non-aggressive frame. Galtung and Hoivik's (1971) notion of a positive peace is one that is led by effecting change after a political settlement has been arrived at and in so doing considers the nature, impact and meaning of other structural concerns. Thus the post-conflict period must aim to shift into a more holistic meaning of harm regarding death, injury and socio-psychological burdens. In addition, a society that remains socially divided and in which social divisions lead to lower life expectancies among the socially excluded, within which such persons are educationally disadvantaged and in which other harms are manifest, requires exploration and challenge. Promoting order and stability out of conflict is not enough and requires challenges to other forms of inequity and social, gendered and racial division. Thus conflict transformation is not solely conflict-related in the sense of resolving armed violence, but is required to seek more universal goals of inclusion and social effect. Decommissioning and the demobilisation of non-State armed groups is only one strategy that is in itself a hollow-signifier if it is not applied and co-joined to societal transformation (Kigma 2001; McEvoy and Shirlow 2009). As Barak (2005: 131–132) makes clear:

> A distinction has been made between 'negative' and 'positive' peace. The former is viewed as stemming from the mere absence of adversarial conflict and violence; the latter, from the presence of humanism, mutualism and freedom from oppression.

Understanding that former combatants have a social justice delivery and demand role not only challenges the structural causes of conflict but signifies that armed opposition was tied to cognitive realisations of multiply constructed societal harms that remain after peace accord-centred settlements. Conflict transformation has and may well develop a more critical edge given that Loyalists, unlike Republicans, have no political movement, in government, to which they must publicly accord corroboration. It is also evident that those who advanced conflict transformation did so to not simply undermine armed opposition but to also critique modes of governance and government that affect social mobility and the inclusion of the Protestant working class, resonant of Väyrynen's argument that those agents involved in conflict transformation have 'interests that change over time as a consequence of the social, economic and political dynamics of societies' (1991: 4). Or, as Mitchell asserts (2002: 1), '... transformation is a process that will make up for the inadequacies of mere resolution'. Schmalleger (1996: 516), in his promotion of peace-making criminology, promotes 'a perspective which holds that crime-control agencies and the citizens they serve should work together to alleviate social problems and human suffering and thus reduce crime' an example here led by those involved with Northern Ireland Alternatives (NIA).

The operation of conflict transformation initiatives is crucial in the delivery of alternative methods and squarely based upon the ushering forth of ideas that evolved in the mid-1970s. Loyalists have been key in the formation of inter-community groups to stop interface violence, have provided seminars to youths to promote anti-violent approaches, worked with Republicans on shared history, harm and other issues, and have developed links with statutory agencies, State combatants and victims groups in order to draw resources into deprived communities, but there is insufficient recognition of this. Moreover, the risks taken for peace, the pursuit of inter-community partnership and the challenge to ethno-sectarianism is virtually unknown in public discourse. Loyalists are partly responsible for this due to their failure publicly to promote positive activities, but there is also a functional form of residual criminalisation, dismissal and intolerance:

> You get to go on the TV or radio to talk about how you are building peace and the first question you are asked is about Loyalist violence, drugs or crime. Then you get

about a second to explain what you are doing and then they sum up by sorrta saying it's all a lot ah balls and what about the victims? There are three things that happen. You think, it was because there were victims that you ended up joining the UVF, that you have served your time inside and that you don't want any more victims. The media are the conflict junkies not me or my mates. I want to move away from that ... I would have been gettin' the same lack of respect from them people if I was beating wee lads and selling drugs outside a primary school. They just see us as scum. (UVF respondent, North Down)

The lack of constructive exposure provided to transitional Loyalist activity appears to be linked to an anchor of illicit Loyalist activity that is firmly attached to positive Loyalist practice within public consciousness. There appears to be no sense that loyalism is in any way dichotomised between those affecting change and those who maintain prohibited social and criminal activities. We here explore two case studies of purposeful Loyalist activity via NIA and the Conflict Transformation Initiative (CTI).

Strengths and limitations of Loyalist approaches to conflict transformation

Limitations that affect Loyalist transformation are linked to a legitimacy afforded by statutory agencies, a problematic relationship with mainstream Unionist parties and the difficulties associated with social capital and weak community infrastructure issues. Despite such limitations, violent feuding and general rejection, Loyalists have and continue to play a valuable role through defined leadership. Contributions to community-based restorative justice programmes, interface work and projects around reconciliation have been vital to the diminution and transformation of localised cultures of violence (Shirlow and McEvoy 2008). Largely underpinning their capacity to do such work is a strengths-based style of conflict transformation based on localised knowledge, intra-community networks, authority to deal with complex issues as a result of their past actions and evident skills and abilities, many of which were developed during incarceration (McEvoy and Shirlow 2009; Ward and Gannon 2006; Ward and Maruna 2007). As McEvoy and Shirlow (2009: 42–43) have argued:

> By working with and aligning themselves in a very public fashion to values of non-violence, human rights, inclusiveness and respect and tolerance for differences, such former prisoners have provided significant small 'p' political leadership in transforming community attitudes to violence. Amongst other benefits, their involvement has also been central to efforts at persuading paramilitary organisations to desist from punishment violence, to refer 'complainants' from the community to the programmes and to consider their own internal organisational attitudes towards violence.

Despite a long history of indiscriminate sectarian attacks against civilians and a well-established proclivity to criminality amongst some, there has been an evident leadership in the transition from violence and a determination to secure transitional and conflict transformation-driven loyalism. Likewise, in 2002, the UVF expelled members in South Belfast who had been involved in racist attacks against immigrants living in the Village area of Belfast, while the UDA in Lisburn undertook significant intervention work to encourage residents to promote good relationships between them and newly arrived Polish immigrants (McAuley et al. 2010).

Mitchell (2008) opines that such leadership has been one of their most important contributions to post-conflict transition. 'Grass-roots' community leadership and stretching members beyond violence and promoting alternative forms of engagement has also arguably contributed to community empower-ment in local areas (Gribbin et al. 2005). Acting both 'within' and 'without' their communities, campaigns for establishing employment and economic development schemes in local areas, the provision of welfare and advice services, children's activities and family projects are valuable examples of this work (Shirlow et al. 2005). Finally, due to their uniquely placed position and skills, Loyalists have played a key role in building bridges with civil society and engaging with alienated and/or harder to reach individuals within their communities (Gribbin et al. 2005). While there are multiple examples of this display of 'moral' or 'transformative' leadership, perhaps the most illustrative, given the discussion below on Loyalist former combatants involved in restora-tive justice schemes and the Conflict Transformation Initiative, is their capacity to dissuade younger generations from becoming involved in violent activity. As Shirlow et al. (2005: 88) have argued, it:

> is precisely because of their violent pasts that many former prisoners are ideally placed to provide leadership For those who have both influenced and been on the receiving end of extreme violence, often it holds little allure. Their rejection of the efficacy of violence as a strategy is itself a powerful exercise in moral leadership and community capacity building.

Using their experience as a deterrent, Loyalists can show the motivations behind violence and how these were misplaced, and the burdens imprisonment placed upon family members. Doing so is an invaluable way of transmitting lessons about the past, dispelling myths[1] and falsehoods and discouraging its repetition. In this vein, the contemporary UVF now regard themselves as 'fourth generation Ulster Volunteers,' but see one of its key tasks as 'the prevention of a fifth generation" (McAuley et al. 2010: 30).

That said, Loyalists have experienced a number of distinct structural and practical limitations. A key problem has been, as noted in previous chapters, dissent within loyalism and the effect of the wreckers and spoilers. The activity of criminal groups who continued to promote ethno-sectarian discord has undoubtedly frozen capacity at key points. In addition, the lack of legitimacy afforded to Loyalist conflict transformation initiatives by statutory agencies – a factor compounded by the tenuous relationship with mainstream Unionist parties and the difficulties associated with the perception that Loyalist communities have poor social capital and a weak community infrastructure – has also hindered efforts. As the case of the CTI highlights, effectiveness has been hampered by the reluctance of a government minister to recognise legitimacy and positive intent (Mitchell 2008). As Gormally (cited in Mitchell 2008: 10) has noted:

> The issue [for the State] is whether to support clearly peaceful activities or to assume that paramilitary leopards will never change their spots and oppose any extension of their influence.

Moreover, there have been double standards about the stance adopted by statutory agencies in their dealings with Loyalists. Gribbin et al. (2005) found that Loyalist respondents were clear in their assertions that they had good-quality co-operative and productive relationships with particular individuals and local offices of statutory agencies, yet such cordiality was rarely extended to official acknowledgement or support in the form of public statements, funding or other resources. This problematic relationship has been further exacerbated by a tenuous relationship with many Unionist politicians and political parties. While many Loyalists have been much more willing to acknowledge their role in the conflict and support the notion that each community has to share responsibility for the past, one of their most commonly expressed grievances is that while some Unionist politicians provided the leadership for and context of violent enactment such persons now reject them out of hand. This is both de-motivating in terms of legitimacy but also motivating in terms of ensuring the independence of more radical thought and actions.

Mitchell (2008) has for example noted that there are various cases of mainstream Unionist politicians privately using former combatants on the ground, while simultaneously denouncing them in the media (Cassidy 2008). This sense of alienation due to de-legitimisation has contributed to an abiding sense amongst those involved in community work that they are working on behalf of:

> a community within a community ... an underclass (marginalised) by middle Unionists, the media ... middle unionism doesn't like [conflict transformation] because they don't want a working class movement. (Shirlow and McEvoy 2008: 138–139)

Loyalist communities also suffer from poor social capital and a weak and fragmented community infrastructure largely borne out of their social location and experiential realities (Cairns et al. 2003; Gribbin et al. 2005). This backdrop inevitably impacts on those engaged in conflict transformation work.

The definition of social capital refers to the social relations and norms that are embedded in any given social structures which engender citizen engagement and mutually designed co-operation and commitment. It is directly related to other forms of capital, such as human capacities and talents, the formation and distribution of wealth, the mode and nature of engagement in cultural renewal and the presentation of agreed symbolic intent. Pranis (2001) argues that a community which has significant forms of social capital has created embedded networks, norms and high levels of social trust that assist co-operation for common benefit and is a place within which citizens feel secure, socially included and have a capacity to influence outside agencies and actors.

As noted above, the suggestion that Loyalist communities suffer from poor social capital has not been uncommon. Cairns et al. (2003) revealed that Loyalist communities contained less social capital than Catholic areas, and experienced a greater reluctance to engage in community development work and greater difficulty with funding proposals, as well as there being an 'apathy' towards and 'lack of confidence' in the ability of Loyalist communities to deal with pressing social issues. Therefore Protestant working-class communities tend to be more fractured, have a lower skill base within the community sector and have both an actual and perceived incapacity regarding conflict transformation initiatives. There are a number of possible subsidiary explanations for these apparent weaknesses, such as that conflict transformation initiatives have tended to focus on single-identity work, and that there have been difficulties applying for European Union funding, a major source of income for nationalist and Republican groups under the Peace and Reconciliation I and II programmes.

Moreover, as Shirlow and McEvoy (2008) note, one possible reason for Republicans' greater success in grant-writing and obtaining funding is their self-confidence in such dealings deriving from their more secure place within their own communities and the nature of their political project, whereas within the Protestant working class there has been a historical culture of subservience and deference to 'big house unionism' fostered by Unionist hegemony during the Stormont era and the conditions of Direct Rule (Cassidy 2008, Spencer 2008). Resultant passivity and ennui has arguably both undermined the capacity of Loyalists to mobilise and create a wider impetus for the progression of strong community leadership (Gallaher 2007). It is perceptible that the socio-political estrangement of Loyalist communities has reinforced their lack of community buoyancy (Spencer 2008), therefore, former combatants have a key role in that they are prepared to set, define and lead challenges to community fracture. Loyalists thus fill a space that appears due to a lack of Unionist leadership regarding inter-community initiatives and practices, a similar role to that promoted by the Republican movement, who led and developed community energy into more positive transactions within their community. However, loyalism has insufficient political verification or mandate to do so. In essence their role is truly processed by internally driven ethics.

Northern Ireland Alternatives

Northern Ireland Alternatives is a community-based restorative justice scheme developed and supported by former members of the UVF and RHC. Marshall (1996: 37, cited in Braithwaite 2002: 11) has defined restorative justice as 'a process whereby all the parties with a stake in a particular offence come together to resolve collectively how to deal with the aftermath of the offence and its implications'. The key principle of restorative justice is therefore to restore individuals and their relationships with their community (Roche 2001). As a consensual and voluntary form of conflict resolution, restorative justice is not a trial process as conventionally associated with traditional retributive justice processes which focuses on determining guilt and apportioning blame and punishment. Instead, the process of restoration is centred upon notions and values such as reconciliation, peacemaking, healing, community participation, respectful dialogue and re-establishment, which affect a triangular relationship between the victim, offender and community (Braithwaite 2002). Such a 'harm-focused' approach to conflict transformation promotes the engagement of multifarious stakeholders via a framework within which the multiple aims of justice – victim service and support, offender rehabilitation and integration, community safety and crime control/prevention and community empowerment and resourcing – are both developed and expressed (Mika and Zehr 2003).

As restorative justice is restitution- or reparation- driven it can deactivate power imbalances between the victim and offender and in turn stimulate mutual appreciation between perpetrator and victim (Johnstone 2002). For offenders, participation can stimulate an appreciation of moral/social accountability, promote reintegration, disassemble vicious cycles of violence and can stimulate self-awareness, active listening, communication skills and emotional literacy (Braithwaite 2002). Finally, restorative justice involves and empowers affected communities, increasing their capacity to recognise and respond to community-based crime, creating non-violent social relationships and aid the building of community pride (Mika and Zehr 2003; Johnstone 2002). As McEvoy and Eriksson (2006) contend, community participation in decision-making processes adds transparency, accountability and legitimacy and minimises the risk of renewed conflict. It also removes institutionalised responses that rarely aid recovery and community restoration (*Journal of Prisoners on Prisons* 1997).

NIA and Community Restorative Justice Ireland (CRJI) grew out of the broader context of peacemaking efforts surrounding the first paramilitary ceasefires in 1994 and latterly the signing of the Belfast Agreement in 1998. In large part, the projects were established to facilitate paramilitary organisations, specifically the IRA and UVF, to move away from violent punishment systems developed over the previous three decades (McEvoy and Mika 2002). This brutal system of 'informal' justice, wherein Republican and Loyalist paramilitaries took on responsibility for 'policing' their areas through punishment beatings, shootings and banishments, saw approximately 2300 people between 1973 and 1998 become the victims of paramilitary punishment shootings and, from 1983 onwards, approximately 1700 individuals became the victims of paramilitary punishment beatings (McEvoy and Mika 2001). Against this backdrop, restorative justice schemes were designed to allow paramilitaries to (in their own terms) 'disengage responsibility' from such acts, handing dispute resolution back to the local communities (McEvoy and Mika 2002: 535). Such projects have made a significant contribution to lowering levels of punishment violence in the communities in which they have operated, have contributed to changing attitudes towards violence in such communities and have enhanced the capacity of local communities to take ownership over local justice issues and to develop the self-confidence for a partnership with statutory agencies (McEvoy and Erikkson 2006).

Against this backdrop, NIA (formerly Greater Shankill Alternatives) was established in 1997 following the completion of a two-year action research project by Tom Winstone, a former life-sentence UVF prisoner, investigating alternatives to paramilitary punishment beatings and attacks. Four specific problems were identified: the failure of the formal criminal justice system; the breakdown of relationships between the community and the statutory sector; antisocial behaviour in the local community; and punishment beatings (North Belfast Alternatives undated). NIA has now grown to encompass six offices with projects in the Greater Shankill Area, North, South and East Belfast and North Down, and is a registered charity and normally employs between 100 and 150 volunteers across Northern Ireland. Table 5.1, taken from the Criminal Justice Inspectorate Northern Ireland's (CJINI) (2007: 6) inspection of NIA, gives an indicative guide to staff and volunteer levels, their geographical distribution and organisational expenditure. Notably, significant shares of employees were on short-term monthly contracts.

The central feature of NIA's intensive restorative justice programme is the development of a contract that specifies how a young person will make amends to the victim(s) of their crime(s) and antisocial behaviour, make reparations to the community for their behaviour, and improve themselves by setting realistic, positive goals. Much of the caseload against which these objectives are structured concerns serious crime and antisocial behaviour, severe and chronic offending youth behaviour and paramilitary punishment violence as well as paramilitary threats and exclusions. Given the success of restorative schemes in decreasing paramilitary punishment attacks, there has also been significant diversification into other areas of community-building and broader

Table 5.1   Employment and expenditure NIA (2006)

	Staff in post	Of whom on monthly contract	Volunteers trained	Volunteers active	Expenditure 2006 (£000s)
Northern Ireland Alternatives	3	1	–	–	133
East Belfast Alternatives	3.5	1	30	10	69
Greater Shankill Alternatives	4	3	100	43	98
North Belfast Alternatives	3.5	2	95	58	64
North Down Impact	2	0	45	16	28

efforts at conflict transformation. NIA's Assistant Director Debbie Watters clearly reflected such an ethos:

> ... restorative justice for me is about healing broken relationships, at all levels within community and society. Justice, for me, in the broadest sense of the word, is about people feeling safe and having a good quality of life. (Payne et al. 2010: 32)

While most referrals to the schemes initially came from paramilitaries, the majority now come from other sources including statutory and voluntary agencies, the PSNI, community activists and families themselves (CJINI 2007a). NIA may also proactively contact children who are known to be causing trouble and may offer to work with them, with the approval of their parents (CJINI 2007a). Reflecting the high standard of work carried out by NIA, in February 2008 the organisation gained accreditation under the Government Protocol for community-based restorative justice schemes (CJINI 2007a). In February 2010, following further inspection by the CJINI, the schemes were found to operate to the standards laid down by the United Nations 'Basic Principles of the use of Restorative Justice Programmes in Criminal Matters'. These criteria included the principles that restorative processes were as follows:

- The scheme should only operate via the free and voluntary consent of the parties (which may be withdrawn at any time);
- That disparities leading to power imbalances, and the safety of the parties should be taken into consideration in referring any case;

and

- Before agreeing to participate all parties should be fully informed of their rights, the nature of the process and the possible consequences of the their decision (CJINI 2010).

Inspectors also sought evidence of the schemes adherence to the *Protocol for Community-Based Restorative Justice Schemes*, published by the government on 5 February 2007. The questions laid out by the Protocol included:

- Are schemes triaging cases correctly and passing appropriate cases to the PSNI?
- Are human rights, the rights of the child and the UN Principles on Restorative Justice observed?
- Is the training of staff and volunteers adequate?

and

- Are proper records kept and stored securely? (CJINI 2010)

The Inspectors found the conduct of NIA to be overwhelmingly positive on all aspects (CJINI 2010). The involvement of Loyalists in restorative justice schemes has been vital to their success as they provide leadership, significant legitimacy and credibility which has engendered an organic and embedded style of local conflict transformation. Inspectors from the CJINI conducting the reports and evaluations of NIA in 2007 and 2010 clearly reflected positively upon this:

> Some of those working in the scheme have a history of paramilitary membership and their history to some extent contributes to their status in their communities and gives them extra influence in dealing with the paramilitaries … organizations such as these are ideally placed to reach those individuals and groups traditionally defined as 'hard to reach'. (CJINI 2010: 4)

Moreover, and in challenging the notion that restorative justice schemes are open to 'capture' and overbearing paramilitary interests and the perpetuation of vigilantism, the CJINI (2007a: 4) reported:

> there is no evidence of Alternatives providing an alternative policing or judicial system … There is no evidence of the schemes being driven by the paramilitaries, and every indication to the contrary.

In 2004 a strident critic of Loyalist violence, the Independent International Monitoring Commission (2009) recognised that community restorative justice programmes operated in an accountable and justifiable manner. Their study showed that between 1998 and 2001, Greater Shankill Alternatives received 129 formal referrals or inquiries related to punishment threats, violent endangerment and exclusion, and that of these referrals, sixty-two young people became involved in the Intensive Programme addressing the harm caused to their victims, their community and themselves. In sum:

- 74% of cases referred to the Intensive Programme were males aged between ten–eighteen, with the bulk of young people aged thirteen–sixteen;
- 42% of referrals came from paramilitary organisations, 27% came from community sources (victims, families and community organisations), 18% from Social Services and 13% from self referrals and Base 2;
- 90% of all cases were under verified paramilitary threat at the time of referral to the programme;
- 31% of cases were referred for stealing, 21% for malicious damage, arson and vandalism, 18% for car theft and 7% for disruptive behaviour or assault at home or school;
- 86% of young people, once referred, formulated a contract in one month or less;
- 64% of contracts were successfully completed in six months or less;
- 64% of cases were on the Programme for a maximum of seven months, with the range extending from one month to seventeen months;
- 76% of cases involved meetings with victims;
- Over 58% of cases involved previous or current statutory involvement;
- Of the cases that were closed during that period, 87% were successfully completed.

In the eight-month period preceding the formation of NIA there were seventeen cases of punishment violence; this figure fell to only three cases over the next four years. A high-ranking police source also credited the work of NIA in significantly reducing rates of crime and antisocial behaviour committed by young people in the Woodvale area and decreased attacks against police officers (Mika 2002). According to Mika, in the period 2003–2005, NIA prevented 71% of potential paramilitary punishments. This has now risen to over 90%. In addition forty-seven community exclusions were prevented and four previously excluded individuals/families were re-integrated into their former communities (Mika 2006: 27). Given both the success of NIAs in decreasing levels of paramilitary punishment violence, the organisation's credibility within the communities in which it works and changing political circumstances, it has successfully engaged in a process of diversification, expanding its remit and furthering the process of conflict transformation. A large proportion of the organisation's work subsequently relates to community development, support for victims and preventive or diversionary work with young people (CJINI 2007a). Moreover, there is a strongly thera-peutic theme to this work, helping young people come to terms with their delinquent behavior, bringing them back into a relationship with older people and setting them off in new directions towards education, training and eventual employment (CJINI 2007a). In 2006 NIA worked with 1035 young people via intensive and preventive youth work and an additional 1267 individuals through victim support work (CJINI 2007a: 14). They remain active in decreasing tensions at a number of 'interfaces' and have been engaged in not only 'policing' the boundaries between Loyalist and Republican commu-nities, but also intervening within youth projects to challenge the 'rationale' of sectarianism (Mitchell 2008; McAuley et al 2010). For example, in Kilcooley in North Down, members of Alternatives successfully facilitated agreement among the four Loyalist paramilitary factions about the flying of flags and the management of the annual 11 July bonfire (CJINI 2007a). Likewise, in the Greater Shankill area of Belfast, staff members helped rebuild relations with the police following the 2005 Whiterock riots which followed the disputed rerouting of an Orange Order march (CJINI 2007b).

The CJINI (2010) follow-up review of NIA's community-based restorative justice schemes (post-accreditation) has led to the Department for Social Development (DSD) currently funding NIA through its Neighbourhood Renewal Programme to help meet the neighbourhood renewal targets in each area. As specified by the DSD, NIA is mandated to deliver intensive youth and family support with young people involved in antisocial behavior; prevention work with groups of young people involved in antisocial behaviour; deliver cultural awareness and mediation programs, crime prevention sessions and a conflict transformation volunteer programme. NIA is engaged in a myriad of other programmes designed to, for example, facilitate community transforma-tion and empowerment, decrease and respond to antisocial behavior and provide counselling and social services. A total of ten projects are detailed in the CJINI (2010) report – Action for Community Transformation (ACT),[3] Pupils and Communities Together (PACT), Mediation and Community Support (MACS) in partnership with the Northern ireland Housing Executive (NIHE), Restorative Adult Practices (RAP) in partnership with the Probabtion Board of Northern Ireland (PBNI), Referrals from Social Services, Pathways Counseling Project, Partnership with Challenge for Youth and the inter-community Terry Enright Foundation, Belfast Outreach Project,[4] and Street-by-Street.[5]

Given the depth and breadth of the work engaged in by NIA, CJINI Inspectors reported that their 'only real concern is NIA's capacity to continue to meet the increasing demands for their interventions and a fear that the organisation over-stretches itself and staff begin to "burn out"' (CJINI 2010: 19). For those who have been involved with NIA, either as a party to a restorative intervention or statutory bodies who have worked closely with the organisation, in the main, their experience has been overwhelmingly positive and high praise has been offered. The perspectives of victims, offenders, their families, community members and representatives of statutory agencies have also been positive.[6]

In echoing[7] positive sentiments and speaking of the capacity of restorative justice programmes to transform the lives of those who participate in their schemes, CJI inspectors who undertook the 2007 pre-accreditation investigation reported that they found:

> remarkable evidence of small triumphs: letters of apology written obviously with enormous labour and difficulty; statements showing that they now had more of an understanding of the consequences of their unacceptable behaviour for other people; statements showing a will to try to do better in future. They met some impressive young people who testified that they had been offenders but that their lives had been turned around by Alternatives. (CJINI 2007a: 15)

Perhaps the greatest testament to commitment and contribution of Loyalists to conflict transformation and peace-building was the conclusion that the work of NIA was:

> a real enabler for young people in understanding what a 'Shared Future' could look like, a society where disputes, disagreements and difference are managed without recourse to violence. (CJINI 2010: 18)

Braithwaite (2002: 572), a specialist in government regulatory innovation, has argued that:

> Northern Ireland actually has a more mature debate on standards and principles of restorative justice than any society I know. It is certainly a more sophisticated debate than in my home country of Australia. I suspect this is because Northern Ireland has a more politicised contest between State and civil society models of restorative justice than can be found in other places. Such fraught contexts are where there is the greatest risk of justice system catastrophes. But they also turn out to be the contexts with the richest prospects for rising to the political challenges with a transformative vision of restorative justice ... I found the restorative justice programmes in both the Loyalist and Republican communities inspiring. Partly this is because of the courage and integrity of the community leaders involved and the reflective professionalism of those in the State who are open to restorative justice.

Despite such conclusions and independent evaluations, McGrattan (2009: 12) has argued, in a somewhat contradictory manner, that despite the successes of such projects 'the failure to appreciate or contextualise the presence of paramilitaries obscures the significance of those findings'. He also argues that 'the uncritical, de-contextualised reproduction of ex-terrorists' ideas often saturates whole research projects' (2009: 14) without providing adequate evidence that they do so or more importantly any appreciation that ideas and approaches among Loyalists and Republicans who work on such projects are neither homogenous or inflexible. In such terms McGrattan merely repeats a clichéd criminalising discourse that appears to detract from reducing the harm of crime among the socially excluded and marking a positive alternative role for former non-State combatants to play. McGrattan offers a misreading that fails to appreciate that projects such as NIA aim to discuss a destabilising past, build relationships with the PSNI and promote the non-return of 'terrorists'.

The Conflict Transformation Initiative

The CTI initiative is renowned following the decision of the former Social Development Minister and SDLP leader minister Margaret Ritchie[8] to stop funding for the organisation and the subsequent judicial review of that decision. McAuley et al. (2010) argue that the IRA's announcement in 2005 that its military campaign had ceased permitted space for the UDA to begin a process of wider engagement with its membership. A Northern Ireland-wide consultation process with the UDA rank-and-file membership was subsequently undertaken, which questioned the role the UDA could play in transforming loyalism and creating a more peaceful and stable society (Hall 2006). As one member put it, 'the reality is that the war has changed. If we don't work out how we go forward to meet that change then we're not going to be effectively defending the interests of our people' (McAuley et al. 2010: 31). An extract from 'A Community Response to Political Instability – A New Reality', a presentation delivered at a UDA consultation workshop, reflected this backdrop:

> In mid-2005 representatives of the UDA, Northern Ireland's largest Loyalist paramilitary organisation, declared the need to develop a conflict transformation initiative which would: seek to address the causes of the Northern Ireland conflict; create an environment which could bring an end to all paramilitary activity; and set in place a community development strategy aimed at addressing the disadvantage and alienation experienced by Protestant working class communities. (Copy held by author)

The consultation process concluded that the UDA wished to move forward to a new future without paramilitarism and criminality, but needed a vehicle to facilitate such transition. The result was the Ulster Political Research Group's (UPRG) *Conflict Transformation Initiative: Loyalism in Transition* and the outline map for conflict transformation articulated in the document *A New Reality*, published in October 2006 (see Hall 2006). This document, in its 'mission statement', made explicit the aim of the initiative:

> *Conflict Transformation Initiative: Loyalism in Transition* is a new and innovative initiative that will assist key Loyalist activists through a process of conflict resolution and community transformation and will ultimately enable Loyalism to emerge

Table 5.2   CTI proposal

Political	Disaffection among Unionist community as result of Belfast Agreement; increased political fragmentation in Unionist community and absence of political leadership at community level.
Community	Limited community capacity within Loyalist communities; 'interface' community in socio-economically deprived areas.
Socio-economic	High levels of deprivation in Loyalist areas; low levels of education and employability aspirations among young people.
Security	The need and desire to end all paramilitary activity within the Loyalist community; desire to live in a society free from criminality.
Deficits in current practice	Current structures have not provided appropriate mechanisms for engagement within loyalism.

out of thirty-five years of conflict to play a full and meaningful role in a process of reconciliation (Hall 2006: 19).

CTI was therefore intended to be a vehicle for transition at two levels – first to address micro as well as macro political issues by providing a mechanism for involving and engaging elements of political opinion within loyalism in an attempt to identify peace-building opportunities, and second, at the 'grass-roots' level, to begin to create an environment that would lead to the improvement of the quality of life within estranged communities. Or:

> Breaking it down into our own words, we wanted to address the causes of conflict and to play a meaningful role in the regeneration of our communities. And thereby create a long and lasting peace. (Hall 2007: 24)

Against this backdrop, the rationale and need for CTI, as set out in the original grant proposal to DSD, centred on five main themes: political change; community development; socio-economic deprivation; security issues; and deficits in current practices within loyalism. Table 5.2, taken from *Loyalism in Transition, CTI, A Proposal to the DSD* (CTI 2005), provides further detail in summary form.

The grant application and proposal based upon administration via Farset Community Enterprises, a well-established community organisation in West Belfast, was approved in March 2006. Following the successful completion of a six-month development stage, in March 2007 the then Secretary of State Peter Hain announced that the CTI project would receive funding of £1.2 million up to April 2010. The Social Development Minister David Hanson initially commented on the success of the development project:

As the Secretary of State identified when he agreed to support the development project, trying to transform parts of society that have suffered most from the grip of paramilitaries and criminality is not easy and not without risk. Working with community representatives and key organisations in six Loyalist areas, this project has begun to develop real working arrangements that are beginning to make a difference and are helping to turn these areas away from paramilitarism and criminality. The development work has led to an action plan that has identified a clear path towards the ending of paramilitary influence and control of communities. This work is a further development of the Renewing Communities Programme announced last year that focuses on freeing communities from the influence of criminality and paramilitarism. I expect that this additional support will deliver a quickening in pace of the work of the UPRG in their conflict transformation work that the latest IMC report identified was required.[9]

The project was subsequently launched in the Stormont Hotel in April 2007.[10] CTI was mandated with the achievement of four specific objectives and four desired outcomes (Hall 2006). The objectives were:

1   To work with key stakeholders, as part of the wider Neighbourhood Renewal Strategy, to identify and address the particular constraints preventing this constituency from playing its part in community cohesion and peace-building;
2   To play a positive role in equipping this constituency (members and supporters of the UDA) with the necessary skills, capacity and abilities to contribute to the end of all paramilitary activity in those communities;
3   To equip this constituency with the necessary skills, capacity and abilities to contribute positively to a demonstrable reduction of crime and criminality;
4   To create an enabling environment where violence is no longer a viable or realistic option and where all paramilitary weaponry is a thing of the past.

The four desired outcomes specified:

1   Hard to reach Loyalist communities will be fully engaged in the peace building process;
2   An end to all paramilitary activity in Protestant working class communities;
3   A measurable reduction in levels of crime and anti social behaviour within target communities;
4   A movement towards conflict resolution, a shared peaceful and prosperous future.

The above four objectives were further broken down into a number of subsidiary aims and the work plan identified twenty associated action areas with outputs and targets for achievement that was estimated for completion within three years. A selection of examples further illustrates the nature of CTI's work. The programme of work included capacity-building, building links with key stakeholders and critical friends with a focus on training, child and youth development and social economic actions including developing inter-community initiatives and working to meet the aspirations of a shared future. These also involved engaging wider civic society with planned and regular meetings with the churches, trade unions, voluntary and community organisations, business, government and all main political parties. In addition, a number of distinct 'Actions' were established that concerned establishing an International Council of Reference, upgrading skills through the creation of 'Community Toolbox' and developing ongoing local constituency consultations. The CTI also aimed to develop and support entrepreneurship programmes and other socio-economic projects.

Quality of life issues were planned through supporting re-imaging and finally converting the UDA into an 'Old Boy's Association'. CTI was also linked to creating an approach similar to NIA, training former combatants to prevent interface violence and developing more support for conflict transformation generally. It was stated that CTI would continue to further the range of conflict transformation projects already in operation, including assisting in the reduction of tension at sectarian interfaces during the marching season, decreasing crime and criminality – especially the widespread dealing of drugs in the community – stopping extortion and the 'justification' for it and visible positive change through control over the display of flags.

The conditions of funding specified that CTI would be monitored by measurable reductions in levels of crime and anti-social behaviour within a target area. Proof would also have to be provided that CTI would not only work with a range of stakeholders to promote an end to paramilitary activity but prove that there was evidence of demobilisation. Such evidence would be sought not from CTI but via the DSD and other sources that would include the PSNI and the IMC. The conclusion of an agency external from CTI was that:

> An important element in CTI's potential is that the motivation for it and design of it has come from the groups and communities involved in and suffering from the issues it addresses. A priceless ingredient to help any change process to be effective. (Letter from Farset Youth and Community Development Limited to Minister for Social Development, 17 August 2007; copy held by author)

The *CTI Development Project Summary Report* (2006)[11] measured the extent to which the objectives outlined by the funder had been undertaken during the interim stage. With regard to processes of engagement with Loyalist communities and stakeholders a total of fifteen consultation workshops had been held across Northern Ireland, with 2471 attendees and 711 evaluation forms completed and returned. Feedback was positive, indicating that CTI was responding to the aim to move their membership forwards within an agreed process. Concerning work with other key stakeholders in the identification of targets for change and their measurement, CTI had hosted a two-way dialogue with the DSD and NIO via weekly meetings and regular meetings with the NIHE, the Northern Ireland Office (NIO), the IMC, and the PSNI. Engagement was also undertaken with the US Consulate and members of the business community and PSNI.

In addition, members of CTI met with the Irish Catholic Cardinal Sean Brady in 2009 and also, as required, hosted an International Foundation Workshop with thirty-three delegates from the UDA, Palestine, Israel, Transniestria and Moldova in attendance. The workshop report, entitled *Learning from Others in Conflict: Report of an International Workshop*, was published in 2007 (Hall 2007). The conclusions offered on the effectiveness of the initial development stage were also illustrative of the achievements and potential of CTI. The achievements specified included increased confidence and self-esteem among activists and the wider Loyalist constituency, a clearer picture of need emerging in Loyalist communities and a developing strategic approach of working in partnership with mainstream government programmes and funding bodies. It was also concluded that CTI had enhanced relationships with a variety of stakeholders, increased trust and understanding and developed the chances of success of their overall transformation and internationally informed strategy. A further evaluation report published in March 2007 (entitled *CTI Development Project. Interim Evaluation Report*), was undertaken by Jane Field who was appointed in November 2006 to undertake formative external evaluation of the Project.[12] She noted the following:

> The Consultants believe that CTI is unique in that it is targeting precisely those communities that other initiatives have failed to reach.
>
> That CTI was working with representatives from other communities representing people who have been affected by the conflict, including representatives from other Loyalist communities, Republicans, nationalists and Unionists. (Field 2007: 14)

Other positive outputs included a willingness to end all paramilitary activity in Protestant working-class communities and that the work undertaken was of a high standard and had engaged significant numbers of people in positive inquiry. In sum CTI was denoted as being 'a considerable success' (Field 2007: 39). However, in October 2007 the Social Development Minister Margaret Ritchie withdrew all funding from CTI.[13] Her decision came against the backdrop of violence between rival factions of the UDA in Carrickfergus and Bangor in July 2007 and her subsequent announcement in August 2007 that unless the UDA decommissioned all its weapons within sixty days, funding for the project would stop.[14] Her reasons for doing so[15] were explained as being tied to the failure UDA to decommission and that:

There is no excuse now for paramilitarism. It is time for all those who subject their communities to thuggery, extortion and violence, under the pretence of defending them, to get off the stage. (Ritchie 2007: 1)[16]

Against this backdrop, in December 2007 Gerald Solinas was granted leave for a judicial review into the Minister's decision. In the supporting documentation,[17] Solinas argued that it was a funding condition that:

The project will work with a range of stakeholders to promote an end to paramilitary activity in Protestant working class areas and also specifically aim to achieve such a reduction in target areas...

It was also a general condition that Farset should:

... ensure that the Grant shall not be used for the purpose of or in any way connected with the promoting of any political party or religious viewpoint.

As Solinas argued:

I do not believe that either of these conditions has been breached.[18]

The Application was made regarding the following:

(a) The Minister failed to consult, adequately or at all, with the employees of Farset who were involved in delivering the CTI, as required by the duty to act in a procedurally fair manner, before making a decision which had the inevitable effect of terminating their employment.

(b) The Minister's decision was pre-determined and any consultation embarked upon by the Minister's officials was therefore nugatory.

(c) In reaching her decision, the Minister took into account irrelevant considerations, namely the failure of the UDA to make a "start to decommissioning" or to conduct (in the Minister's view) 'meaningful engagement' with the Independent International Commission on Decommissioning. Such considerations were legally irrelevant as they formed no part of the contractual arrangements between the Minister's Department and Farset.

(d) In reaching her decision without the agreement of the Executive, the Minister acted in breach of paragraphs 1.4, 2.4 and 2.5 of the Ministerial Code and thus unlawfully by virtue of sections 20(4), 28A(1) and (10) of the Northern Ireland Act 1998 (as amended).

(e) In reaching her decision the Minister took into account further irrelevant considerations, namely:

(i) The activities of what the Minister knew, or ought to have known, was a breakaway or splinter group of the UDA; and/or

j) The activities of the UDA in areas which were not targeted by the CTI funding which the Minister terminated.[19]

Commencing in November 2008 and ruling through to April 2009, the High Court judge Mr Justice Morgan ruled that Ms Ritchie acted erroneously when cutting CTI's funding as she had breached the ministerial code, which required all ministers to support and act in accordance with all decisions of the Executive and Assembly – all at a cost for the court of c£300,000 (BBC 2009b). The UPRG argued that they had and were involved in meaningful engagement with the Independent International Monitoring Commission, although that was not a condition of funding, and that their group had held nearly forty meetings over the previous three months – before the suspension of funding – with the police regarding crime and criminality. In a subsequent judicial review of the decision taken by Ms Ritchie to remove CTI funding, the validity of that decision was subsequently struck down by the current Lord Chief Justice Sir Declan Morgan on the grounds that she had failed to consult properly with her Executive colleagues in making her decision.[20]

The SDLP had previously been engaged in quite determined political struggles with Sinn Fein over projects concerning former political prisoners. In that instance, tussles centred on the issue of community-based restorative justice programmes, many of which were managed and staffed by former IRA prisoners (McEvoy and Eriksson 2006). Prior to Sinn Fein joining the Policing Board in 2007, such conflicts between the SDLP and Sinn Fein were a reflection of the political contest within nationalism concerning divergent political approaches. Sinn Fein had accused the SDLP of having 'jumped too soon' and therefore reducing the bargaining power of nationalists and Republicans. The SDLP (2006) countered such a position through arguing that restorative justice projects represented Sinn Fein aiming to maintain their own 'private army' in the areas in which they were electorally robust. In the case of the funding of a UDA-linked project, where Sinn Fein were publicly supportive of the funding of the project and the SDLP against, the withdrawal of funding to CTI allowed the SDLP to flex their muscle and indicate that it would deal with Loyalist paramilitarianism. Ultimately, the CTI were caught in a political conflict which was divorced from any objective judgement as to the quality of the work engaged in.[21]

In response to Ritchie's actions CTI activists made three counter-arguments; first, there was a strong refutation of any suggestion that the CTI was linked to the ongoing UDA activity.[22] Second, the withdrawal of the funding represented a failure to appreciate the tentativeness needed to ensure all members of the UDA could move forward. The UPRG spokesperson Frankie Gallagher for example expressed concern that:

> Everybody is trying to double their efforts to maintain the peace process and if this derails the peace process because a minister connects social need with decommissioning, then we are in a disastrous place. (Newsletter 2007)

Similarly, Gerald Solinas argued that:

Playing games with people in hard to reach Loyalist communities, with their social needs, isn't really the best. (BBC 2009b)

Third, Gallagher also linked the withdrawal of funding to the perception that 'mainstream' politicians did not want to see working-class Loyalist communities develop:

> I believe that all those politicians who are misrepresenting this to the public do not even know what the project is about ... What is it that they are afraid of? A resurgent, articulate and vibrant Loyalist community that can't be pulled like rabbits out of hats when they need them? (Newsletter 2007)

Speaking of the relief brought about by the court's decision, Solinas remarked that the decision would bring more certainty to the group and the communities it helped (BBC 2009b). He also made the following post-judgement statement:

> If you asked me would I give £1 million to the UDA I would say no, as would most people would. But if you asked would you give money to help Northern Ireland's most socially deprived areas, reduce interface violence, promote education and youth development, well then most people would say yes.
>
> The problem is Loyalist communities were already suspicious of the political institutions and this decision just reinforces that Stormont had nothing to offer them. It's going to take a lot of hard work to reverse that belief. (*Irish News* 2009)

Notes

1 One myth located within loyalism is that of the Cruithin as the original stock of Ireland driven out by the Celts. Therefore, the Plantation of Ireland was a reclaiming of a homeland. Much of that work has been produced by Adamson (1991). There is no archaeological evidence for such a people.

2 Base 2 is a voluntary project that aims to remove punishment violence and help those who have been victims of such violence. It operates via crisis and long-term intervention with those at risk or who have been victims of paramilitary assault. Base 2 also aims to build better relationships between communities and the statutory sector.

3 Action for Community Transformation is a conflict transformation programme designed to work specifically with former paramilitaries of the UVF and RHC of all ages. It is also designed to work with young men within the community who are on the fringes of paramilitary groups or violence within the community, such as interface rioting (CJINI 2010).

4 Belfast Outreach Project is a partnership between NIA and Challenge for Youth funded by Belfast Community Safety Partnership and aimed at dealing with anti-social behaviour. The programme delivers a combination of detached youth work, group work and drop-in facilities in designated hotspot areas of Belfast and works closely with the PSNI and NIHE (CJINI 2010).

5 Street-by-Street is a project delivered by East Belfast Alternatives and involves an outreach team of staff and volunteers working mostly at night and at weekends

with the Walkway Community Centre. The programme provides reassurance to elderly residents and works with young people gathering at identified anti-social behaviour 'hot spots'. The team works closely with the PSNI, Neighbourhood Wardens and existing youth groups (CJINI 2010).

6   The following extracts are taken from the 'in house' publication 'Greater Shankill Alternatives: The Story' (undated: 27). Views of programme participants: 'I think hoods would even think the best about Alternatives. You would do what you could for them to thank them. Even for just listening to you. No one usually wants to listen to a hood. It's made me think a lot now, but it wasn't like that when I just started it, then I just thought, I've got out of another situation, I've saved myself from getting beat. But as you go through it you start to wise up a bit.' Views of parents of programme participants: 'I'm a parent and my son was in trouble and came to Alternatives and went on the programme and it completely changed him. It learned him to respect other people and their property. He's no angel, but he has completely changed.' Views of victims involved with the project: 'Meeting with him [offender] was hard but very worthwhile. I got my stuff back and also got answers.'

7   For example, representatives of the Community Relations Council told inspectors that Alternatives was viewed as a 'safe pair of hands' and 'a legitimate, authentic group that has made the journey without damaging their credibility with the difficult communities from which they originate' (CJINI 2010: 7). They are also regarded by Atlantic Philanthropies as one of the voluntary and community sector's real success stories: 'an organization that has managed to get its work mainstreamed, built effective partnerships and proved resourceful and innovative and no longer reliant on Atlantic Philanthropies' (CJINI 2010: 8). The dedication, integrity and professionalism of NIA was also confirmed by representatives of the Belfast Regeneration Office and Belfast City Council: 'NIA are by a long way the most professional community group that BRO deal with. They are responsive and provide very detailed financial and practice feedback' (quotation from representative of the Belfast Regeneration Office, cited in CJINI 2010: 9)

8   The former DUP MEP Jim Allister (2008) has also opposed funding of such groups.

9   Department for Social Development Press Release, 22 March 2007. 'Government expects end to paramilitarism'. Available at http://sluggerotoole.com/2007/03/22/in-return-for-the-funding-the-government-wants-to-see/ (last accessed 10 November 2011).

10   'Farset employee invites minister to "come see work we've done"'. *Irish News*, 1 May 2009.

11   Copy on file.

12   Copy on file.

13   In the opinion of Gerald Solinas, a Farset employee, ceasing CIT funding was a way for the Minister to 'launch' her political career (Interview with Gerald Solinas, 25 October 2010).

14   'Statement by Margaret Ritchie MLA, Minister for Social Development to the Northern Ireland Assembly on the future of the CTI'. Northern Ireland Executive press release, 16 October 2007. Available at www.dsdni.gov.uk/index/publications/ministers_speeches/offps-ministers-speeches-archive/future-of-the-conflict-transformation-initiative.htm (last accessed 10 November 2011).

15   The Alliance Party also demanded an end to such funding in an article entitled, 'Alliance Leader demands end to Loyalist funding after police shooting' (23 July 2007). Available at   http://allianceparty.org/article/2007/002900/alliance-leader-demands-end-to-loyalist-funding-after-police-shooting   (last   accessed   10

November 2011. See also BBC, 'UDA is in "last chance saloon"' (10 August 2007). Available at: http://news.bbc.co.uk/1/hi/northern_ireland/6939636.stm (last accessed 10 November 2011).

16 Conflict Transformation Initiative – statement by Minister Margaret Ritchie, (2007), available at www.dsdni.gov.uk/conflict-transformation-initiative.htm (last accessed 10 November 2011).

17 All documentation held by author.

18 Application by Gerald Solinas for leave to apply for judicial review.

19 Application in full at www.courtsni.gov.uk/NR/rdonlyres/C3F76DCB-13AB-440B-9ACB-889B38E514E6/0/j_j_MOR7497Final.htm (last accessed 1 June 2011).

20 See Re Solinas Application [2009] NIQB 43.

21 For example, in the Solinas judgement, Lord Chief Justice Morgan notes that Ms Ritchie 'made it clear that she has no criticism to make of Farset'. Farset is the community development organisation which received £135,000 as part of the CTI initiative.

22 Interview with Gerald Solinas, 25 October 2010; 'Funding is for Loyalist communities … not paramilitary pockets' (*Belfast Telegraph*, 5 August 2007).

When Adair and them ins' got into to murals
I just thought I need to get a brush and paint,
start painting different things from that shower.
(UDA respondent)

6 Beyond enclosure: re-imaging and the challenge to 'self'

The embedding of ethno-sectarianism was achieved via the fabrication of discursive formations, which created a systematic and conceptual framework capable of defining 'truth' and other forms of propaganda (Burton 1978). Increased ethno-sectarian enclaving was achieved through violence and the growth in levels of residential segregation which in turn stimulated discursive formations that enclosed ideas, images and 'moral' inflection. Those inflections, that appeared via wall murals, aimed to solidify purpose and present practices that were, with regard to the ethno-sectarian 'other', offensive and purposefully exclusionary. Murals performed the task of defining ethno-sectarian allegiance and regulated the form of community space and the system of ethno-sectarian demarcation and in so doing visually asserted the nature of localised power relationships (Connerton 1989; Jarman 1992, 1997).

Early wall murals produced in Protestant working class communities were linked to forms of a sublime stewardship of place that had been achieved through an emotive dimension within which 'the homeland' was seen as having been protected through the sacrifices of the 'elect' people. This was generally reproduced through the commemoration of the Williamite Wars (1689–1690) in Ireland. Ethnic election and the 'right' of residence in Ireland were attached to an obligation to defend stewarded place, a key concept within Orangeism. As the conflict of the late 1960s evolved wall muraling drew more specifically upon Loyalist paramilitarianism and the invoking of the power of armed resistance and also a singular narrative of the persecution of an innocent and beleaguered community (*Combat* 1996, 1998).

This form of resistance was constructed around the immediacy of political turmoil and an epistemology that was linked to righteousness, moral order, the legitimacy of violence and potential triumph. Ultimately previously aggressive and militaristic images aimed for and reproduced discursively driven spatial enclosure. The allegories and mythic representation that were chosen during conflict were the product of a discursively fabricated classifications of Loyalist belonging and interpretation. Murals outlined a Loyalist interpretation of localised power relationships and the 'rights' of resistance toward those with an alternative discourse of community-centred identification (Hall 2007). Undoubtedly, resistance as displayed via wall murals was centred on realising and promoting mythic traditions and the presentation of ideological concerns, a situation which echoes Harvey's supposition that:

> Social practice may invoke certain myths and push for certain spatial and temporal representations as part and parcel of their drive to implant and reinforce their hold on society. (1989: 216–217)

Anderson (1991) has identified how ethno-centrism and its various imaginings are tied to the promotion of exclusive practices that sustain unproven forms of motivation such as the presentation of pseudo-history that is synthesis of action and violent enactment. However, it is also the case that 'myth makers' also make claims that are factual and justified such as the nature of their persecution and endurance (Archard 1995). There is no denying that the realities of ethno-sectarianism and place-centred conflict stimulated a cause to 'defend' even if the promotion of a discourse of protection aimed for territorial enclosure, assault upon the 'other' community and increasing exclusivity around Protestant culture.

However, the demand and requirement of defence ultimately subverted other realities, such as the harm caused to the 'other' community and wider interpretations that would have led to conflict transformation. Wall murals became a visible product of a bind between territorial control and the perpetuation of conflict, or what Sack (1998) would identify as impermeable sites. As Feldman has stated, the overall intensification of ethno-sectarian segregation 'managed violence in and through spatial devices' (1991: 36). Spatial and discursive enclosure aimed to enact the meaning of Loyalist identity and action and co-join ideas into the objectification of time and space. The narratives, images and reality of protecting place, when in fact most violence was linked to assaulting the 'other' community, was in itself an interlinked mechanism in the whole performance and enactment of violence and conflict (Aughey 1985). Murals and their exclusive renditions aimed to extol and laud place-centred uniqueness against any form of topographical concord. Such subjective and territorially designed sentiments and representations required images that formed Loyalist identity into a process of inclusive and exclusive power relationships.

Murals were incessantly produced in order to constantly reconstruct territorial division and allegiance through summarised but discrete, eulogised notions of devotion that aimed to pinpoint the contrary nature of Loyalist places in comparison with Republican communities (Bairner and Shirlow 1998). As Kong observes, landscapes 'are ideological in that they can be used to endorse, legitimise, and/or challenge social and political control' (1993: 24). As such, a politicised and cultural landscape is a concept of tension, anxiety and ultimately division (Duncan and Duncan 1988), part of the overall problematic related to the selectiveness of iconographies that were:

> serving particular interests and ideological positions. Just as memory and identity support one another, they also sustain certain subjective positions, social boundaries, and, of course, power. (Gillis 1994: 2)

Place during conflict was socially and culturally refabricated into idiosyncratic understanding of it and community and aimed to stimulate and manifest support for Loyalist practice and authority. Wall murals became a crucial insight into the production and reproduction of conflict and the modes and meaning of resistance to the power of the 'other' community (Karanga 2000). Conflict stimulated and reproduced not only acts of resistance, via wall murals, but also provided for the significance of identity-securing strategies in the reproduction of violent discord (Nordstrom et al. 1992). The illegality of wall murals also testified to the nature of unofficial discourse and narrative and in addition murals also aimed to guard identities from their professed 'powerlessness' and the consequences of the reproduction of conflictual power-centred relationships. As a result, language, murals and meaning came to constitute the form of discourse that gave acts and forms of violent resistance a uniqueness of character (Finlayson 1999). Given the restricted meaning of the wall murals presented during conflict and the limited vocabularies allied to them it is evident that in terms of effect they were important modes of cultural deployment and political contestation. Loyalist murals presented simplified texts of 'loyalty', 'patriotism' and 'truth', and a visual celebration of the narrative and embodiment of the uni-dimensional evaluation of conflict and the appropriate affiliations and perseverance required (Connerton 1989).

Remembering, for Loyalist organisations, had become an operative process in which place and identity were manipulated and utilised in order not only to maintain but also rationalise conflict and the need to continually resist the collective 'other' (Jarman 1992, 1997). To establish a collective memory there is a compulsion to originate and occasion images, which are decontaminated of other histories. During conflict symbols were designed both to 'inform' a community about who they 'were' and as the warrant required to aid their survival as the collective 'self'. This involved an imperative-driven ideological use of violence and myth, in a situation where there was a real or perceived threat to the security of the Protestant community. This invariably meant promoting elements or ideas within a collective symbology that was determinedly restricted and removed elements of previous inter-community cordiality and reason. Thus a complex mosaic of socio-political and cultural homogeneity within loyalism was reduced to an ever-repeating cycle of menace, symbolic cordoning, confrontation and defined antagonism. The siege mentality, which defined the nature of previous Loyalist resistance, was indebted to the conception of precedent and the construction of an allegoric narrative. Myths in their purest form abridged, performed, sensationalised and synthesised the bond for action and the right to enact violence. This was generally construed around the notion of an ancient and historical enemy, that being Irish Catholics. Such historiography simplified the complexities of conflict and reduced the harm caused by Loyalists as either invisible or triumphant.

Wall murals are a noteworthy facet of unofficial custom that is rooted in the cultural landscape and narratives of local and politicised identity in Northern Ireland (Loftus 1994; Rolston 2003a and b; Santino 2001). Research has traditionally focused upon the contrasting nature of Republican and Loyalist wall murals and their role in representing both traditions, but there has been virtually no analysis of the role played regarding the re-imaging of Loyalist iconography as both a sign and act of conflict transformation. Such transformation aims to reduce or remove the iconic elements of the Northern Irish cultural landscape in order to resignal Loyalist pursuits and remove the persistent symbolism of contention and divisiveness. Evidently place and the mode of symbolic intent therein are usually linked to narration or under-standing of community devotion, collective action and socio-cultural modifi-cation (McCormick and Jarman 2005). However, the themes and nature of Loyalist wall murals have now been exposed as essentially temporal with previous forms that were overtly militaristic or ethno-sectarian and which aimed for 'spatial enclosure and forms of socio-spatial demarcation that created fear and hate of others, and push in the directions of inequality and justice' (Sack 1980: 254) being rejected and redrawn.

Academic deliberations appear to have ignored the process of re-imaging and the removal of overtly ethno-sectarian murals across the landscape of loyalism, which is peculiar in that most Loyalist murals have been recast away from the celebration and commendation of violence. Loyalists have generally removed themselves from a 'resistance to hybridization' (Graham and Whelan 2007: 479) within which they had been fully implanted. They have also removed themselves from what were contended as 'spaces of hate' (Graham and Whelan 2007: 494) as they have aimed for a more inclusive social narrative of inclusion and inter-community engagement. Graham and Whelan (2007) are correct in their study of the nature of the commemorating of the dead but some Loyalists have also come to the conclusion that exclusively rendered murals were insufficient cultural signifiers that reproduced ethno-sectarianism. A significant part of the process of altering such images was based upon the recognition that:

> We claimed to be off the people but then as things cooled down and the Troubles
> sortta ended like, those people were saying 'we don't like paramilitary murals'. So
> I suppose you thought that not everyone round here's a paramilitary. So you also

thought about how to connect with them people. So it was logical then to re-image as you knew then that you were reconnecting with people. So for me and my ones that was about healing and findings ways of celebrating the community without offending people no more. (UVF respondent, North Down)

What Loyalists were effectively recognising was that imagery, its classification and application, was creating chains of correspondence which tied subjects within both an ethno-sectarian and also utterly self-possessed and self-referential notion of identity, material practice, habituation and community devotion (Morrill et al. 2003). Foucault's argument that 'practices ... systematically form the objects of which they speak' (1972: 49) designates how discourse can function in both a constrained or cathartic manner, especially in the process of either embedding socio-cultural entrapment or promoting renewal and more collective senses of community cognition. In addition, it can be contended that Loyalist identities within a post-conflict environment are no longer, in symbolic terms, unified by the same sites of conjecture or concern. There has been an as-yet uncompleted but no less significant process within which Loyalists are aware both of the complex heterogeneity of place and that any further representations had to include women, older people, youth and the socially vulnerable as well as celebrating community achievement. Conceptualisations of multiple identities and non-militaristic themes is clearly relevant as a mechanism in conflict transformation as it pinpoints how Loyalists have accepted that monolithic depictions are insufficient, atavistic and essentially not required in a process of peace-building and community renewal. Ignoring the symbolic recoding that has taken place undermines the understanding of Loyalist transformation and this socio-cultural modification.

The development of new symbols and the de-militarisation of murals aims to lift loyalism out of isolation, undermine its self-referential nature and merge community via an more agreeable symbolic landscape. What Foucault (1972) termed counter-memory linked to what becomes a more unconventional view of the past which challenges the dominant representation of the community 'self', its future intent and possibilities. The process of re-imaging that is taking place has emerged slowly due to a lack of confidence to debate and study identity from within, the growth in the political success of Sinn Fein, Loyalist feuding and a fear that challenging Unionist authority would weaken pan-unionism. It was in a self-understanding of Unionist hybridity and that transitional Loyalism required self-sufficiency in terms of legitimating and validating itself that the process of renegotiating Loyalist imagery was to begin haphazardly in the late 1990s, accelerating in the early 2000s. Loyalists themselves came to understand that promoting a brutish landscape of fear and absolutism was invalid and rejected the requirement to present more sufficient and empathetic notions. That does not mean that Loyalist wall murals do not reproduce the notion of Loyalist victimhood at the hand of Irish Republicans, but it also concerns understanding that Loyalist communities have been undermined by marginalisation from within unionism and the British State. Self-imaging increasingly means more about a people's history than discourses of dupery, betrayal and Unionist rejection. Therefore, it is now more difficult to contend that 'the Loyalist guns were still around to prevent anything which could be interpreted as a Republican victory' (Rolston 2003a: 7).

In broader terms transformative Loyalists are concerned with senses of exclusion and alienation and the loss of position and labour market status. This implies, although subtly, that working-class Protestant and Catholics share the immediacy of poverty and social exclusion and that more can be located in the unison of experience. Although some murals depict a romanticised loss of heavy industry and pre-Troubles working-class history, it is the selection of images that are non-militaristic from which lessons to be drawn. The extent of re-imaging goes some way to disproving Graham's (2004: 498) previously correct assertion that:

> It does seem profoundly depressing that Ulster Loyalists seem intent on reinventing micro-scale versions of the zero-sum trap of the ethnic nation-State more than a century after Gaelic nationalism began its evolution into the ideological basis of the post-partition and exclusivist Catholic Irish State.

There has been a more organic and sufficient re-imaging of Loyalist murals that aims to present loyalism as inclusive, community-centred and appreciable. That process has been tortuous with regressive Loyalists arguing that re-imaging is a 'giving up' of Loyalist identity and serves a wider non-Loyalist agenda. As noted by a UDA respondent from Foyle:

> I won't support the re-imaging as we have given up too much of our history already. Those who are doing the re-imaging are playing to a tune set by others and at the end of the day it's against what I see as loyalism.

In simple terms the scale and level of re-imaging would suggest that more progressive elements are slowly subverting what were primarily ethno-sectarian discourses. However, as indicated in the next section, Loyalist rejectionists during the period of peace-building aimed for alternative symbolic and discursive routes.

Symbolic intent: enclosure or disclosure in the Lower Shankill

In the run up to the Shankill feud the use of images became part of the fragmentation between progressive and regressive elements. In the period between the Belfast Agreement and the eventual demise of C Company and Johnny Adair's authority the symbols and notion of history became linked increasingly to a division between ethno-sectarianism and the location of alternate images and histories. Identity formation for the PUP and UVF was increasingly based upon a process of re-identification and in particular locating non-sectarian elements of identity construction, whereas C Company's painted wall murals remained ever dedicated to the reproduction of a standard ethno-sectarian discourse. The selection of images and meaning occurred to such an extent that the overall design of murals within the Shankill area was either increasingly attached to a process of identity-seeking (although not complete) or a fundamental desire to present anything but Loyalist tradition and in so doing contend that positive re-imaging was a process of betrayal and unfaith-fulness to the Loyalist 'cause'.

The UVF in the Shankill area, after 1994, began a process within which they started to present images, one of which used the Irish language, to encourage a class-centred ethos of affliction and remembrance. As Jarman forcefully argued the UVF utilised the Battle of the Somme in order to evoke

> a confrontation between contemporary values and traditional meanings and, as such, are part of an internal Unionist discourse. The realty that Irish Catholics also fought for Britain in World War One is also important. (Jarman 1997: 216)

In this instance, resistance was not predicated solely around the 'otherness' of Irish Republicanism but also against a class system within which working-class Protestants remained socially subjugated and their loyalty unfulfilled. For the UVF, the Somme was reborn as an unofficial 'people's history' that was not beholden to middle-class control and construction. Moreover, the Somme could be utilised as a site within which there was no evident or infected sectar-ianism more commonly linked to the Battle of the Boyne mythology. Unlike C Company the UVF aimed to challenge Unionist leaderships that had

> used the Protestant working class as their personal army. Used us to do the dirty work. Never said thanks for that but instead treated us as felons and scum. (UVF respondent, West Belfast)

Ultimately, the UVF aimed to present a value system within which the working classes could 'own' a history that was pre-conflict and more impor-tantly post-conflict. The Somme provided an ability to point to loyalty to Britain but at the same time ask, as one UVF respondent in West Belfast noted:

> Why did returning wars heroes end up living in poverty and squalor? You can't blame the Republicans for the way we were abused by the Unionist elite in the 1920s and 1930s.

Such senses of betrayal, as noted previously, were paralleled by a desire to empower the working classes in order that they could reach a point of political and cultural autonomy. The PUP and UVF were in effect walking on a cultural tightrope as they were prepared to denounce Unionist hegemony and the perfidious nature of the British State, but at the same time search for a positive way in which to express their Britishness and certain Irishness. This latter point is illustrated by the use of Irish in a RHC mural located on Lawnbrook

Avenue. In claiming the Somme for the working-classes the UVF aimed to define a part of that unofficial history of the Protestant people denied to them by the Stormont regimes and the cult of Britishness implanted through an education system that excluded Irish history. As noted by a UVF activist from West Belfast:

> Men of my age, I'm sixty-one, were never taught about the Somme or other aspects of working-class history. We learnt about the Empire, Clive of India and the like. But we never learnt anything about our own people. We aim to correct that by showing our people that we have a history of our own.

Yet the Somme is also important as a potential symbol of reconciliation between Protestants and Catholics. As noted by a PUP activist in West Belfast:

> We aren't like the UFF. We seek to present Unionist and Irish history. We want the Protestant people to know that Catholics also fought for Britain. Most Prods wouldn't have a clue that Catholics were in the British army.

One mural in particular, located on Berlin Street, presented four UVF members breaking down the door of a house as they aimed to gain entry to the home of their victim. The removal of this and other similarly vicious images was tied to a desire to present less odious representations. As noted by a UVF respondent in North Belfast:

> We used to paint murals which were like, 'Look we are the UVF and we shoot people we don't like. We are going to keep shooting them because that's what we do.' As I was looking at those sorts of things other voices were saying things like 'we need to stop the shooting of Catholics' or some were saying 'is that all we are a group of people who terrorise Catholics?'
>
> When peace, sort of came, those voices got stronger. It became a process of 'Is that the only history we have? Is that the only type of things we paint?' There was a process of sitting down and saying 'Right OK let's get beyond the sectarian thing. Let's do something that doesn't encourage sectarianism. Let's not take pride in having shot some innocent Catholics in the back of the head.

Such people believed that through organic-led education a non-sectarian history could be harnessed into an empowering network of contrary activity and belief. The intense and competing nature of identity-building in the Shankill at that time reflected above all the fragmentation of loyalism and the desire to distinguish a particular locale, not necessarily from Republican areas, but also from its adjacent Loyalist neighbourhoods and specifically those controlled by C Company.

After the Belfast Agreement of 1998 the location of murals in the Lower Shankill area dominated by C Company had worked in a very different direction, a process that was intensified after the feud in 2000 when UVF murals located in the Lower Shankill (Hopewell Avenue and Townsend

Street) were defaced. Two other UVF murals in Shankill Parade and Agnes Street were painted out and replaced with C Company murals. The painting out of another group's murals was an activity that had rarely happened before without an agreement concerning such operations – prior to this there had been a purposeful sharing of space, most notably at the junction of Northumberland Street and the Shankill Road during the existence of the CLMC, an organsiation which aimed to uphold the Loyalist ceasefires. This road junction had been persistently used to indicate Loyalist unity via the planned sharing and presentation of both UVF and UDA murals.

However, after 1998, C Company's murals worked in a variant manner as they remained dedicated to the reproduction of a standard sectarian discourse. The murals painted during C Company's 'supremacy' within the Lower Shankill were characterised by a number of key themes. Many were suggestive of a 'religious resistance' that was aligned to ethnically supremacist and ultra-nationalist modes of political practice. Religion and the 'persecution' of the Protestant community were central themes in which suffering was tied to the premise of 'resistance' not only to Republicanism but also toward Catholicism. One mural depicted the killing of Protestants during the Catholic uprising of 1641; close by another offered support for the 'rights' of Orangemen to march at Drumcree. In both cases persecution of the Protestant community was a central theme. Essentially the underlying argument being made was that Protestants were caught up in an infinite struggle against the forces of Catholicism. This message was made more clearly in the mural dedicated to Oliver Cromwell and his statement that:

> Catholicism is more than a religion it is a political power. Therefore I am led to believe there will be no peace in Ireland until the Catholic Church is crushed.
>
> Our people clearly persecuted and our Protestant churches desecrated. Also our Protestant people slaughtered in their thousands.

Beside the mural of Cromwell was that of William III, triumphant at the Battle of the Boyne. The victory of William and the ensuing Act of Settlement, which institutionalised Anglicanism as the official religion of Ireland, is placed in such a way as to invoke the memory of Protestant triumphalism. Evidently, the Williamite victory was depicted as a continuation of Cromwell's desire to suppress the 'heathen' and provide glory to the 'faithful', a continuation that was historically incorrect. Loyalty to the Crown was also a theme strongly represented in the murals of C Company with two murals depicting Elizabeth II and Princess Diana. The painting of these murals was not simply a reflection of loyalty to the Crown but was undertaken as there were, at that time, no such murals in the Mid and Upper Shankill areas and so represented a crude but effective way of claiming that the people of the Lower Shankill were more 'dedicated' to an institution much 'beloved' by many Shankill residents. In 2002 muralists on the Mid Shankill responded by painting larger and more sophisticated images of the Queen Mother and a dedication to the Golden Jubilee of Elizabeth II's reign, effectively undermining the uniqueness of the images of monarchy that existed in the Lower Shankill.

The most common theme painted in the Lower Shankill was that of the 2nd Battalion C'Coy (C Company) of the UFF. Most of those murals depicted hooded gunmen with arms at the ready. Such an image of preparedness was not paralleled in UVF murals painted in the Shankill area after 1998; by way of contrast these depicted men whose guns were pointed downward as if at rest. Within this context C Company aimed to represent the 'reality' that they were continuing the 'struggle' against Republicans and the Catholic community. As noted by a member of C Company the central goal of such images was to make explicit statements concerning the contemporary role of their organisation:

> We are making it clear to the Prods that we have not given up and that we will not sell them down the river. We are not like the UVF. We are here to fight and to ensure that Ulster remains British. We are the defenders of our community. We trust no one but ourselves.

The defence of community was also depicted in two murals which operationalised crude visual images. One image, which was borrowed from the cover of rock band Iron Maiden's album *The Trooper*, depicted a skeleton dressed in army fatigues carrying an assault rifle. Below his feet lay burned ground and grave markers which depicted the names of Republicans, two of whom were still alive. The grim reaper in the background accompanied the overall apocalyptic message. Nearby a cartoon-style mural depicted a British bulldog resembling Johnny Adair kicking a rat-like Gerry Adams, President of Sinn Fein, out of the Lower Shankill and down a road signposted to Dublin. The background clearly depicted the wall murals and buildings that surrounded the viewer. Such localisation of an image denoted that it was only the 'Loyalists' of the Lower Shankill who would deal with the Republican 'scourge'. As with other murals, Johnny Adair was pinpointed as the 'true unwavering patriot'.

In addition C Company, unlike the UVF, re-presented images linked to the culture of Orangeism via a historical sense of defence depicted through the use of a scene from the siege of Derry in 1689. This mural portrayed the Apprentice Boys of Derry locking the gates of the city to the forces of King James II. The siege of Derry is an emotional and strong metaphor of defence and deliverance, which depicts how it remains possible through loyalty to defeat the forces ranged against the Protestant people. In this sense C Company depicted itself as the modern day Apprentice Boys in a city within which the growth of the Catholic population was heralded as a modern-day form of besiegement. Thus, many of their murals aimed to mobilise images of the past as a metaphor for present struggles and as part of a broader strategy of contemporary legitimisation.

Two murals, however, aimed to confront the UVF in a more direct manner. One of these commemorated the life of a UFF member Jackie Coulter. Below his image were the words, 'Murdered by the UVF'. The dedication of a mural to Billy Wright was used to represent the struggle within contemporary loyalism. The image of Wright as a 'true' Loyalist was a defiant gesture towards the UVF. Ultimately, C Company's murals aimed to operationalise two forms of resistance. In general terms they presented themselves as being tied to an unwavering cultural devotion and the defence of what they construed as ethnic purity, kinship and a self-reflexive interpretative framing of power. In more specific terms they were designed to excluded the UVF in a manner that indicated their ability to control the near singular production of images within the Lower Shankill.

Shortly after the feud several walls throughout the Shankill area were painted with the words 'Reserved UVF' or 'Reserved C Company'. The claiming of vacant walls was also part of the process of demarcating Loyalist places. An abundance of graffiti also appeared. This included denouncing C Company on the basis that its members were engaged in criminality and in response to this C Company produced graffiti claiming that the PUP and UVF were betraying the Loyalist 'cause' and that the PUP MLAs, Ervine and Hutchison, were 'MI5 informants' or 'Republican sympathisers'.

The demise of Adair and C Company led to the UDA re-imaging ten of the murals previously presented by C Company. The mural depicting the events at Drumcree was replaced with an A–Z of the new wall murals in the Lower Shankill. A C Company mural on Peter's Hill is at the time of writing the position of a 'Welcome to the Shankill' message that depicts lost buildings such as mills and sites of employment. The Siege of Derry mural now reflects a depiction of local boxing legends, young people and women. Moreover, a previous mural that promoted the idea of ethnic cleansing has been replaced by a mural that demands 'Sustainable employment required for all' with a nearby mural erected concerning 'Children's Rights to Play'. A mural dedicated to the Scottish Brigade of the UDA has been replaced with images concerning what is known locally as the 'Brown Square Gold Rush' – an event in the late 1960s when golden coins were found in the demolished home of a former money lender that sparked a search for additional hidden bounty. On Beverly Street next to the Falls Road a large UFF mural was replaced by the Hidden Treasures mural that depicts, set against an old treasure map, a journey across Belfast and the celebration of key buildings and the story of *The Lion, the Witch and the Wardrobe* written by C.S. Lewis, a native of the city. The re-imaging of that mural, in particular, was set within the context of being painted and designed by youths from Loyalist and Republican backgrounds. In 2011 a mural was dedicated to Irish suffragettes in a commemoration and dedication to women's issues. In sum, the Lower Shankill, with the exception of the mural linked to Oliver Cromwell, at the time of writing depicts murals concerning gentrification, youth suicide, equality, sustainable employment and community cohesion. In one mural the attic of a house contains the tools for repair in the form of a paint can, brushes and a hammer, a subtle hint that a place more commonly linked to the storing of weaponry has been re-established as a site of potential renewal.

The Re-Imaging Communities Programme

Loyalist re-imaging was to accelerate after 2006. The Re-Imaging Communities (RIC) Programme was launched on 10 July 2006 by David Hanson MP[1] and Maria Eagle MP.[2] It opened for application in October 2006 and up to 2010 had funded 154 projects throughout Northern Ireland. It was initially conceived as a three-year project with an investment of £3.3 million. Although suspended at one point due to lack of capital a further £500,000 was provided to restart the programme. The Arts Council of Northern Ireland (ACNI) now runs the programme through funding from the Special European Union Programmes Body and the International Fund for Ireland (IFI).[3] The Programme has funded a diversity of projects across Northern Ireland, including public art and the clean-up and regeneration of neglected sites, alongside the replacement and transformation of paramilitary and ethno-sectarian murals.

Funding was initially provided by the Shared Communities Consortium (SCC) which was made up of representatives of the ACNI, the DSD, the IFI, the NIHE, the Community Relations Council (CRC), the PSNI, the Society of Local Authority Chief Executives and Senior Managers (SOLACE) and the Office of the First Minister and Deputy First Minister (OFMDFM). The programme is principally aimed at District Councils in order to develop and support their Good Relations Strategies and to build on work already undertaken in local communities that will broaden community participation across age groups and genders. Applications can also come from constituted community and voluntary organisations as long as they can demonstrate that the proposal has the support of a public authority such the Housing Executive, Local Strategy Partnerships, Health and Social Services Trusts or Community Safety Partnerships. All projects are assessed and must meet all five of the strategic themes of the programme.[4] These are:

- *Shared Future*: Working to achieve a normal civic society rooted in mutual recognition and trust;
- *Community Relations*: Working to embody the richness and diversity of our society and improve the quality of relationships within and between communities;
- *Community Cohesion*: Working with communities to provide opportunity for more stable, safer neighbourhoods and developstrong, positive relations between people from different backgrounds;

- *Regeneration through the Arts*: Working with communities wanting to develop more inclusive civic and cultural identities through the production of high quality artwork and design for the public realm;
- *Neighbourhood Renewal*: Working to complement the existing Neighbourhood Renewal programmes and policy.

The Arts Council was given the responsibility of managing and taking the programme forward and an evaluation of the Programme was carried out over the first two and a half years of the programme by Independent Research Solutions (IRS), as commissioned by the ACNI. The Re-Imaging Programme is rooted in a wider agenda of social, economic and cultural regeneration/modification in Northern Ireland. This particular programme was established as an important element in the process of converting and transforming visible signs of ethno-sectarianism and inter-community separation with a particular emphasis on transforming paramilitary murals. In fact, this programme has initiated approximately thirty-nine projects involving murals and as such constitutes the most significant attempt to change wall murals. The intention of the programme is to encourage communities to consider the way imagery reflects on their community and how to plan to replace 'divisive' imagery with images that promote neighbourhoods in a positive manner with the potential to develop the concept of shared space. The ACNI describes the Re-Imaging Programme as being fixed within the rebuilding of a shared future and the promotion of murals and images that are nonviolent, socially wide-ranging, agreed as reflecting community spirit and founded upon partnership building, equity and tolerance. Therefore, the aim is to free public space from images that are threatening, ethno-sectarian, racist or in any manner aggressive and exclusionary.

The origins of the programme are founded on *A Shared Future* (OFM/DFM 2005), the policy framework to promote the development of good relations. One section in the document addresses 'Visible Manifestations of Sectarianism and Racism' and speaks of the importance of releasing the public realm (including public property) from displays of sectarian aggression through:

- Active promotion of local dialogue involving elected representatives, community leaders, police and other stakeholders to reduce and eliminate displays of sectarian and racial aggression;
- Using the police, in conjunction with other agencies, acting to remove such displays where n` o accommodation can be reached. (2005:19)

The document identifies flags, murals and painted kerbstones as the most obvious examples of such displays. It also makes clear that the best way to approach this process is through:

a common project with agencies working collaboratively with the police, elected representatives and local communities as part of environmental improvements with a view to enhancing the areas economically and building trust (2005: 19).

In January 2007, the action plan, *Making it Happen – Implementing the Policy and Strategic Framework for Good Relations in Northern Ireland*, was produced. Priority Area 1 of the paper raised the issue of 'Tackling the Visible Manifestations of Sectarianism and Racism', and involved a commitment to working in collaboration with communities and other agencies to found a programme that removed the sectarian painting from kerbstones and the hosting of murals, flags and graffiti in public housing estates so as to reduce the sectarian casting of place.

OFMDFM's current strategy for *Cohesion, Sharing and Integration* (CSI, OFM/DFM 2010) includes the issue of murals as one of its long-term goals in political leadership/community engagement. This includes the establishment of a ministerially led panel which will tackle:

> the multiple social issues effecting and entrenching community separation, exclusion and hate; and cultural identity, including issues around flags and emblems, murals, bonfires, cultural expression, language and popular protest. (OFM/DFM 2010: 9)

Murals are also a key aim of the 'People and Places' section of the CSI document, in that the display of flags and emblems, graffiti or murals, parades or public assemblies or festivals it is contended should be held in an environment which respects individual and community rights. When the Re-Imaging Communities Programme was first introduced, the language used in publishing the programme emphasised the importance of addressing problems in disadvantaged Protestant communities with funds being allocated for a tracking programme to ensure that it was benefitting such places. This prompted a response from the SDLP which stated that the programme was a pay-off to paramilitaries and emphasised the fact that as murals are illegal that they should simply be removed. Sinn Fein added that that this was 'the latest in a long line of crude attempts by the British government to portray Unionist areas as somehow more disadvantaged than nationalist ones' (Romens 2007: 10).[5] In response to this, the ACNI revised grant guidelines to stress that funds were available to all communities seeking to replace murals and graffiti with politically neutral imagery. However, significantly more projects have taken place in predominantly Protestant areas (61), compared with predominantly Catholic areas (23) or even within shared districts (39).

Re-Imaging Communities was not the first attempt to re-image murals. In 1977, according to Romens (2007: 8), '"Spruce-Up Belfast" was a State-sponsored initiative between the Northern Ireland Office and the local arts councils designed to integrate students from the Belfast College of Art and Design into local communities with the aim of producing politically neutral murals that would reflect local identity'. Romens also argues that guidelines stipulated that all murals had to avoid any topics that could ignite sectarian division or prompt demands for increased social services, therefore when any political themes were attempted they were swiftly stopped. An article at the time described such impediment as follows:

> Even when the tenants groups attempted to give some political bite to the paintings, to comment on rent increases or housing conditions, their ideas failed to re-emerge from the City Hall consultation process. (Redpath 1983: 21)

Several of these murals were successful in depicting community ideas without being overtly political, concentrating on activities such as football and boxing. However, most were incompatible with notions of community identity and included fairy tales and children's entertainment characters, circus and jungle scenes, one even depicting a barbarian, which was insulting to the local community (Romens 2007: 6). The NIO considered this programme as successful and continued to fund it, but by 1981 communities had stopped applying for funds. The campaign of the late 1980s entitled 'Brighten Up Belfast' was similarly constructed and returned to the themes of children, nursery rhymes, cartoon characters and rural scenes. As Romens (2007: 8) states, 'most of the murals from these two campaigns no longer exist as they were irrelevant in terms of encouraging local ownership and were in conflict with more assertive representations'.

Up to April 2009 there had been eleven rounds of applications and 177 project applications. The majority of these (123) were successful with grants awarded and conditions accepted (as of November 2010, 154 projects have been funded, however statistics on these further thirty-one projects have not been analysed and categorised). Awards have declined for a number of reasons such as a perceived lack of support from external sources, the belief that the community was not prepared to accept the removal of certain symbols, the appearance of a conflict of interest between groups within the community and occasional disagreements with the provision of the award.

There are three levels of award. Awards categorised as 'small' represent a grant of £15,000 or less (thirty-nine awarded thus far), 'large' grants are between £15,000 and £50,000 (thirty-eight awards) and 'multiple' awards above £50,000 (forty-six awards). Of these thirty were multiple applications from six councils with the remaining sixteen emanating from six community groups. There are several types of projects funded. Thus far 106 projects were production projects, where the intention was to produce, change or create an object or community-related artefact, mainly a sculpture or a mural. Of these fourteen were feasibility projects, where the possibility of taking on a production project was explored, two concerned project management and one was a combined feasibility and production project.

Projects can be divided into 'shared space' projects and 'shared space plus'. Of the production projects forty-two were shared space projects, which normally involves the engagement of each section of the community, for example, in cleaning or tidying up a neglected or derelict piece of ground, removing graffiti and making the space available for recreational or reflection purposes. Shared space plus projects (sixty-four production projects) develop and deliver more challenging objectives such as replacing or removing displays of an oppositional or offensive nature, often including paramilitary symbolism in the form of murals, flags, emblems and painted kerbstones. Shared space plus projects are mostly delivered by community organisations (forty-four of the sixty-four) as these groups either include former combatants or contain the capacity to communicate with local paramilitary groups and therefore gain the approval to remove or replace a mural. The majority of production projects are based in a specific location and of these 73% are within areas categorised as being within the most deprived areas in Northern Ireland.

The ACNI has organised support activities to promote the programme in these areas, including a seminar in June 2007 for Good Relations Officers and Arts Officers from local Councils and a roadshow in October 2007. In addition they have also visited and talked to various council representatives, almost half the projects are located in the Belfast area. Thus far 102 projects have been completed or have determined the outcome of the project. The most popular forms of artwork are murals and sculptures which together account for 69% of the total. The aim of programme has been to contribute to the general aims of the 'shared future' policy by increasing the number of existing examples and levels of usage of shared space by negotiating the removal of displays of a sectarian and divisive nature or by changing the content of displays and symbols. The Northern Ireland Department of Culture, Arts and Leisure in support of the programme has stated that 'public art of this kind has a key role to play in raising aspirations and in promoting positive community identity and cohesion' (2006: 1).[6]

Tigers Bay: a case in point

Tigers Bay, a place of significant UDA presence, is located in North Belfast, less than one mile from the city centre. It is neighboured by the New Lodge (a predominantly Republican community) and is within the top 10% of the most deprived wards in Northern Ireland. The area had been a site of interface violence that led to the death of Glen Branagh a member of the UDA, in 2001. As Henry McDonald (2001: 1) stated after Branagh's death:

> As low-level sectarian attacks continued in north Belfast, despite the ceasefires, the UYM[7] became the teeth of the Loyalist hydra, a new army of terrorists waiting for their chance to emulate the likes of Johnny Adair.

A further impetus for change and community redirection came in 2008 when two young men, who it was alleged had been using drugs supplied by a local UDA member, committed suicide. This motivated local women in the community to demonstrate against drug-dealing and, as noted by a community activist when interviewed:

> In Tigers Bay especially, when things happen, it's the women who come out. It's the women who spearhead change.

The senior UDA linked spokesperson Frankie Gallagher was to openly state that 'all of the drug dealing that's going on in Tigers Bay is by people in Tigers Bay' with a conclusion that those involved would have to be removed from influence.[8] The horror of these deaths, which included one young man hanging himself from a railing along the Limestone Road, provided an opportunity for the ACNI to approach the Tigers Bay community to explain the purpose and procedures of changing the whole visual aspect of the neighbourhood.

Consultations started with local groups including the Tigers Bay Concerned Residents Association, the North Belfast Community Development Centre, local paramilitaries and Tiger's Bay Community Voice (a group of local women) who together decided to work in partnership with Groundwork Northern Ireland to apply for funding. They were awarded £125,000 in early 2008 to work on a combination of displays – two wall-mounted artworks (murals) and one sculpture. Groundwork Northern Ireland facilitated completion of the application and held project funds on behalf of the community, however, responsibility for allocating the use of funds and designing the project itself rested with the community.

In order to choose the direction for artwork, the community groups visited several other completed re-imaging projects in Twinbrook, a Republican area, and Broughshane. Although the murals were under the control of the Loyalist organisations it was agreed and envisioned by them that the new murals would have to become community designed and owned, a symbol in itself of a shifting power dynamic. As noted by a UDA respondent in North Belfast:

> They were the organisation's murals but it was up to the community what went in its place.

The first step in consultation was to appoint an artist. This was undertaken by collecting portfolios from several artists recommended by the ACNI and choosing the most suitable. The artist chosen was Ross Wilson.[9] Those involved interpreted a need for young people to be involved in the design and creation of proposed artwork and it was decided that primary school children from the local school (Currie Primary School) and a local youth group would work on two murals while other community members would be involved in developing a sculpture.

The primary school children worked on the most famous mural in Tigers Bay on Cultra Street, which portrayed two gunmen flanking a huge tiger's head with a UFF emblem to the left and UYM badge on the right. It was decided that the image of the tiger should be kept as it was synonymous with Tigers Bay and the children worked on re-imaging the tiger's head by creating a series of smaller images. The new mural has a specially made tiger's head mounted on the wall with the words 'community', 'pride' and 'culture' above it.

The second mural was designed and painted by Mountcollyer youth group and was placed in Upper Mervue Street. In the first consultations with the artist, the young people mainly presented a desire for an image of George Best, the Manchester United football player born in the city. However, as the group included more females than males, the theme of 'women in the community' began to emerge, especially related to the demonstrations held by women after the death of Dean Clarke. Therefore, the 'Mother, Sister, Daughter' mural was painted onto boards that were placed at the heart of Tigers Bay, a significant example of de-masculation of Loyalist imagery through the presentation of women at the centre of family and civic life.

The final piece of artwork was a bronze sculpture which was placed in a children's garden on Halliday's Road in December 2010. Local people donated items to represent their family and these items were pressed into the sculpture, making it personal to the community. The eventual scripture was that of a male angel symbolising a watchful eye over the community and also representing a messenger of hope. The sculpture's jacket is decorative, with tiger cubs and symbols of youth, hope, grace and truth included within it. The back of the angel is adorned with the objects of identity and family supplied by Tigers Bay residents as an expression of their faith in the future. Ross Wilson had a very positive experience working with the local community on this artwork and stated:

> I was very surprised how radical the people in the area were in terms of their attitudes towards changing them [murals]. Paramilitary leaders were very positive about it. (*Belfast Telegraph* 2010: 1)

Tigers Bay now has removed or re-imaged all five of its paramilitary style murals[10] as well as painted over two kilometers of kerb painting. In the main, the reaction to the re-imaging project has been positive, with those from the local community feeling that the area is more welcoming and a better environment for children to grow up in and those from outside the community feeling that a less intimidating environment has been created.

One of the most successful aspects of the programme has been the procedural aspect for communities. Discussions with those involved have stressed the importance and significance of the process of dialogue, debate and negotiation that has been an important element in the evolution of the projects. The programme provided a safe space where communities could come together to debate their identity and its representation and create a more coherent view of their own community. This also brought a sense of ownership to the community as previous murals had been controlled, maintained and decided upon by Loyalists as opposed to wider resident cognition. This is not to say that the process was fluid, in many cases it was a long-drawn-out series of negotiations, with a certain amount of suspicion and uncertainty about the removal of certain symbols and what imagery was allowed under the programme (especially related to the use of weapons on murals). The fact that the process was lengthy was important for some participants as it stressed the importance of the project and the fact that it encouraged participation of the whole community.

Conclusion

The success of re-imaging stretches beyond government funding and in some places murals have been re-imaged through using locally generated funding. In one instance a social economy enterprise was linked into re-imaging and this spun into a decorating business, with profits from that enterprise being used in various ways and somewhat emotionally to provide headstones for graves for those families who cannot afford them, especially when the deceased is a child.

Evidently re-imaging is not about producing a non-emotive or contested past but instead remembering in more positive and inclusive ways. Its power lies in the de-masculation of identity and the movement of Loyalists away from being designers of identity to facilitators of it. The shifts that are taking place with regard to representation are linked to producing other forms of memory but also of action. The non-militaristic murals remain as a guide but to an alternative form of meaning that is driven by community pride, restoration and congruity. Importantly Loyalists no longer produce murals to a passive audience but instead include residents in their construction and display. Thus re-imaging is a self-cognitive process within which distortion and allegory are removed. Meaning is no longer concentrated upon conflict but instead has managed a more fluid and inclusive dynamic, tied to a process of moving from the imagined to more collectively constituted expressions of community. Re-imaging is a process in which groups aim no longer to 'map myths' (Till 1999: 254).

Notes

1 Minister for Social Development.
2 Minister for Culture.
3 Based on conversation with Re-Imaging Community staff member.
4 ACNI Guide to Re-Imaging Communities, www.artscouncil-ni.org/award/forms/re_image/re_image_guide.pdf (last accessed 10 November 2011).

5 Breakingnews.ie, 'Outrage at £3m funding for removing murals' 10 July 2006, http://saoirse32.blogsome.com/2006/07/10/p8831/ (last accessed 10 November 2011).

6 Department of Culture, Arts and Leisure, '£3.3m Re-Imaging Communities Programme Launched', DCAL, 10 July 2006, http://archive.nics.gov.uk/cal/060710i-cal.htm (last accessed 1 June 2009).

7 The UYM or Ulster Young Militants are the youth section of the UDA.

8 At an event hosted, and attended by the author, in Tigers Bay on 7 February 2008 a UVF spokesperson stated 'I am not here to hide the facts or air-brush over the facts as an organisation, the UVF holds its hands up: We fully acknowledge that in the past a minority of our members have flaunted our zero tolerance stance on drugs ... We have repeatedly said that the time is now for Protestant and Catholic communities across Ulster, to unite with the single agenda of ridding our streets of drug dealers'. In 2010 Loyalist community activists closed a marijuana operation in Mount Vernon and two drug houses/brothels in Sandy Row. In addition Loyalist magazines have also published photographs of homes from which they contend drugs are being sold.

9 The artists had also worked on other RIC projects including one at Mosside in Ballymoney, www.artscouncil-ni.org/news/2008/new01122008a.html (last accessed 10 November 2011).

10 However, near to the 'Mother, Sister, Daughter' mural there remains a 'First Flute' band mural. Although this may not be an official paramilitary mural, it may be perceived to have links to paramilitaries from those within and outside the community.

7   The problem with Loyalists or Loyalists' problems?

The essence of general thinking concerning Loyalists is that they operated as death squad cabals who merely shifted from a sectarian murder campaign into drug-dealing and the control and maintenance of extensive criminal empires. Such general depictions aim to maintain the notion and practice of felon-setting and obscure other realities, such as the role Loyalists played in developing and more importantly sustaining peace-building and supporting inter-community interaction. It is evident that the media finds it easier to sell copy if it plays upon the standard image of the Loyalist wrong-doer. Such persons are easy to locate and identify. Some, involved in crime, even claim to be members of Loyalist organisations when they are not. Moreover, several who have been involved in racism, racketeering and drug-selling have been ousted and removed from their parent organisation, some others have even been killed. A feature of some Loyalist leaders in certain places has been to expel and condemn those involved in illicit activities. As noted by a RHC respondent in North Down:

> The reason why I am involved is for two reasons. I want to help my community and see if people can have better lives. The other reason is to stop the blank cheque for bullies. To help those who are getting rid of those who use the cover of our organisation to scare and make people afeared [sic]. Those Loyalists, and there not Loyalists at all, who think they have a blank cheque to do what they want.
> Like last week we threw people out who were fighting in a pub. They threatened people that they would use the Commandos [RHC] to get back at the ones they were fightin'. That was wrong, it was a personal thing and nothing to do with us. So once we heard that they were misusing the organisation for their own ends and purposes they were out. They can't threaten people full stop. So we are the ones dealing with the people like that, nobody else bothers themselves.
> You said about the newspapers. See that story would end up being about Loyalists doing this and that and bullying others. But you wouldn't see nothing

about them ones being thrown out. So we are doing the right thing but we get no credit for it. For me it is about ending the blank cheque for bullies.

That sense of doing the 'right' thing concerning the removal of those involved in nefarious activities does vary from place to place and is linked to variant leadership styles and abilities across Northern Ireland. However, knowledge of strong and positive leadership appears rarely in public discourse and the wider societal benefits that concern the removal of unsavoury elements is virtually invisible. There appears to be a general frustration among Loyalists that they are left to cope and deal with criminal elements and that the PSNI play an 'insignificant' role in terms of prosecuting and controlling rogue elements (McKittrick 2002a, 2002b). In addition to these understandings of an increasingly positive role in terms of internal policing a further problem is the universality of the tag of 'criminal' attached to Loyalists. As noted by a UVF respondent in Mid-Ulster:

> I stepped outside the law as I took up the gun, but I never was involved in crime or anything like that. Some were but I wasn't and I can swear on my grandkids lives that I only ever broke the law as a paramilitary who took up the gun. Jesus Christ, I always had a TV licence, paid m' bills, taxed the car and all that. I came from decent people, good decent parents and I respected that an awful lot. My kids were brought up the same. But that counts for nowt, it counts for f all squared. You have a tag and that's it, you're a bully, a druggy, a bad lad etc. Not all Loyalists are the same but no one wants to hear any of that.
>
> But here's something you have to put in your book. Put this in! Why were the ones who tried to wreck the peace process all touts and in cahoots with Special Branch? They were a plague on us and our communities, selling drugs and bullying people, and we were asking at the time of the feuds and all that about why isn't he lifted, why isn't he scooped, why is he still on the streets? You know why? Them types was being protected.

The evidence that has emerged from the Police Ombudsman when combined with event such as the Holy Cross dispute, the Shankill feud and the killing of Bobby Mofatt further illustrates the manner in which positive Loyalist intent remains submerged by negativity – both from within and beyond. That negativity is burned into the consciousness of the citizens of Northern Ireland who have an imprecise knowledge of Loyalist diversity with regard to variant discourses and behaviours. In general, the primary 'signifier' of Loyalists is of persons involved in collusion or criminal activity. The reality is that as C Company and the Mount Vernon UVF were 'upping the ante', other Loyalists were trying to build peace and were taking responsible actions to sustain a future without violence. Generally neglected and hidden from view are such positive realities that are obscured as they sit too awkwardly with the more public resonances of criminality and violence. The instructive lesson from this is that the analysis of positive and transformative loyalism has insufficient public appeal in a society seeking the corroboration of the various, and at times valid, prejudices that they hold. As contended:

> That diversity results in not being very sexy to the media, because the media like a straight story, down a straight line, know exactly where we are to put it across in a news bulletin or a programme or whatever they are doing. But because loyalism is so diverse and everybody is giving their own options and own opinions, it doesn't make good programmes and will also be misinterpreted as being all over the place, stuff like that. That results in a negative image and the media don't like it, the media can't cope with it and the media don't want to try to work it out … (UVF respondent, West Belfast)

Loyalists enjoy less of the laudable type of recognition that appears to be more common in Republican communities. They obviously evolved without the same distinct movement-based cognition of the IRA and the obvious movement-centred aspects of it. Republicans have sensed achievements, such as the collapse of Unionist hegemony, social mobility within the Catholic community and the articulation of a positive role within constitutional politics. As noted by a UDA respondent from North Down:

> It's like they [IRA] get the lottery numbers every time. They end their war and get to be ministers in government … They are control freaks but I wish we could be like them.

There is no doubting that the role of the IRA is identified as a positive feature of community-based loyalty and devotion. That is not to say that Loyalists never had supporters but corroboration was, in comparison with the IRA, on the low side and was never formalised into a coherent social or political movement, especially as the *raison d'etre* for loyalists was generally contingent upon the existence of the IRA. If anything, as shown below, there have been significant consequences of being a Loyalist combatant, and having not developed a unique system of practice or an acceptable ideological authority in which they defined the nature of their discourse. Although, that has been partly achieved through the model of conflict transformation, the failure to garner a positive reception regarding reformist-driven loyalism significantly undermines any appreciation of it beyond very narrow confines.

If anything Loyalists appear to have the same emotional and other problems associated with State combatants regarding the sense of being used for the State's ends and then returning to a civilian life in which few people are aware of what has been endured. Again Republicanism has turned struggle into plays, novels, poetry and song. It has harnessed the energy of volunteers throughout and ensured that many feel part of a solidified and concrete cause. That project is neither complete or without its critics, but more than anything Republicans were mindful of claiming, restoring and developing the concept of legitimacy and articulating that to a global audience, compared with, as one Loyalist asserted:

we would be tellin' people on the Shore Road or Tiger's Bay, that we was fightin' their cause. We never thought to tell anyone outside them types of places what we were aiming for. We are crap at explaining ourselves to outsiders. (UDA respondent, North Belfast)

A significant case in point concerned the media reaction to Bobby 'Beano' Niblock's play *A Reason to Believe*. This black comedy, regarding two aging paramilitaries, aimed to disprove the allure of conflict and imprisonment. The play drew upon the futility of wasted time, lost hope and the fatal illnesses of both characters. The play was first performed during the West Belfast Festival in 2009 in an attempt to bridge relationships between Republican and Loyalist West Belfast. It was then performed in the Spectrum Centre on the Shankill Road. The latter performances aimed to encourage community bonding and indicate the capacity of drama-making within a beleaguered, socially deprived and fractured community. Indeed at the first performance in the Spectrum Centre several members of the audience spoke of never having seen a play, never thinking that people within their community could write a play and that the play itself, although depressing in its conclusion, had been an uplifting experience. The fact that Bobby Niblock was a former RHC prisoner who had been involved in the killing of fellow Loyalist Robert Thompson (who was brutally killed in South Belfast in February 1975) became the central feature of media reporting concerning the play. Writing in the *Belfast Telegraph*, Lindy McDowell (2009: 12) reported the following under an article entitled 'Are we in danger of losing the plot over violent past?' As stated:

> Scene One: Niblock is busy in rehearsals for the play when he is approached by a young man who cries out 'Beano!' Niblock hurries towards this stranger. Who can it be? His face falls as recognition dawns (and this is surely an uncomfortable moment for our leading man[1]). The newcomer is in fact the brother of a murdered 23-year-old pal of Niblock's. The young man was mercilessly beaten and stabbed 52 times by Niblock and a gang of others. The brother has only recently been told the full details of this terrible story by his aunt. He tells Niblock he wants to know why his brother was murdered. Niblock refuses to even discuss it. Scene Two: later that evening the brother and his aunt show up at the opening of the play. They are denied entry. Scene three: The family go public. They give newspaper interviews describing their suffering and call for Niblock to meet them. The brother demands that any money made from the play should go to charity. With heartfelt words he describes the awful pain his mother, in particular, suffered following her son's murder.

Although McDowell was to also add that:

> I don't doubt Bobby Niblock is sincere in hoping his play serves as a warning to young people about getting sucked in to paramilitary gangs.

She concludes:

But odd, isn't it, that our process has encouraged us to applaud the killers who have 'moved on' while primly drawing a line under the terrible stuff from which they have moved on?

But, one wonders, who is applauding? The Niblock case illustrates a central tension for Loyalists. In public terms a positive act based upon positioning the futility of conflict, engaging with the Republican community and using a play to forewarn the young about the 'allure' of violence, appears diminutive compared with a previous act of brutality. Without doubt the Thompson family deserves closure and explanation. If that had not been forthcoming the question is, do Loyalists who aim to resolve a complex past have to remain anchored within it and not engage in playwriting? It seems in public terms that they must, even if their intent is to frame a more positive future. In sum, there is reason to McDowell's commentary but also reason in using Loyalist resources to move onward and to fashion a stable future out of a destabilising past, especially when Loyalists have publicly presented challenges to the pernicious effects of their own actions. Interestingly, the play could be accepted in a Republican community that had borne the brunt of Loyalist violence, but was, in media terms, generally seen as questionable by those writing in what would be construed as a Unionist-leaning newspaper.

Even in accepting that the Republican community is built upon various imaginings we can still view the creation of that imagination upon a congruent and managed process in which suffering sat at the core of group oppression and everything that was done to aid Republicanism was counted as support whether that meant engaging in violence, placing money in a prisoner welfare collection tin, buying *An Phoblact* or talking a discrimination case. Everything that showed resistance to British and Unionist authority was part of that cause. However, for Loyalists they were unable to locate the same substantiation as they were fighting, in relative terms, a civil-sectarian war, had generally the same political ideology as Unionist politicians and some sections were embroiled in criminality that was unpopular, especially when it involved prostitution and drugs. They were in many ways legitimacy-constrained. Furthermore, critics of Loyalists do not permit any sense of Loyalist suffering to be explained if it does not equate with the victims of their violence, despite the reality that the majority of them unlike most people in Northern Ireland, had a friend or family member killed during the conflict (Shirlow and McEvoy 2008).

The media have taken the easy route of explaining loyalism as deficient and find it compelling to write about the drug barons and their like akin to the television programme *The Sopranos*. They have easy fodder in that many like Adair and the Shoukris played to the media gallery, a situation that reflected more about their personalities than any dedication to a cause or more importantly aiding the redefinition of Loyalist non-violent activity. More serious analysis should, as it has elsewhere, be dedicated to examining the 'ordinary' combatant and how their lives have, as like other combatants elsewhere, been shaped by experiences of conflict and conflict-related phenomena. It seems at present that they remained framed within legal and moral forms of criminalisation, based upon a perpetual burden of wrong-doing.

In the gaze that is fixated upon the tattooed and heavily muscled Loyalist 'thugs' there has been insufficient attention paid to the different dimensions of life that affects many former Loyalist combatants. As most of those persons are now into their forties and beyond there is now a capacity to view them as having lives that have run parallel with the conflict and its variations, movements and directions and also how their life course has developed in an emergent post-conflict landscape. In general, there is compelling evidence that many Loyalists have few places into which they can seamlessly integrate themselves, due to 'criminal' convictions and hostility to them. As shown below many Loyalists suffer from the consequences of conflict as evidenced by poor physical and emotional health, while some who have fared better mask the realities of their pasts in an attempt to avoid the casting of deviance and putative allegations. Evidently, the Loyalist 'thug' has more complex realities to cope with and in terms of status and stature they evoke the opposite lifestyle to the imagined discourses of brutal drug lords and criminal barons. The life course of many is dissimilar to the perspective generated by sections of the media and the ridiculous depiction of Loyalists as Mafioso living with and benefitting from criminal empires, driving BMWs and financing long holidays in the Caribbean sun. The evident trap is one of pinpointing the problem of loyalism as opposed to opening up a mature debate on Loyalist problems and how these subvert the process of meaningful post-conflict-led human value.

A contrary image: hardship and endurance

Research conducted by the author and Jamieson and Grounds aimed to investigate the issue of well-being and the relationship between conflict and issues regarding the social and economic inclusion/exclusion of politically motivated former prisoners (PMFP) in a post-conflict scenario (Jamieson et al. 2010). That research employed triangulated research methods that included a well-being survey, focus groups and in-depth interviews in order to garner descriptive and diagnostic information on former combatants and the issues that they encounter (Gibbs 1991). The results of that work, especially the survey on well-being, was whenever possible linked to comparable data to benchmark comparators between PMFP and other citizens. In 2008 the health and well-being survey was completed by a total of 190 PMFPs: 117 Republicans (of whom 23 were women) and 73 Loyalist men. Their average age was 52 years.

The survey aimed to determine the economic circumstances, health (both physical and mental health) and social well-being, including financial and familial issues, with a spotlight on issues relating to ageing. The study assembled a representation of how PMFPs, both Republican and Loyalist, were coping, adapting and responding to post-imprisonment and the various other changes, opportunities and challenges that influence their lives. These were evaluated within each constituent group and across them. The data itself was then presented in focus groups and in one-to-one interviews in order to determine how respondents understood the issues explored and in what ways the structures of criminalisation endured and if they offered significant impediments to their inclusion. Those interviews utilised a biographical narrative format to discover how an individual's own familiarity, experience and sense of conflict and imprisonment had affected their life course, sense of purpose, and how they constructed the meaning of well-being and importance or otherwise of social and familial relationships (Dewilde 2003; Kaufman 2002).

Evidently, PMFPs have life courses that have been disrupted by imprisonment and that can involve a sense of life being distorted, with many respondents reflecting negatively upon time having been lost and of time now being too partial and insignificant in terms of being able to turn their life around. Imprisonment can also, especially regarding legislation that debars former prisoners from employment, undermine social well-being and weaken the capacity to save for the future. In sum, imprisonment can undermine the capacity to not only integrate but to participate in virtually all facets of life given that it significantly alters the life course. Zoellner et al. (2002) have contended there is a strong correlation that exists between experiences of injury, emotional and physical trauma and imprisonment and the likelihood of enduring high levels of social exclusion. In general it is most probable that a person subjected to extreme forms of stress, such as imprisonment, victimisation or having caused harm are more likely to endure emotional difficulties. These experiences may well create an impaired ability to adopt or acclimatise to everyday stresses in a post-imprisonment environment.

Several academics and practitioners have been strong proponents of the argument that as Prisoners of War (POWs) age, many symptoms of their traumas are exacerbated by the problems associated with becoming older (Shephard 1997; Engdahl et al. 1999). Traumatic experiences encountered when in conflict can be coped with due to initial protective mechanisms such as bonding, resilience and ideological commitment but can emerge later as former combatants cope less well with long-term penury, loss of family relationships, developed emotional problems and the dilution of social bonding with other combatants. In addition, poor medical health symptoms can also emerge as protective factors become allegoric and memory-based and combatants begin to reflect upon time lost, especially as the conflict becomes a social memory and society moves on, even if it does so imprecisely. As Mikulincer and Florian (2000: 262) argue, the imprisoned political prisoner can emphasise differing attachment styles due to the impact of imprisonment as they can lose a sense of habitual regulation:

On this basis, we claim that a basic component of a person's attachment style is the habitual regulatory strategies he or she employs in coping with different sources of distress. The basic hypothesis here is that people differing in attachment style would differ in the strategies of affect regulation that they employ when facing stress. These strategies would shape the management of negative emotions and coping with life stressors, and would have meaningful repercussions on the individual's mental health.

The positive attachment experiences of secure persons may create the basis for the formulation of a salutary pattern of reality appraisal. These person may find out that distress is manageable and that external obstacles can be overcome … In this way secure persons could develop optimistic beliefs regarding stress management, a sense of trust in others' responses, and a sense of self efficacy in dealing with distress.

Neria et al. (2000) offered a detailed analysis of captured POWs and showed how the variety of their backgrounds can affect coping mechanisms post-incarceration. In a further study Zakin et al. (2003: 820) pinpointed how a sense of their being someone close to 'on the outside' may affect the capacity of the imprisoned to 'master' psychological well-being:

The importance of both a sense of autonomy, control, and active coping strategies, and of interpersonal bonds and support in coping with the ongoing and repeated traumatisation of captivity. The ability to affect daily schedules and to find outlets for their skills helped the prisoners to gain a relative sense of mastery. Helping other prisoners, sharing feelings with them, and fantasising future encounters with close people back home helped to alleviate the hardships of captivity.

All of these studies and others indicate that senses of 'guilt' in its various forms can impact upon any trauma endured, and that being involved in death and injury can affect and stimulate senses of depression and acute feelings of nervousness and misapprehension which can form as emotive concerns that are dealt with via self-medicating and a negative use of alcohol. In addition, it would appear that PMFPs become or are acutely aware, as time goes by, that one-time fellow inmates can enter a cycle of depression even leading to suicide or premature death. This can, in turn, engender a negative cycle of feeling trapped in a self-reinforcing world of negativity in an imprisoned 'self' among the formerly co-imprisoned. What one respondent identified as 'sitting in the pub all day, talking about the aul days, how hard things become and not, just not moving on. Living in what I call our own trap' (UVF respondent, South Belfast).

In addition, the wider literature on POWs also indicates that they are more likely than the general population to suffer from depressive and anxiety-based conditions and that the effects of those disorders can pertain long after being released from incarceration. It would also appear that these conditions are at their most acute among men who, after incarceration, live on their own (Zoellner et al. 2002). A higher proportion of Loyalists (50.7%) reported that they took prescription medication for anxiety or sleeping difficulties (sedatives and tranquillisers) compared with Republicans (35.0%) (Jamieson et al. 2010: 42). The higher prevalence rate for sedative or tranquilliser use among Loyalists is five times the Northern Ireland average for men (8.2%) (Jamieson et al. 2010: 42). That level of prescribed medication use can be linked to higher level of marital breakdown, with nearly twice as many Loyalists (38.4%) compared with Republicans (21.6%) stating that they were divorced or separated. With regard to those respondents who had been in an adult relationship prior to imprisonment more Loyalists (42.5%) than Republicans (28.2%) were no longer in those relationships.

There has been some four decades of academic work that has evaluated the return of men after incarceration, the stigma families bear due to a member's imprisonment, and the impact, usually negative, upon family life (Carlson and Cervera 1992; Morris 1964; Girshick 1996). Recent analysis promotes the role that families can play, through a social capital model, regarding effective resettlement (Mills and Codd 2008; Murray 2005) and as shown here there is a link between mental and physical good health (usually among those who had a home to return to) and poor mental and physical health (usually those who could not fit back into a family relationship). Academic analysis of the partners of political prisoners has also been linked to how women coped with a partner brutalised by torture, sensing betrayal and feeling emotionally worthless (Herman 1992). Those analyses consider how some females had to cope with male partners who suffered from mental health problems and emotional stress – and especially the masking of it – and had to adjust to a partner returning to an environment that had become alien to them.

Much of the distress dealt with concerned women feeling that their authority was undermined when men returned, that some of the men who returned were immature and had insignificant parenting skills and that some were not prepared to take on a role of responsibility (Boss 2002; Cohan at al. 2005; Dent et al. 1998; Dekel 2007; Dekel and Solomon 2006; Hall and Malone 1976; McCubin et al. 1975). Also many males were ashamed of the burden they placed on their families, especially as their imprisonment had led to penury. Among female respondents we spoke to there was an admission that some men were not prepared for a return to family life with some over-rewarding their children, others not being able to bond with them and some turning to domestic violence. In some instances there was a relatively seamless re-entry into family life. However, an additional problem for many Loyalists (49.3%) is that they many appear to have a stronger sense than Republicans (34.2%) that their imprisonment has caused moderate/severe harm to their families (Jamieson et al. 2010: 83).

The break-up of relationships, often an emotive situation, may be compounded, in emotional terms, if the break-up occurs during imprisonment (Alway 1995). What Zakin et al. (2003) identified as the 'fantasizing [over] future encounters' with family life may lead to immediate distress. As noted, not returning to a family home but to a more isolated habituation produced sensitive issues that Loyalists had to contend with. As stated by a UDA respondent (East Antrim), the reaction of a fellow prisoner when he found out that his wife was leaving him was shattering:

> There was a big man on my wing. He was as tough as they came. He came back from a visit on day and [a relative] told him that his wife had taken up with another man. It was all 'he has a good job', 'he treats her right', 'he's well liked about the town' all of that type of stuff.
>
> So he goes back into his cell and cries like I never heard a man cry before. I have never seen, well I didn't see it, I mean heard the likes of his crying and moaning. Like from a big man like him. It was a real shock to hear that. I can tell you now that man was broken. Not even the IRA or the screws could have broken that man. But he was a good father and husband and that's all he had to look forward to and then all of a sudden that hope, those dreams about the home waiting for him were gone. Snapped out of him, the rug pulled from under him, a big slap in the teeth.

And as noted by a UVF respondent (North Down):

> As a lifer I got to know a lot of Republicans. It seems that your numbers there is telling me what I already knew. Many of our ones' wives never stuck with them. Their wife's family would tell them to get on with life that the likes of us had made our choices and they shouldn't suffer for it. The IRA ones seemed to have wives who stuck with them more, supported them through thick and thin and maybe them ones felt proud of their men.
>
> Can you imagine what it was like thinking they [Republicans] had family support and we did, some of us, I mean didn't? Some did but it was another thing. You just felt that the Provies were always more together. It was that all the time. Even if they [Republicans] were nasty shits to each other they all stuck together. But although it was tough on us maybe them women was right. Why sit and wait why not get on with it? It was showin' some sense in a sortta way. Hard on some of the men but them women, who gave up on their men, they had lives to get on with.

Obviously having a relationship to return to or being able to return to a relationship was probably an important variable in sustaining a more seamless re-entry into life. Furthermore, home ownership can provide a sense of emotional and financial value and can also sustain access to credit and borrowings. Although, some 43.7% of respondents owned or were buying their homes, a higher proportion of Republicans (50.4%) than Loyalist (32.9%) did so (Jamieson et al. 2010: 23). As expected a higher proportion of Loyalists (61.7%) than Republicans (31.8%) lived in rented accommodation or in homes that they neither owned nor were buying (Jamieson et al. 2010: 23). Such evidence appears to point to different contexts of support and cognition. Also rejection came automatically and as explained:

Yes we was more likely to be left behind. You had fellas who had brothers in the RUC. Those brothers never spoke to them again. You had fathers who were the types of men who just couldn't cope with what their sons did. Mothers usually stuck with the men but even that could be very difficult at times, in the visits always askin' about 'why did you do that?' 'Why did you bring shame on the family?' That aul Prod thing about saying what you think and always worrying about what others think about you and your ones. I think the families did what they felt was proper and right as they saw it.

Some gave a lot of time to support and others were ashamed. Some of the Da's and Ma's were very against what Loyalists did. They just couldn't get it, but that was their way of being. You never tried to tell them they were wrong. It was up to them, there was no code book. Like them [IRA], we didn't tell people how they should think. We stepped outside the law and was being punished. Fair enough is what I thought. I understood it, it was up to others to think what they thought and to do what they did. (UDA respondent, Mid Ulster)

Or in some cases rejection was purposeful in order to lessen the burdens on family members. At times prisoners would stop families visiting them and attempt to control a fragmenting family life. In one case:

The first time she and the kids came to see me was just after I had a hiding in Castlereagh. I was like a Panda bear, with two big black eyes and big massive swollen wrists. Like someone stuck a tennis ball on them. I saw the shock in her face and the kids were in some state.

She had a good job, well enough paid job to and all that and the kids were really bright, and good at school, they went on and got the eleven-plus and are in big jobs now. So I said to her that she had to look after her own interests. I didn't spell it out but she knew what I meant, to be straight with you I think she had already worked out an escape from it all. She came back for the first few years and then less and less and then she went off with someone. I was gutted but because I took control of it and made the decision for her then when she did go off with another man that was easier. Most never took control like that but I knew her and what she was like and knew she could get on with life and also she never knew I was involved so why should she be burdened with it all? (UVF respondent, North Belfast)

In some cases the protection of others was more controlled and based upon other forms of protection.

I told my mother not to come near me. She would stand out on the Crumlin Road waiting for the visits. I knew people driving past would see her. She also was very decent and I knew she hated all the searches and being treated like shit stuck to your shoes, by the screws. She was a decent woman and I couldn't have her being treated like that. I told her not to come near me and that we would write. I am OK, not screwed up about it, because we kept in touch and I didn't have to care about what people thought of her. But I would have been even more screwed up if she was trekking up and down to the Crum. She was too decent for that.

You see all the writing made me brighter and I was able to go on and get good qualifications. So you think I'm odd saying this, but when I told her to stop coming it brought us together and also made me write and then gave me something to do with my time (UVF respondent, North Belfast).

However, in other cases there was a blunter conclusion concerning family break-down:

She didn't take too long to run off with another man. A mate of mine too, he was a really slimy shit. I'll never forgive them for that. Never in my life! Every minute of the day that annoys me. People say never mind 'n all that. Aye right, that's just not the way of it. I could never trust a women again, never wanted to be marrying and all that shit. Never wanted to be left alone again. Yes, people like me are screwed up, effing screwed up. (UDA respondent, Lagan Valley)

However, for some family rejection was less problematic and as noted by a UVF respondent from Mid Ulster:

Your parents are decent, church going and hard working and all that. You go to gaol and they tell you that you have broken their beliefs and that you are being punished. No pat on the back, but just their way of being honest and in your face. It never bothered me, but other ones were devastated, took it real bad. I think it fair to say lots of ones with problems never got over that type of being put out of their family.

A lot of us ones who went in early weren't political but just angry at the situation. So you had a brother and he and you who were both victims of Republican terror, and he did nothing and you fought back. Then he's a great lad and you're a scumbag. I'm fine with that it's their right to feel that way, I made my own decisions.

If you were going into Dungiven [a predominantly Republican community in County Derry] in the 70s it would have been the opposite. I got 'why did you pick up the gun?' and they probably got 'why haven't you picked up the gun?' Prods are just different, they just don't like the violence thing unless you're wearing a uniform.

Respondents who appeared to have fared better after imprisonment often spoke of supportive wives or family members. Their capacity to fit back into life was pronounced as were senses of reacting differently to situations of emotional distress compared with others, with a recognition that a positive reaction to a negative event was feasible with family support. There appeared to be a strong sense that Loyalists were aware of their family's commitments and the problem of their imprisonment upon them, but in many instances the sense of being betrayed and left behind is a major component in feeling deserted, unwanted, socially redundant and discarded. Unlike Republicans, as the first generation of Loyalists who served time in prison there was no designed or experienced emotional scale within which to posit imprisonment. For some however, and those who stated good mental health, there was an undoubted appreciation of people standing by them. One would tentatively suggest that the maintenance of family bonding helped to shore up well-being. Women in particular who maintained homes are viewed with pride and those who broke relationships are viewed with a mixture of appreciation of their plight but at times anger and recrimination.

In some instances those who were more politicised and who could reason why they were involved in violence appear to have coped better, have remained close to other combatants and have become more involved in community/voluntary activity. Seemingly, finding a purpose to add onto the life course appears to be linked with emotional well-being, although this may be a chicken and egg type issue, given that these more positive individuals may have had a strong sense of purpose prior to incarceration. For many Loyalists there is an understanding that those who coped better were generally emotionally different from the outset compared with those who coped less well (Green 1998).

Criminalisation and work

Despite the higher levels of Loyalists on anti-depressants and other medication a higher proportion of Loyalists (35.5%) than Republicans (25.6%) reported that they were working full time. Three times as many Republicans as Loyalists were working part time (17.1% compared with 4.1%) and twice as many Republicans as Loyalists were self-employed (11.1% compared with 5.5%) (Jamieson et al. 2010: 23). Around one in four (25.8%) respondents were unemployed, 15.8% were in receipt of some sort form of sickness or disability benefit, 4.7% were retired and a mere 0.9% were on a training scheme (Jamieson et al. 2010: 23). Loyalists (20.5%) were much more likely than their Republican counterparts (12.8%) to be receiving some form of incapacity benefit, this compares with an estimated 10% of people of working age in Northern Ireland receiving Disability Living Allowance (DLA) in 2006 (Jamieson et al. 2010: 23). So, although both groups were more likely than others in Northern Ireland to be on DLA, Loyalists were twice as likely to be receiving this form of social support.

In measuring the impact of criminalisation, survey respondents were questioned on whether they had been refused employment due to them possessing a conflict-related conviction. Over half (54.7%) stated that they strongly agreed/agreed with the statement '*I have been refused employment due to imprisonment*', with slightly more Loyalists (61.7%) than Republicans (50.4%) concurring (Jamieson et al. 2010: 28). It could also be postulated that those who neither/agreed disagreed may have not even bothered seeking employment due to a sense of fatalism that the chances, due to restrictive legislation, would be negligible – the absence of statutory protection from employment discrimination on the grounds that possessing a 'terrorist'-related conviction places many former combatants in an invidious position. The experience of many is that being open about holding a conviction curtails not only their own employment opportunities, but also those of their family members. For that reason, some respondents do not, when applying for jobs, affirm their convictions and then have to live with the consequent fear of being 'found out', especially now that criminal record checks are increasingly mandatory for many forms of employment. A particular issue for some Loyalists is the experience of family members who have been affected by their imprisonment, even in circumstances when those family members are distant from them but are debarred for employment, especially in security-related work, due to a relative's conviction. As stated by a former UVF former prisoner (West Belfast):

> You will hear this sortta thing a lot. My niece got through all her exams and was doing really well and all she had to do was pass an interview for to get into the police, somewhere over in England, one of them big cities. I don't know the wee girl from Adam. Haven't seen her in years and knows not much about her. At the interview she was told she was doing well, getting on the best and passing exams, the sort of thing you know about. Then a file on me was put in front of her. That was that and she didn't get it. How's that fair? Why did that happen to her? The Troubles is over, she hardly knows me and that's what they did. So who feels bad about that? Me, not the fella who threw her out after she tried so hard to get on in her life.

Another respondent reported that he had been dismissed from a job in factory after he had worked there for two days:

> Went to this factory and told the boss that I had been in gaol and all that. Made it all very clear to him. Worked there for a couple of days. Was OK, although bored the tits of me. He came to me the last day of the week and says 'sorry you have to go. They don't want you here, you're dangerous'. I said 'look I was up front about it all and never hid anything'.
>
> It didn't matter. I walked out past the others and felt angry. It was a Prod place too and there they were all too ashamed to say it to my face. I was going to do the aul, I fought for your lot, speech and just thought 'screw it!' What was the point? It will only prove them to be right in their thinkin'. I just thought, look it was simple, it was going to be tough and they had their way of thinking and that was all that ever came to. I never hid the fact I was inside and people could like it or lump it or stick it up their arses or whatever. They weren't going to shame me. (UVF respondent, East Antrim)

The low levels of employment reported is undoubtedly also influenced by legislation that permits the non-employment of those, as stated in Section 2(4) of the Fair Employment and Treatment (Northern Ireland) Order 1998, whose political opinions: 'approve or accept the use of violence for political ends, connected with the affairs of Northern Ireland, including the use of violence for the purpose of putting the public or any section of the public in fear'. In sum, an employer can legally disbar any person convicted of a conflict-related offence or can remove from employment any person who when applying for a job did not state, when asked, if they held such a conviction. Moreover, the recent heightened concern to protect children and vulnerable people has lead to a significant growth in employers seeking information regarding criminal convictions, not least to identify potential employees who are sex offenders. This legislation is viewed by former combatants as a form of criminalisation that is intimately connected to discrimination in general, and the reality that employers and employment agencies hold information regarding former prisoners at their disposal. Although no formal legislative proposals designed to tackle discrimination against such person have yet been tabled, a govern-ment-led task force produced a voluntary code in 2007 for employers and others to assist them in dealing with people who have conflict-related convic-tions (OFM/DFM 2007).[2] That document advises that:

> conflict-related convictions of 'politically motivated' former prisoners, or their membership of any organisation, should not generally be taken into account [in accessing employment, facilities, goods or services] provided that the act to which the conviction relates, or the membership, predates the Agreement. Only if the conviction, or membership, is materially relevant to the employment, facility, goods or service applied for, should this general rule not apply. (OFM/DFM 2007: paragraph 2.5)

This employers' guidance goes on to indicate that conflict-related convictions should not bar PMFPs unless the conviction was 'manifestly incompatible' with the job, facility, goods or service in question. The onus of demonstrating incompatibility would rest with the person making the allegation and the offence would not, per se, constitute adequate grounds. Any applicant affected by a negative decision should have a right of appeal and 'it is expected that only in very exceptional circumstances that such grounds could be successfully invoked'. (OFM/DFM 2007: paragraph 2.8). As well as practical advice to employers on making assessments of decisions as to conflict-related convic-tions, the document also provides for an appellate body known as a Tripartite Review Panel. That Panel, which will have a part-time secretariat, will be able to receive complaints from individuals and will be required to produce an Annual report to the Secretary of State. However, the same document concludes that:

> if there is evidence that the voluntary arrangement is demonstrably not working it is the view of the Government that the voluntary arrangement should be put on a statutory basis. (OFM/DFM 2007: paragraph 6.2)

At the same time as the employers' guidance was introduced the Northern Ireland Executive indicated that there was to be a review of the effectiveness of the voluntary code after eighteen months of operation. However, it was almost three years later before the review of the code's effectiveness was begun. Despite the existence of the employment voluntary code, it is evident that former political prisoners still confront the outworking of a series of policies, processes and practices that sustain and entrench residual criminalisation. As a result of this, many continue to be barred legally or informally from a significant number of social and economic positions. Such residual criminalisation is not merely symbolic as it has very real material and social effects on the life chances of both the formerly imprisoned and their families (Hunt and Robbins 2001). Given a combination of all of the factors outlined above it is unsurprising that 80.8% of Loyalist respondents stated that they were experiencing financial problems since their release (Jamieson et al. 2010: 32). Far from being a finding which supports the contention that Loyalists are mostly drug barons overseeing criminal empires, this indicates that this image is both exaggerated and clichéd.

Health and emotional well-being

Many more formerly imprisoned combatants suffer higher rates of mental health problems than the general population in Northern Ireland. About one in three rated their general health as good, very good or excellent with less than 30% rating their health as poor. Those who reported poor health tended to cite gastro-intestinal problems, hypertension or joint pain. The indicators used within the survey to assess mental health included the GHQ-12 standardised test that allowed respondents to self-report on medication (sedatives/tranquillisers or anti depressants) usage, the experiencing of trauma-related symptoms (intrusive thoughts and dreams, avoidance of reminders or anxiety and panic attacks), the tendency towards suicidal thoughts and prevalence of self-medication with alcohol.

It was found that 41.1% of Republicans and 38.0% of Loyalists had GHQ-12 scores above the threshold that indicates that mental health problems are likely. Such persons are twice as likely as other men in Northern Ireland to score above the GHQ-12 threshold for probable mental health problems (Jamieson et al. 2010: 39). A significant proportion of survey respondents also reported experiencing trauma-related symptoms such as having *anxiety/panic attacks*, *intrusive thoughts/dreams*, or avoiding reminders of terrible scenes witnessed. More Loyalists (65.8%) in comparison with Republicans (48.8%) agreed to trying to control for *avoidance of reminders*[3] which may suggest a symptom of not coming to terms with conflict-related incidents and an attempt to circumvent difficult and emotive issues (Jamieson et al. 2010: 49). As noted by a Loyalist from Mid-Ulster:

> I wake every night covered in sweat thinking about the pain I caused to others ...
> I wrote to the family of my victim and they wrote back saying they respected that.

But the sweating and bad dreams never stopped. I'm sorry for what I done, but that doesn't help. When the head goes it just goes.

In terms of analysing the impact and meaning of depression and depressive disorders respondents were asked to consider *since release there have been times of … either feeling seriously depressed* or *not wanting to go on living*. Some 38.4% of Loyalists stated that there had been times of *not wanting to go on living* (Jamieson et al. 2010: 51). Similar shares of Republicans (55.5%) and Loyalists (53.5%) stated having felt at some point seriously depressed since their release from imprisonment (Jamieson et al. 2010:.43). As stated by a UVF respondent from Upper Bann:

> It's a strange way that it hits you. I believe in what I did in my heart, but my head won't accept it. It's like my body is fighting the Troubles everyday inside itself. I just see the eyes of the man I killed all the time. He is always there in my head. If I hadn't done it to him he wouldn't be there. I'm responsible for that, but knowing that doesn't help. I had an aul Uncle, an aul harmless soul of a man, who used to say 'being sorry is never enough, as the good Lord knows it all'. Well I know it all, I can tell you that!

A common theme among Loyalist former combatants is the desire to seek psychiatric help with regard to their condition and the problems encountered regarding legislation and the reporting of crime. Under Section 5 of the Criminal Law Act (Northern Ireland) 1967 any person who knows of any other person who has committed an arrestable offence who has no lawful authority or reasonable excuse shall be guilty of an offence if they do not report it to the authorities (see also Dickson 1995 on emergency powers). No person, GP, psychiatrist or otherwise enjoys legal privilege, and they may be liable to legal prosecution if they do not report a crime or are expectant that what they are have been told may lead to a crime being committed. As several Loyalists contended they were able to talk to their GP and psychiatrist about offences that they had committed for which they had been prosecuted, however:

> When you get brave enough to go an see a 'head' doctor [psychiatrist] and tell him that you are all messed up and he turns around and says 'we can't talk about any crimes that you didn't do time for'. Then you just shrink back into a bubble and wonder to yourself how can you talk to anyone when the reason you go to see them is not allowed for to be said. You can't take apart every incident of the whole story of why your heads gone the way it is. You would think the likes of the man I went to see would have had more sense. It's that word you used, what was it, that's it, more traumatic … when I left seeing him I just gave up. I just gave up and thought that I would have to be being punished for the rest of my days. You know what I said before. The way it is like this you aren't allowed to move on. Even if I begged for forgiveness the people of this place wouldn't let me move on, not even a man who is supposed to help me. (UVF respondent, South Belfast)

Given the levels of psychological distress reported, it was not surprising to find that some respondents were dealing with their problems by 'self -medicating' with alcohol. The survey utilised two widely used standardised tests to screen for problems with alcohol, namely the FAST test screens for *hazardous drinking* and the CAGE test screens for *alcohol dependency*. Although, more Republicans than Loyalists scored over the FAST threshold for hazardous drinking, more Loyalists scored at the high end of that scale than Republicans (32.8% v. 27.7%), with Loyalists being twice as likely to have a maximum CAGE score (30.1% v. 16.2%) (Jamieson et al. 2010: 53). So although fewer Loyalists than Republicans were hazardous drinkers or alcohol dependent, a significant number were drinking excessively and are serious problem drinkers. The UK comparator for the FAST test screens for *hazardous drinking* and the Northern Ireland comparator for CAGE test screens for *alcohol dependency* were both four times lower than the averages pertained for those surveyed (Jamieson et al. 2010: 53).

Former combatants (particularly Loyalists) reported that the conflict and their imprisonment had resulted in some harm across all areas of emotional and social well being. In addition, many PMFPs, especially Loyalists, reported feeling isolated in their own communities. The survey included specific items relating to past exposure to traumatic events, changes in personal and social relationships, and experiences of being an ex-prisoner. In determining present circumstances and future expectations 35.2% of all respondents disagreed or strongly disagreed that they have found a sense of purpose since their release, with 54.1% of Loyalists disagreeing or strongly disagreeing that the peace process has made it easier for them to cope (Jamieson et al. 2010: 81). Many more Republicans (44.1%) agreed with the statement *I think in old age I will look back with a sense of achievement* compared with 26.0% of Loyalists (Jamieson et al. 2010: 87).

The depressive state in which many survey respondents are or have been located appears to be influenced by either repeated or persistent recollections of traumatic events in which they harmed others, were harmed or witnessed others being harmed. There also appear to be forms of psychological anaesthetising or processes of being unable to cope with the effects that psychosomatic disorders such as anxiety, self-doubt, low self-worth and self-esteem produce. For some the ability to express senses of fatalism and depression was limited by the masking of emotional distress and self-censorship, especially when imprisoned with men whose performed masculinity may have furthered senses of personal inadequacy.

It would appear that those who admitted, when interviewed, that they had endured emotional distress did so via a series of performances in which they denied stress and a lack of emotional well-being to themselves. This first stage was then compounded by further masking that distress to other inmates and also family members. In the first instance masking was driven by not wishing to appear weak and inept in front of peers, but with family members it appears to have been linked to not wanting others to worry, or to have placed burdens upon them. Masking emotional pain in front of the authorities was seen as a less difficult terrain and was co-joined into a sense of not allowing weakness to be exploited by the less sympathetic prison officers. However, Loyalists were also of the opinion that they would have been more likely to have sought anti-depressants from prison GPs than was the case with Republicans.

One of the obvious burdens of masking is that it has continued, for some, beyond the confines of prison. The refusal publicly to admit to mental ill-health appears to be driven by the constant yearning to be identified as masculine, stoic, non-emotional and never frenzied. The sense of enduring and not discovering solutions and problem-solving mechanisms for emotional distress appears to have been limited as Loyalist PMFPs age. Societal changes also explain some of the desire to seek help or recognise emotional ill health, but two factors in particular have presented a sense of foreboding and that has been the early death or former comrades and, more harrowingly, the suicide of others.

The suicide of former UVF prisoner Billy Giles is instructive of the emotional scale that has been experienced. Billy, who died aged forty-one, had secured a degree in prison, had produced a play entitled *Boy Girl* and was a strong advocate for peace, but had been unable to secure employment. Prior to his death he wrote an articulate four-page statement and ended it with the emotional line 'please let the next generation live normal lives'. Like others, including a former UDA prisoner who hanged himself in a public park whilst wearing his 'Sunday Best', Giles had performed acts of hopelessness in a significant and ritualised manner. In a situation in which such grief is unbounded such acts had the positive effect, among some, of leading to enquiries into practical ways to cope with depressive disorders.

For many Loyalists there was a sense that once they had engaged in violence they had lost control over their lives, and that the rejection of them by loved ones and members of their community was an additional burden. Doubts, especially regarding the harming of others, the sense of having been duped by loyalty, and that the community 'served' did not respond, corroborate or accept the Loyalist role in 'defending' it, is at times a site of uncertainty and recrimination. This can then be exacerbated by the post-imprisonment period when new hostilities, forms of exclusion and the loss of a solidarity with fellow inmates can present a confusing time within which the rebuilding of life appears daunting and the responsibilities of coping become, for some, immense. Some appear to be perpetually bounded emotionally with former fellow inmates and at times become caught up in a vicious cycle of negativity, spending their time in near daily discussions about loss, and feeling deserted and alienated.

An additional mask

The psychological impacts of conflict are obvious, but there are other fears and ambiguities affecting former combatants that concern how the direct experience and exposure to criminalisation and resentment leads to the acquisition of complex behaviours related to an attempt to escape public judgement. In having conducted research for many years with Loyalists a surprising and constant observation arose with regard to masking financial well-being. This involves an adaptation of lifestyle within which the behaviour of Loyalists and their families is based upon hiding material well-being from public view and rejecting forms of conspicuous consumption. Learning not to display well-being is based upon the nature of an environment and how that environment operates in terms of public criminalisation. The refusal to display well-being in terms of consumption or even family-based success is for some a complex emotional reaction over which they sense that they have no control.

As with fear the response of some is to avoid any potential for others to judge and make allegations about them and the spending of their or others' income. This masking of financial well-being is centred upon cognitive appraisal, making the correct decisions, the adoption of performances that deny economic well-being, the affect of criminalisation and the active misinterpretation of all Loyalists as a cabal of drug-dealers and criminals. But most of all the moderating role tied to being afraid to behave in ways that may lead to an individual being judged in a putative and hostile manner is dramatic and asserted (Ervine 2002b). In this instance, we refer to Loyalists who refuse to use income or savings in any way that may lead to their neighbours suspecting them of being involved in nefarious activities. As noted by a UVF respondent (South Belfast):

> When I got out I went back into the same sort of job I had been doing before. It was good money and I got a few promotions and the likes. My wife worked and we put one of our three through university. We paid our bills and put a bit away as best we could for that rainy day. So it comes to a point that me and her has a bit put away and the kids are reared, married and the house paid of n'all. So we goes off on one of them cruises, nothing fanciful or that. We had a relative who saw a cheap deal on the web, that's how we knew.
>
> When we come back she is showing the neighbours photos of the trip and one of them says 'how you get the money for that, is your [name of respondent] selling drugs?' See the woman who said that, thought it was funny.
>
> Is that what people think of me and her? The way of it is, that people round her put you in a box and think you're a drug man or something. I wouldn't know one end of a drug from the other, but that's not the way people think of it. Like they think if you have a few bob you must be up to bad things.

According to another respondent:

> Me and her has a wee nest egg and I was always thinking of getting a wee conser-

vatory or something on the house for her to sit out in and read her books and stuff. We was about to do it and then a mate of mine who was inside with me tells me that he bought a decent wee caravan and he got lots of stick about being a drug dealer and the like. So that was that, there was no way that I was going to have people thinking me and her was up to anything. Like for her, I couldn't have had her not being, you understand, holding her head up in the street if people thought we was selling drugs. To be honest there won't be anymore thinking about spending our money, it'll just sit there for the kids. You know when those ads come on the telly about over sixties going on cruises and holidays and buying second home? Those ads turns my stomach. (UDA respondent, East Antrim)

The manner in which these Loyalists evaluate the frame in which they aim to control how others describe and understand them, in this case through not being conspicuous in terms of spending, is reminiscent of Goffman's (1959, 1961, 1972, 1974, 1981) work on how individuals negotiate and certify their position through discourses attached to the meaning of the opinions of others (Wootton 1988). The presentation of self (and more importantly female partners) as indicated above, is that of trying to control the criminological frame, not through resistance to, but via acceptance of emotional negativity and the presentation of a front of 'decency'. Playing, as it here, the customs of acceptability even when no wrong-doing has been evident or desired. Such interaction with the non-imprisoned is centred upon an interpretation of acceptability even when the provision of it is undermined by labelling. It is in many ways a futile attempt to undermine the reproduction of what essentially are unconstructive and negative presumptions. Therefore, there is a craving to be viewed as morally unblemished, a perception that ultimately bonds some Loyalists to a process in which they control their behaviour and in effect perform self-criminalisation. Goffman (1981, 1964) viewed performance as a series of techniques linked to preparing, creating and performing a public persona and an acceptable front based upon the fear that being labelled would create unbearable burdens. Of course, many other Loyalists may care little what others think, but evidently some wish for them and in particular their families to be uncontaminated by gross and prejudiced explanations and opinions of them. Thus public criminalisation creates a desire to protect others from the stamp of their criminalisation. As noted:

I don't give a shit what they think about me, but I will go to the end of the earth to make sure I don't do or say anything that will mean that my kids are tarred with the same brush as me. (UVF respondent, Mid-Ulster)

Or more emotively:

I did my degree inside and then my two did theirs' a while back. I didn't want to go to their graduation as people might have worked out who I was and I never wanted people to know that I was their Da.

> The only time my daughter ever swore at me was then. She was angry that I worried about that. So I went and spent the whole day, up where you work, you know, you know, eating strawberries on the lawn, all la de dah. It was a lovely day for all of us. The weird thing was there were Republicans I knew from prison and even a few cops. They all said hello and we talked about our kids n' all.
>
> Let's just say there were tears on the way home. (UVF respondent, North Belfast)

Again the theme here is about the judgement of acceptance and the fear that being at an event, such as a graduation, is risk laden. Of course, the actuality of being recognised is probably less than the perception of being so, but the fear of recognition is vast given the failure to control the potential interpretation of the father and thus more importantly, the implication upon a daughter. Goffman (1981) distinguishes the process of information being 'given' but what we observe here is information being controlled. Not simply to cover deviance or wrong-doing but instead to appear virtuous or to hide away from a social event. The role of many Loyalists, regarding their daily lives, is to ensure that information does not 'leak' through. This is not simply to do with shame but the powerlessness with regard to controlling generalisable perspectives and allusion – a similar process to that involving sectarianism and the formation of concrete assertions that the 'other' is hostile, That denying any assertions of individual uniqueness. Loyalists, it seems, can rarely be promissory characters and must remain as depictions of a wider reading of them. This is noteworthy because Loyalists have not only acquired an understanding of their significance through their own observations and communications, but mcuh of their social awareness also comes from the judgements of others (Glover 1999).

Notes

1 Niblock was not the leading actor but the playwright.
2 The then head of the Northern Ireland Civil Service, Nigel Hamilton, and Sir George Quigley, former permanent secretary and Chairman of the Ulster Bank, co-chaired the working group. In addition to Loyalist and Republican former prisoner groups, it included representatives from the Confederation of British Industries, the Irish Congress of Trade Unions and relevant government departments.
3 This relates to, for example, not entering places where violence or traumatic issues were encountered.

There will be no end to loyalism, just rebirth
into something good this time around.
(UVF respondent)

8 Conclusion:
the end of Ulster loyalism?

Loyalists are divided between progressive and regressive elements. There will be no end to the former, but there is a desire/requirement for the removal of the latter. What is now required is a 'coalition of the willing' prepared to remove past organisational structures and create a new loyalism upon the foundations of key and social justice-driven principles. Some Loyalists have clearly supported the tenets of what would be understood as peacemaking criminology. Beginning with a reaction to the 'signs of alarm' they have purposefully stated that such signs no longer exist. They have upheld and part-designed the architecture and structure of the Belfast Agreement and have placed faith in the institutions that emerged from it, despite significant social and cultural rejection. Their far-sightedness with regard to realising that republicanism was no longer threatening has bolstered the overall peace process and guided wider transitions. However, the organisations themselves require removal combined with alternative structures being created. Without that loyalism will appear and remain read, paraphrasing Billy Hutchinson, as tattooed and muscular men with a dog in a T-shirt. For positive loyalism to continue and develop, it requires the (re)production of 'responsible participants' whose role would be driven by introspection and explicit reflection upon positive transitional opportunities. Without the control of Loyalist actions, whether they are positive or regressive, the motivation for transformative loyalism will remain hidden and determined by external and hostile commentary (McAuley 2005).

Reasons for acting in ways that are regressive are too fixated upon the habitual regularity of unthinking preferences and imprecise deliberation. Without doubt regressive Loyalist acts that remain, such as extortion or drug-dealing, influence criminalisation, rejection and political usury, but they are also predisposed by a rejection of positive loyalism. Progressive Loyalists cannot cover the transgressions of others and expect and demand participation in the manner that they aspire to. Undoubtedly positive and transformative-seeking Loyalists identify themselves as those most capable of 'turning' their unsavoury comrades around, but this must now be set within a specified temporal frame. Progressive loyalism has to at some point concede to its own selflessness and drive itself forward either with or without the burden of an unwavering bandwagon. As Schroeder (2007: 82) states regarding the processes of reflection:

> Every act of reflection starts somewhere, and the first thought that begins reflection is not chosen on the basis of reflection.

Reflection in whatever form it emerges has to be centred on introspection, and therefore an expulsion of criminal elements. Irredentist elements that remain are unlike transformative Loyalists as they do not possess the same ability to reflect upon a destabilising past and is so doing forge the requirement to shift into supporting community and societal transition. Progressive or transitional Loyalists have challenged the erroneous nature of previous fealty and directed their ire away from ethno-sectarian asperity and in several instances have dealt with wreckers and spoilers. Yet they have not rooted out all elements that retard their progress. This is an insufficiency that anchors capability, reproduces the stigma of loyalism and undermines the capacity to deliver the credentials of change and transition.

There is insufficient time left for the spontaneity of some to be tolerated or understood as a problem. Loyalists who are progressive-minded should not ultimately ditch their regressive elements due merely to societal pressure but because they chose to do so for the development of their own potential. The negatives within loyalism of drug-dealing and other criminality impede transitional loyalism as much as the excessive external criminalisation of them. The place for progressive Loyalists should not be in the middle between the camps of criminal elements and those who criminalise, but elsewhere, in a place within which they can build on the sufficient architecture of capacity that they have developed thus far (Hutchinson 1995). As Habermas notes, democracy is 'reconceived under the conditions of complex societies' (Habermas 1998: 7).

Positive Loyalists are aware of the conditions under which they operate but they must step onward and detach themselves from regressive elements. The immediate capacity of Loyalists after 1994 was tempered by the wreckers and spoilers but most of these excessive elements have now gone. The spectacle of Adair and Wright clearly impeded a positive trajectory but so too has the drag of the less obvious regressive elements. Such elements will remain as long as they can use the badge of parent organisations to 'legitimise' extortion and other criminal activities. Ultimately organisations such as the UDA and UVF must civilianise completely – the removal of the blank cheque for the bully. The power of usury of organisational structures will merely continue until those structures have gone. The cessation of the UVF and UDA, as organisations, would ultimately mean that a Loyalist involved in extortion would no longer be a Loyalist extortionist but simply an extortionist. A shift to that scenario would create the reality of a societal problem as opposed to an internal Loyalist predicament.

There is no fundamental problem in that progressive elements are aware of the reasons and structures for alternative socio-political change and the proper conduct of collective life and responsibilities, but there is an issue of drag upon such assertions. Northern Ireland Alternatives and the re-imaging of murals clearly highlights the realisation of Loyalist intention and capacity. Such persons involved in such activities aim for social transformation and civic inclusion, and are those who understand the difference between the various fictions and facts regarding the future of Protestant working-class communities. Those involved in such groups and actions are at the pinnacle of democratic accountability and change, but are generally unrecognised given the draw of less conscientious, unreliable and assiduous elements. Such regressive elements viz-a-viz those committed to positive change not only increasingly occupy different positions and responsibilities within social space but are circum-scribed by contrary positions and habitus. Loyalists, as they have been for some time are subject to classification and the distinctions between the acceptable and the unacceptable, the capable and the dystopian and the liberating and the destabilising. The antithesis between the two can be measured and qualified but that is an act of calculation that has virtually no meaning or acceptance beyond loyalism – a clear example being the element within the East Belfast UVF who orchestrated rioting in June 2011. Within that element and up to the rioting positive UVF mural re-imaging was replaced by the return of murals of armed and hooded gunmen. Several weeks before the riot Protestant youths had daubed paint on the St Matthew's, a Catholic Church in the small Republican enclave of Short Strand. Progressive loyalist elements had raised funds and provided the labour to remove the paint – a sign of good intentions viewed by regressive elements as an act of de-masculation. Such a positive act was buried by the rioting that was to occur.

Society does not, through the act of criminalisation, submit to interpreting and understanding such complexity of classification. The consumption of Loyalists is driven by tabloid media to such an extent that the signs of progressive change have been submerged. The most significant and meaningful act that Loyalists can achieve is to create and control their own image – such as task of civilianisation must deny the function of regressive elements. There is no longer a requirement to maintain common ground between those active in positive change and those who are not. The conflict may well have solidified disparate elements and made tolerable those that were unsavoury in the execution of violence, but the structure and immediacy of armed conflict has gone and ultimately the assertion of a common ground must not now been subscribed to if it maintains dysfunctional umbrella organsiations. A blunt assertion from the progressive element that it has detached itself from regressive sections both privately and then publicly is required via clear and unambiguous statements of intent.

It may be that media-driven depictions are excessively generated but any mark upon which the regressive and stunting forms of Loyalist activity remain will never permit such accounts to evaporate. It is within the development and explanation of the actual conditions of progressive and forward-thinking loyalism that the formation of judgments will be both performed and delivered – a task that is complex but can be founded upon the question, 'Why is loyalism relevant?' That relevance lies in community renewal, acting against educational disadvantage, encouraging non-sectarian histories, building restorative justice and seeking order and inclusion for socially marginalised communities. In 2002 a sign of that social conscience was stated in the UVF's Remembrance Day speech with regard to the outplaying of the peace process:

> To date, our communities, our people and our constituencies, are yet to witness any benefits from the peace process. All across Belfast we see the property developers making a 'killing'. In Protestant working-class areas, our schools are run down, hospital services are run down and communities are run down – we have gradually become the underclass.[1]

Those committed to progressive loyalism must fully embed themselves in a community/voluntary structure that deliberately seeks to challenge socio-economic exclusion within an evolving post-conflict landscape. Relevance can only be achieved from the ground upwards. The sentiment of having protected the people must now be shifted into the response of delivering their social and educational evolution. Loyalists possess the vocabulary and intent to do so, but they require a structure to embolden such efforts. This must be the primacy of their efforts if they are to ditch the hollow signifiers of rhetoric over action. As argued by Barak:

> The 'battle' to develop a fuller and richer mutualism as well as the challenge to reign in and to control our adversarial tendencies, especially when they are destructive of others and ourselves, involves individuals, families, communities, nation-states and ultimately, the planet, all working together to alter traditional as well as international patterns of social interaction. These struggles for peace-making and nonviolence over warmaking and violence are not about negating conflict and competitiveness per se. After all, at various levels of individual and collective interaction, conflicts are normal and to be expected. In this sense, conflict can be defined as what results from the existence, real and imagined, of incompatible beliefs, interests, goals or activities. (2005: 139)

A fundamental problem, more generally, that relates to Northern Ireland is the desire to abandon a contested past or to leave it to remain within the margins of society. There is insufficient desire to comprehend the remaining legacies of conflict or dwell too long on alternative paths and trajectories that could radically reassemble Northern Ireland into a more stable and democrat-ically driven society. What has emerged relatively unscathed out of conflict is the capacity of the constitutional question to uphold ethno-sectarian contention. For Republicans Northern Ireland is in a holding position, whereas for Unionists the future is undetermined. Transitional and progressive Loyalists remain committed to the Union but see no purpose in arming against Irish unification. Instead their energies are aimed at developing a less rhetorical version of Northern Ireland plc through challenging what is represented as democracy and the myth of order, equality and classlessness. They have realised that for their responsible participation to be effective it must create a community sphere that is progressive and aims to develop the discourse and meaning of citizenship. However, that task is incomplete unless they influence wider external readings of them, a task set against an insufficient knowledge of their role and the corrosiveness of remaining criminality. The concerns of transformative Loyalists, such a poverty, exclusion and social truncation, ring hollow if there is any opportunity to demonise such persons by pointing to others linked to them who are involved in nefarious activities. In addition Unionist politicians have effectively watched as the Protestant working class has fallen into demographic, educational and labour market decline. As made clear by Howe:

> 'Resisting', though, with few resources and little confidence. The essential cultural difference between Loyalism and its foes is indeed that while Republicans conceive of themselves as having an inherited, densely woven tradition – however thoroughly and recently reinvented that 'tradition' may really be – Loyalists have to make it up as they go along. If the result of that heterogenous improvisation is a kind of untheorised postmodernism, it is the postmodernism of despair. These are the fragments they shore up against their ruins. (2005: 4)

Northern Ireland is a society within which 24% of children live below the poverty line and are twice as likely to be living in persistent poverty compared with those living in Britain. Moreover, a fifth of children aged five to fifteen have a moderate to severe mental health disorder requiring mental health service support (Bradley 2000). Between 1997 and 2007 there was a 61% increase in suicides of which 22% were persons under the age of 25. In 2007 the median male wage in Northern Ireland was £424.80, or £3822 less than the UK median annual wage. In 2006 24% of working age adults in Northern Ireland possessed no qualifications compared with 14% in England. A mere 8.5% of those on free school meals in the Controlled non-grammar (generally Protestant) schools sector achieved two A-levels compared with 21.2% in Maintained Catholic non-grammar schools. Just under twice as many pupils (not on free school meals) in Catholic Maintained (38.0%) schools gained two A-levels compared with those in Controlled Schools (19.6%). A socially disadvantaged pupil on free school meals in a Catholic (Maintained) school will have a one in five chance of going to university compared with a similar pupil in a Protestant (Controlled) school, who has a one in ten chance (Purvis 2011). At the launch of the report into Protestant educational disadvantage in 2011 a grand total, excluding Dawn Purvis, of one Unionist MLA was in attendance compared with at least three Sinn Fein MLAs, including the Deputy First Minister. Unionist political representatives remain fixated upon defending the transfer test as opposed to seeking alternative modes and means of learning that would undermine the Protestant working class's largely fatalistic attitude to education. Such indifference encourages loyalism to remain and consider the position of a Thirdspace (Soja 1996, 2000).

The capacity to influence the public sphere is a difficult enough condition for any group committed to civic and social inclusion as it requires challenging the status quo of public opinion that is already predicated upon bourgeois indifference, the related desire of class separation and the outpourings of increasingly privatised market-driven economies. In the period of late capitalism the social construct is more emotionally driven by demonisation-driven discourses within which the socially excluded are at fault for their own social position. Those who push for civil inclusion are burdened by wider societal indifference, similar to Bourdieu's (1984) sense of a developing and socio-culturally defined elitism and the intent of social displacing via symbols, language and class asperity. This complexity of class dislocation hampers meaningful democratic assertion, all the more so when those aiming for social inclusion are read as being unsavoury.

The goal of transitional loyalism must be linked to developing unconventional forms of political accountability and enhanced social challenge and concern. It must challenge the mythic trappings of rule-based consent and the limitations therein. The primary motivator has to be a meaningful demand for inclusive democracy which can only be pursued with a morality that challenges the rhetorical sphere of hegemonic geared 'consent'. That should be linked to a five-part typology which is based on the following recognition:

- That equality-driven policies are not the same as social inclusion;
- That there are reasons for the rejection of Loyalists acts, and in particular the Loyalist 'self' must pursue an uncontaminated moral good;
- That social interests which affect the socially excluded in a dramatic fashion are more important than national identity;
- That the influence required to alter the readings of Loyalists are not merely contingent upon seeking redress from statutory agencies;
- That challenging the claim to full accessibility to society for marginal members is the key point of activism.

Part of the progressive discourse must also challenge the rendition of the efficacy of labeling. In the past senses of implied exclusion linked to constitutional conflict initially led Loyalists into reproducing the inequality of power relationships. Obviously, some have now realised that social stratification and the call to arms from beyond the working classes simply mimicked social-class positions. In enacting violence Loyalists endured imprisonment and rejection and fell into a trap of class labelling and denunciation. Thus the conflict only reproduced social stratification and unequal positions in a post-conflict situation. Republicans earned their political empowerment through acting free from or in opposition to social constraint. In terms of alternative lifeworlds the Catholic working class has earned cultural and political representation whilst their counterpart in general has failed to draw upon their social as opposed to their cultural condition. The pressure of socio-economic truncation has for the Protestant working class been amplified. With an inexact leadership from within unionism they not only lack equal access to civic society but also the material means of inclusion. The space of Protestant working-class abandon-ment has produced an autonomy that could either garner a challenge and rejection of such social discord or deepen it more broadly. Any deepening would have severe societal outcomes.

If progressive loyalism is to continue to make a contribution that is positive it must invoke and demand participatory parity which is not centred upon discourses of rejection but instead the denunciation of negativity itself. Needs that are tied to social justice must not remain inchoate. The application of energy for political and social adjustment cannot simply be framed by counter-discourses aligned against the State, unionism or Republicanism as there is a requirement to offer a discourse that is more socially liberating. Ideas cannot be recast along an oppositional cannon of rejection that in any fashion is tied to resource competition, a platform that only reproduces ethno-sectarian diatribe and gains the morsels of social potential. Instead it should be fashioned around explicitly challenging subaltern-producing agendas, anti-egalitarianism and all forms of hegemonic impositioning (Shirlow and McEvoy 2008). That entails pinpointing the reproduction of separatism within its many guises. As Barak (2005: 145) contends:

> Mutuality does not strive to end tension but to cultivate those tensions that produce growth and pleasure. Indeed, there is also tension in mutuality. But it is not the tension of confrontation and defeat; it is the tension of efforts to expand and to connect. In other words, it is about the tensions involved in finding alter-natives to the unnecessary destructiveness fostered by adversarial assumptions and practices. It is also about finding out how to relate to others and nature as friend rather than foe. Ultimately, it is about finding out how to live a 'life of balance' rather than a 'life of excess'.

Loyalists have done many positive things in terms of community restoration and conflict transformation. Persons allied to the UDA helped turn the Glencairn estate in West Belfast from a 'dump' estate into a place in which there is now a healthy waiting list for homes. Work at sectarian interfaces has led to significant declines in inter-community violence and members of the UDA met Catholic Cardinal Sean Brady in an act of obvious reconciliation. Such developments echo Barak's concept of mutualism. Some have also worked to aid the lives of economic migrants. As noted in the *Principles of Loyalism* (2002: 12):

> It is the duty of the volunteers to co-operate with the political process by ensuring that our political and community activists have a safe environment within which to work, and that our communities are safe and secure and free from all that would harm the personal, social or economic welfare of our people.

Therefore, with such principles, to what extent do we require an end to Ulster loyalism? Positive and grounded community intervention will remain a key goal for Loyalists as it is the arena within which a spirit of dedication to place-centred communities and their future can be realised. For them, Unionist politics offers a lack of sufficiency which undermines their desire to remove themselves from the stage. Yet any reproduction and insertion aiming for social justice in marginalised communities must remain as a goal of Loyalist inter-vention. However, Loyalist interaction must be attached, as much of it is, to inclusion, verification and community corroboration. To aid that there must also be a cessation of external renditions that obscure positive Loyalist inter-ventions.

There is a wider commitment, beyond loyalism, that must uphold and support the positives within a post-conflict society. However, in the final stages of a post-conflict process positive Loyalists must emerge out of a wider sloth-like body that has impeded their potential. It is not an end to Ulster loyalism that is required, but the cessation of de-stabilising elements and actions from within. To be a volunteer or defender should never be a rhetorical guise but an earned title tied to inclusive actions that aim for justice, inclusion and social emancipation. Loyalism cannot, as a discourse, organisation or set of ideas remain as a one-size-fits-all body when some participants do not embrace or abide by socially transformative principles. Promoting and sustaining an alter-native set of practices within which criminalising discourses are starved of the oxygen of wrong-doing is the ultimate test. In sum, for some, loyalism's end is its ultimate future.

Note

1 Copy of statement held by author.

Bibliography

Adair, J. (2007) *Mad Dog*, London: John Blake.

Adamson, I. (1991) *The Ulster People*, Bangor: Pretani Press.

Allister, J. (2008) Submission on: Draft Programme for Government 2008-2011, http:// www. pfgbudgetni.gov.uk/allister_jimqcmep.pdf (last accessed 27 November 2008; paper copy held by author).

Alway, J. (1995) *Critical theory and Political Possibilities*, Anchor: Greenwood Publishing Group.

Anderson, B. (1991) *Imagined Communities: Reflections on the Origins and Spread of Nationalism*, London: Verso.

Anderson, C. (2002) *The Billy Boy: The Life and Death of LVF leader Billy Wright*, Edinburgh: Mainstream Publishing.

Anderson, J. and Shuttleworth, I. (1994) 'Sectarian readings of sectarianism: interpreting the Northern Ireland census', *The Irish Review*, 16: 74–93.

Archard, D. (1995) 'Political philosophy and the concept of the nation', *Journal of Value Inquiry*, 29: 379–392.

Arendt, H. (1969) *What is Authority?* Cleveland and New York: World Publishing.

Aretxaga, B. (1997) *Shattering Silence: Women, Nationalism, and Political Subjectivity in Northern Ireland*, Princeton, NJ: Princeton University Press.

Ashe, F. (2006) 'Gendering the holy cross dispute: women and nationalism in Northern Ireland', *Political Studies*, 54: 147–164.

Aughey, A. (1985) 'Between exclusion and recognition: the politics of the Ulster Defence Association', *Conflict Quarterly*, 1: 40–52.

Aughey, A. (1997) 'The character of Ulster Unionism', in P. Shirlow and M. McGovern, (eds) *Who Are 'The People'? Protestantism, Unionism and Loyalism in Northern Ireland*, London: Pluto Press.

Aughey, A. and McIlheney, C. (1984) 'Law before violence? The Protestant paramilitaries in Ulster politics', *Eire-Ireland*, 19: 55–74.

Azaryahu, M. and Kellerman, A. (1999) 'Symbolic places of national history and revival: a study in Zionist mythical geography', *Transactions of the Institute of British Geographers*, 24: 109–123.

Bairner, A. (1996) 'Paramilitarism', in A. Aughey and D. Morrow (eds) *Northern Ireland Politics*, London: Longman.

Bairner, A. and Shirlow, P. (1998) 'Loyalism, Linfield and the territorial politics of soccer fandom in Northern Ireland', *Space and Polity*, 2: 163–177.

Ballymacarrett Think Tank (1999) *Puppets No More*, Newtownabbey: Island Publications.

Barak, G. (2005) 'A reciprocal approach to peacemaking criminology', *Theoretical Criminology*, 9: 131–152.

BBC (2003) 'Loyalist commisssion – Loyalists should end rackets', http://news.bbc.co.uk/go/pr/fr/-/2/hi/uk_news/northern_ireland/3193050.stm (last accessed 20 October 2011).

BBC (2007) 'Loyalist drug dealer "untouched"', http://news.bbc.co.uk/1/hi/northern_ireland/7078554.stm (last accessed 20 October 2011).

BBC (2009a) 'Loyalist weapons put beyond use', BBC Northern Ireland, 27 June.

BBC (2009b) 'Ritchie case cost taxpayer £300k', BBC News, 30 April.

Bean, K. (1995) 'The new departure? Recent developments in Republican strategy and ideology', *Irish Studies Review*, 10: 2-6.

Belfast Telegraph (2007) 'Funding is for Loyalist communities … not paramilitary pockets', 5 August.

Belfast Telegraph (2010) 'Belfast's murals: Off the wall?', http://www.belfasttelegraph.co.uk/lifestyle/features/belfasts-murals-off-the-wall-14764361.html (last accessed 20 October 2011).

Bew, P., Gibbon, P. and Patterson, H. (1979) *The State in Northern Ireland 1921–72: Political Forces and Social Classes*, Manchester: Manchester University Press.

Bew, P., Gibbon, P. and Patterson, H. (1995) *Northern Ireland 1921–1994: Political Forces and Social Classes*, London: Serif.

Bhabha, B. (1994) *The Location of Culture*, London: Routledge.

Billig, M. (1995) *Banal Nationalism*, London: Sage Publications.

Bjorgo, T. (1995) *Root Causes of Terrorism: Myths, Reality and Ways Forward*, London: Routledge.

Boss, P. (2002) 'Ambiguous loss in families of the missing', *The Lancet*, 360: 9–40.

Boulton, D. (1973) *The UVF 1966–73: An Anatomy of Loyalist Rebellion*, Dublin: Torc Books.

Bourdieu, P. (1984) *Distinction: A Social Critique of the Judgement of Taste*, London: Routledge.

Bourke, R. (2003) *Peace in Ireland: The War of Ideas*, London: Blackwell.

Boyce, J. (2002) 'Aid conditionality as a tool for peacebuilding: opportunities and constraints', *Development and Change*, 33: 1025–1049.

Bradley, M. (2000) *Post Traumatic Stress Disorder in North Belfast*, Belfast: North Belfast Trauma Study Team.

Braithwaite, J. (2002) *Restorative Justice and Responsive Regulation*, Oxford: Oxford University Press.

Bruce, S. (1986) *God Save Ulster! The Religion and Politics of Paisleyism*, Oxford: Clarendon Press.

Bruce, S. (1987) 'Ulster loyalism and religiosity', *Political Studies*, 35: 643–648.

Bruce, S. (1992) *The Red Hand: Protestant Paramilitaries in Northern Ireland*, Oxford: Oxford University Press.

Bruce, S. (1994a) *The Edge of the Union: The Ulster Loyalist Political Vision*, Oxford: Oxford University Press.

Bruce, S. (1994b) 'The politics of Loyalist paramilitaries', in B. Barton and P. Roche (eds) *The Northern Ireland Question: Perspectives and Policies*, Aldershot: Avebury.

Bruce, S. (1995a) 'Northern Ireland: reappraising Loyalist violence', in A. O'Day (ed.), *Terrorism's Laboratory*, Aldershot: Avebury.

Bruce, S. (1995b) 'Paramilitaries, peace and politics: Ulster Loyalists and the 1994 Truce', *Studies in Conflict and Terrorism*, 18: 187–202.

Bruce, S. (2000) 'Loyalist assassinations and police collusion in Northern Ireland: an extended critique of Sean McPhilemy's "The Committee"', *Studies in Conflict and Terrorism*, 23: 61–80.

Bruce, S. (2001) 'Terrorists and politics: the case of Northern Ireland's Loyalist paramilitaries', *Terrorism and Political Violence*, 13: 27–47.

Bruce, S. (2004) 'Turf war and peace: Loyalist paramilitaries since 1994', *Terrorism and Political Violence*, 16: 501–521.

Bryan, D., Fraser, T. and Dunne, S. (1995) *Political Rituals: Loyalist Parades in Portadown*, Coleraine: Centre for the Study of Conflict.

Brysk, A. and Gershon, S. (eds.) (2007) *National Insecurity and Human Rights: Democracies Debate Counterterrorism*, Berkeley: University of California Press.

Burton, F. (1978) *The Politics of Legitimacy: Struggles in a Belfast Community*, London: Routledge.

Cairns, D. (2000) 'The object of sectarianism: the material reality of sectarianism in Ulster loyalism', *Journal of the Royal Anthropological Institute*, 6: 437–446.

Cairns, E., Van Til, J. and Williamson, A. (2003) 'Social Capital, Collectivism-Individualism and Community Background in Northern Ireland', OFM/DFM: Belfast.

Calhoun, C. (2007) *Nationalism*, Buckinghamshire: Open University Press.

Capoccia, G. and Kelemen, R. (2007) 'The study of critical junctures: theory, narrative, and counterfactuals in historical institutionalism', *World Politics*, 59: 341–369.

Carey, S. (2007) 'European aid: human rights versus bureaucratic inertia?', *Journal of Peace Research*, 44: 447–464.

Carlson, B. and Cervera N. (1992) *Inmates and Their Wives: Incarceration and Family Life*, Oxford: Greenwood Press.

Cassidy, K. (2008) 'Organic intellectuals and the new Loyalism: re-inventing Protestant working-class politics in Northern Ireland', *Irish Political Studies*, 23: 411–430.

Cavanaugh, K. (1997) 'Interpretations of political violence in ethnically divided societies', *Terrorism and Political Violence*, 9: 33–54.

Clapham, A. (2005) *Human Rights Obligations of Non-State Actors*, Oxford: Oxford University Press.

Clayton, P. (1996) *Enemies and Passing Friends: Settler Ideologies in Twentieth Century Ulster*, London: Pluto Press.

Cohan, C., Cole, S. and Davila, J. (2005) 'Marital transitions among Vietnam-era repatriated prisoners of war', *Journal of Social and Personal Relationships*, 22: 777–795.

Cohen, S. (1972) *Folk Devils and Moral Panics: The Creation of the Mods and Rockers*, Oxford: Martin Robertson.

Cohen, S. (1996) 'Government responses to human rights reports: claims, denials, and counterclaims', *Human Rights Quarterly*, 18: 517–543.

Cohen, S (2001) *States of Denial: Knowing about Atrocities and Suffering*, Cambridge: Polity Press.

Cohen, J. and Arato, A. (1992) *Civil Society and Political Theory*, Cambridge, Mass.: MIT Press.

Cohen, S. and Young, J. (1981) *The Manufacture of News: Deviance, Social Problems and the Mass Media*, 2nd edn, London: Sage.

Combat (1975) 'The futility of violence', June.

Combat (1977) 'From the cages', June.

Combat (1987) 'Booked any good reds lately?', September.

Combat (1995) 'Loyalists break new ground', January.

Combat (1996) 'Progressive Unionist Party conference', December.

Combat (1998) 'Pantomime in Portadown', December.

Combat (2003) 'All links severed', January.

Connerton, P. (1989) *How Societies Remember*, Cambridge: Cambridge University Press.

Cooke, D. (1996) *Persecuting Zeal: A Portrait of Ian Paisley*, Dingle: Brandon.

Cornell, C. 'The other community: Northern Ireland in British television, 1995', *New Hibernia Review*, 1: 37–47.

Cory, P. (2004) *Cory Collusion Inquiry Report*, London: The Stationery Office.

Coulter, C. (1994) 'The character of Unionism', *Irish Political Studies*, 9: 1–24.

Coulter, C. (1999a) 'The absence of class politics in Northern Ireland', *Capital and Class*, 99: 77–100.

Coulter, C. (1999b) *Contemporary Northern Irish Society: An Introduction*, London: Pluto.

Crawford, C. (1999) *Defenders or Criminals? Loyalist Prisoners and Criminalisation*, Belfast: Blackstaff Press.

Crawford, C. (2003) *Inside the UDA: Volunteers and Violence*, London: Pluto Press.

Crenshaw, M. (1983) 'Introduction: reflections on the effects of terrorism', in M. Crenshaw (ed.) *Terrorism. Legitimacy and Power: The Consequences of Political Violence*, Middletown, CT: Wesleyan University Press.

Crenshaw, M. (1990) *Theories of Terrorism: Instrumental and Organisational Approaches*, University Park, PA: Pennsylvania State Press.

Criminal Justice Inspectorate (2007a) *Northern Ireland Alternatives: Report of an Inspection with a View to Accreditation Under the Government's Protocol for Community Based Restorative Justice*, Belfast: Criminal Justice Inspectorate Northern Ireland.

Criminal Justice Inspectorate (2007b) *Restorative Justice Ireland Report of a pre-inspection of schemes in Belfast and in the Northwest with a view to accreditation under the Government's Protocol for Community Based Restorative Justice*, Belfast: Criminal Justice Inspectorate Northern Ireland.

Criminal Justice Inspectorate (2010) *Northern Ireland Alternatives: A Follow-Up Review of the Northern Ireland Alternatives Restorative Justice Schemes*, Belfast: Criminal Justice Inspection Northern Ireland.

Criminal Law Act (NI) 1967 (1967) www.statutelaw.gov.uk/content.aspx?activeTextDocId=1186125 (last accessed 20 October 2011).

Crothers, J. (1998) *Reintegration – the Problems and the Issues*, Belfast: EPIC.

CTI (2005) *Loyalism in Transition, CTI, A Proposal to the DSD*, copy held by author.

CTI (2006) *CTI Development Project Summary Report*, copy held by author.

Cusack, J. and McDonald, H. (1997) *UVF*, Dublin: Poolbeg.

Cusack, J. and Taylor, M. (1993) 'Resurgence of a terrorist organisation – part 1: the UDA, a case study', *Terrorism and Political Violence*, 5: 1–27.

Darby, J. (1976) *Conflict in Northern Ireland: The Development of a Polarised Community*, Dublin: Gill and MacMillan.

Davis, R. (1994) *Mirror Hate: Convergent Ideology of Northern Ireland Paramilitaries*, Aldershot: Dartmouth.

Dekel, R. (2007) 'Posttraumatic distress and growth among wives of prisoners of war: the contribution of husbands' posttraumatic stress disorder and wives own attachment', *American Journal of Orthopsychiatry*, 77: 419–426.

Dekel, R. and Solomon, Z. (2006) 'Secondary traumatization among wives of Israeli POWs: the role of POWs' distress', *Social Psychiatry and Psychiatric Epidemiology*, 41: 27–33. ·

Della Porta, D. (1992) 'Institutional response to terrorism: the Italian case', *Terrorism and Political Violence*, 4: 151–70.

Dent, O., Tennant, C., Fairley, M., Sulway, M., Broe, A., Jorm, A. and Creasley, H. (1998) 'Prisoner of war experience: effects on wives', *Journal of Nervous and Mental Disease*, 186: 231–237.

Department of Culture, Arts and Leisure (2006) '£3.3m Re-Imaging Communities Programme launched', www.grant-tracker.org/news/re-imaging-communities-programme-launched (last accessed 21 November 2011).

Deutsch, M. (1969) 'Conflicts: productive and destructive', *Journal of Social Issues*, 25: 7–41.

Dewilde, C. (2003) 'A life-course perspective on social exclusion and poverty', *British Journal of Sociology*, 54: 109–128.

Dickson, B. (1995) 'Criminal justice and emergency laws', in S. Dunn (ed.) *Facets of the Conflict in Northern Ireland*, London: Macmillan.

Dillon, M. (1990) *The Dirty War*, London: Arrow Books.

Dixon, P. (2001) *Northern Ireland: The Politics of War and Peace*, Basingstoke: Palgrave MacMillan.

Douglas N. and Shirlow P. (1998) 'People in conflict in place: the case of Northern Ireland', *Political Geography*, 17: 125–128.

DSD (2007) 'Government expects end to paramilitarism' (press release), Belfast: DSD.

Duncan, J. and Duncan, N. (1988) '(Re)reading the landscape', *Environment and Planning D: Society and Space*, 6: 117–126.

Dunn, S. and Morgan, V. (1994) *Protestant Alienation in Northern Ireland. A Preliminary Survey*, Coleraine: Centre for the Study of Conflict.

Edwards, A. (2009) 'Abandoning armed resistance? The Ulster Volunteer Force as a case study of strategic terrorism in Northern Ireland', *Studies in Conflict and Terrorism*, 32: 146–166.

Edwards, A. and Boomer, S. (2004) *A Watching Brief? The Political Strategy of Progressive Loyalism Since 1994*, Belfast: LINC.

Elshtain, J. (2001) 'Bonhoeffer on Modernity: Sic et Non', *Journal of Religious Ethics*, 29: 345–366.

Engdahl, B., Dikel, T., Kuskowski, M., Eberly, R. and Pardo, J. (1999) 'Regional cerebral blood flow during script-driven imagery in combat-related PTSD: A PET study', in B. Engdahl (ed.) *Neuroimaging and PTSD: An Update*, Miami, FL: International Society for Traumatic Stress Studies.

English, R. (2009) *Terrorism: How to Respond*, Oxford: Oxford University Press.

Eolas Project (2003) *Consultation Paper on Truth and Justice*, Belfast: Relatives for Justice.

EPIC (2004). *Truth Recovery: A Contribution from Within Loyalism*, Belfast: EPIC.

EPIC (2005) *Truth Recovery: A Contribution from Loyalism*, Belfast: EPIC.

Eriksson, A. (2009) *Justice in Transition: Community Restorative Justice in Northern Ireland*. Devon: Willan Publishing.

Ervine, D. (1995) 'Beyond betrayal', *New Times*, 18 February.

Ervine, D. (1998) 'Consent the only way forward', *Belfast Telegraph*, 12 May.

Ervine, D. (1999) 'Responsibility begins at home', *Belfast Telegraph*, 15 March.

Ervine, D. (2000) 'No surrender', *Corrymeela Connections*, 2: 8–10.

Ervine, D. (2002a) 'Redefining loyalism', in J. Coakley (ed.) *Changing Shades of Orange and Green*, Dublin: University College Dublin Press.

Ervine, D. (2002b) 'Loyalist groups re-arming' BBC News, http://news.bbc.co.uk/1/hi/northern_ireland/1977895.stm (last accessed 27 October 2011).

Farrell, M. (1976) *Northern Ireland: The Orange State*, London, Pluto Press.

Farset (2007) *Letter from Farset Youth and Community Development Limited to Minister for Social Development*, 17 August, copy held by author.

Feldman A. (1991) *Formations of Violence: The Narrative of the Body and Political Terror in Northern Ireland*, Chicago: University of Chicago Press.

Field, J. (2007) *CTI Development Project. Interim Evaluation Report*, copy held by author.

Finlay, A. (2001) 'Defeatism and Northern Protestant identity', *The Global Review of Ethnic Politics*, 1: 3–20.

Finlayson, A. (1997) 'Discourse and contemporary Loyalist identity', in P. Shirlow and M. McGovern (eds) *Who Are 'The People'? Unionism, Protestantism and Loyalism in Northern Ireland*, London: Pluto Press.

Finlayson, A. (1999) 'Loyalist political identity after the peace', *Capital and Class*, 69: 47–76.

Follis, B. (1995) *A State Under Siege: The Establishment of Northern Ireland 1920–1925*, Oxford, Oxford University Press.

Foucault, M. (1972) *The Archeology of Knowledge*, London: Tavistock.

Friedrichs, D. (1998) *State Crime*, Brookfield, VT: Ashgate.

Gallagher, M. (1995) 'Beyond the Bullwark? The fringe Loyalist parties and the future', *An Phoblacht/Republican News*, 19 January.

Gallagher, T. (1981) 'Religion, reaction, and revolt in Northern Ireland: the impact of Paisleyism in Ulster', *Journal of Church and State*, 23: 423–444.

Gallaher, C. (1997) 'The religious right and identity politics: hiding hate in the landscape', *Antipode*, 29: 256–277.

Gallaher, C. (2007) *After the Peace: Loyalist Paramilitaries in Post-Accord Northern Ireland*, London: Cornell University Press.

Gallaher, C. and Shirlow, P. (2006) 'The geography of Loyalist paramilitary feuding in Belfast', *Space and Polity*, 10: 149–169.

Galliher, J. and DeGregory, J. (1985) *Violence in Northern Ireland: Understanding Protestant Perspectives*, Dublin: Gill and MacMillan.

Galtung J. and Hoivik T. (1971) 'Structural and direct violence: a note on operationalization', *Journal of Peace Research*, 7: 5–13.

Garland, R. (2001) *Gusty Spence*, Belfast: Blackstaff Press.

Gibbs, J. (1991) 'Environmental congruence and symptoms of psychopathology: a further exploration of the effects of exposure to the jail environment', *Criminal Justice and Behavior*, 18: 351–374.

Gillespie, G. (2001) 'Loyalists since 1972', in D. Boyce and A. O'Day (eds) *Defenders of the Union: A Survey of British and Irish Unionism since 1801*, London: Routledge.

Gillis, J. (1994) 'Memory and identity: the history of a relationship', in J. Gillis (ed.) *Commemorations: The Politics of National Identity*, Princeton, NJ: Princeton University Press.

Girard, R. (1979) 'Mimesis and violence: perspectives in cultural criticism', *Berkshire Review*, 14: 9–19.

Glover, J. (1999) *Humanity: A Moral History of the Twentieth Century*, London: Jonathan Cape.

Girshick, L. (1996) *Soledad Women: Wives of Prisoners Speak Out*, Westport, CT: Praeger.

Goffman, E. (1959) *The Presentation of Self in Everyday Life*, New York: Doubleday

Goffman, E. (1961) *Asylums*, New York: Doubleday Anchor.

Goffman, E. (1964) *Stigma: Notes on the Management of Spoiled Identity*, Englewood Cliffs, NJ: Prentice-Hall.

Goffman, E. (1972) *Relations in Public: Microstudies of the Public Order*, New York: Harper Colophon.

Goffman, E. (1974) *Frame Analysis: An Essay on the Organisation of Experience*, New York: Harper and Row.

Goffman, E. (1981) *Forms of Talk*, Oxford: Basil Blackwell.

Gomes Porto, J., Alden, C. and Parsons, I. (2007) *From Soldiers to Citizens: Demilitarisation of Conflict and Society*, Farnham: Ashgate.

Gormally, B., Maruna, S. and McEvoy, K. (2007) *Thematic Evaluation of Funded Projects: Politically-Motivated Former Prisoners and their Families* Monaghan: Border Action, 2007.

Grabosky, P. and Stohl, M. (2010) *Crime and Terrorism*, Los Angeles: Sage.

Graham, B. (1998) 'Contested images of place among Protestants in Northern Ireland', *Political Geography*, 17: 129–144.

Graham, B. (2004) 'The past in the present: the shaping of identity in Loyalist Ulster', *Terrorism and Political Violence*, 16: 483–499.

Graham B. and Shirlow, P. (2002) 'The Battle of the Somme in Ulster memory and identity', *Political Geography*, 21: 881–904.

Graham, B and Whelan, Y. (2007) 'The legacies of the dead: commemorating the Troubles in Northern Ireland,' *Environment and Planning D: Society and Space*, 25: 476–495.

Greater Shankill Alternatives (undated) *Greater Shankill Alternatives: The Story*, Belfast: Greater Shankill Alternatives.

Greater Shankill Alternatives (2001) *Greater Shankill Alternatives Evaluation 1998–2001*, Belfast: Greater Shankill Alternatives.

Green, M. (1998) *The Prison Experience: A Loyalist Perspective*, Belfast: EPIC.

Greenwood, C. (2010) 'Organised crime gangs outwitting police', www.independent.co.uk/news/uk/crime/organised-crime-gangs-outwitting-police-2025348.html (last accessed 20 October 2011).

Gribbin, V., Kelly, R. and Mitchell, C. (2005) *Loyalist Conflict Transformation Initiatives*, Belfast: OFM/DFM.

Grounds, A. and Jamieson, R. (2003) 'No sense of an ending: researching the experience of imprisonment and release amongst Republican ex-prisoners', *Theoretical Criminology*, 7: 347–362.

Guelke, A. (2000) 'The triumph of ambiguity: Ulster's path towards peace', *Global Dialogue*, www.worlddialogue.org/content.php?id=110 (last accessed 20 October 2011).

Habermas, J. (1973) *Theory and Practice*, Boston: Beacon Press.

Habermas, J. (1975) *Legitimation Crisis*, Boston: Beacon Press.

Habermas, J. (1984) *Observations on the Spiritual Situation of the Age*, Cambridge, Mass: MIT Press.

Habermas, J. (1987) *The Theory of Communicative Action, Vol. 2: Lifeworld and System: A Critique of Functionalist Reason*, Boston: Beacon Press.

Habermas, J. (1992) *The Philosophical Discourse of Modernity*, Cambridge Mass: MIT Press.

Habermas, J. (1998) *Between Facts and Norms: Contributions to a Discourse Theory of Law and Democracy*, Cambridge, Mass: MIT Press.

Hall, M. (1994) *Ulster's Protestant Working Class: A Community Exploration*, Belfast: Island Pamphlets.

Hall, M. (1995) *Beyond the Fife and Drum*, Belfast: Island Pamphlets.

Hall, M. (1996) *Reinforcing Powerlessness: the Hidden Dimension to the Northern Ireland 'Troubles'*, Belfast: Island Pamphlets.

Hall, M. (1998) *At the Crossroads?*, Newtownabbey: Island Pamphlets.

Hall, M. (2002) *An Uncertain Future: An Exploration by Protestant Community Activists*, Newtownabbey: Island Publications.

Hall, M. (2006) *A New Reality?* Belfast: Regency Press.

Hall, M. (2007) *Learning from Others in Conflict: Report of an International Workshop*, Belfast: Regency Press.

Hall, R. and Malone, P. (1976) 'Psychiatric effects of prolonged Asian captivity: a two-year follow-up', *American Journal of Psychiatry*, 133: 786–790.

Hamm, M. (1994) 'A modified social control theory of terrorism: an empirical and ethnographic assessment of the American neo-Nazi skinheads', in M. Hamm (ed.) *Hate Crime: International Perspectives on Causes and Control*, Cincinnati, OH: Anderson.

Hamm, M. (2002) *In Bad Company: America's Terrorist Underground*, Boston, MA: North Eastern University Press.

Hart, P. (1996) 'The Protestant experience of revolution in Ireland', in R. English and G. Walker (eds) *Unionism in Modern: New Perspectives on Politics and Culture*, Basingstoke: MacMillan Press.

Harvey, D. (1989) *The Condition of Postmodenity. An Enquiry into the Origins of Cultural Change*, Cambridge, Mass: Blackwell.

Herman, J. (1992) *Trauma and Recovery: The Aftermath of Violence: From Domestic Violence to Political Terror*, New York: Basic Books.

Horowitz, D. (1985) *Ethnic Groups in Conflict*, California: University of California Press.

Howe, S (2005) *Mad Dogs and Ulstermen (Part 1)*, www.opendemocracy.net/globalization-protest/loyalism_2876.jsp (last accessed 20 October 2011).

Hunt, N. and Robbins, I. (2001) 'The long-term consequences of war: the experience of World War II', *Aging and Mental Health*, 5: 183–190.

Hutchinson, B. (1995) 'A Loyalist perspective', *An Phoblacht/Republican News*, 2 February.

Hyndman, M. (1996) *Further Afield Journeys from a Protestant Past*, Belfast: Beyond the Pale Publications.

Independent International Monitoring Commission (2004) *Third Report of the Independent International Monitoring Commission*, London: HMSO.

Independent International Monitoring Commission (2009) *Eighteenth Report of the Independent International Monitoring Commission*, London: HMSO.

Independent International Monitoring Commission (2010) *Twenty-Third Report of the Independent International Monitoring Commission*, London: HMSO.

Independent Research Solutions (2009) *Evaluation of the Re-Imaging Communities Programme: A Report to the Arts Council of Northern Ireland*, Belfast: Arts Council for Northern Ireland.

Innes, M. (2004a) 'Reinventing tradition? Reassurance, neighbourhood security and policing', *Criminal Justice*, 4: 151–171.

Innes, M. (2004b) 'Signal crimes and signal disorders: notes on deviance as communicative action', *British Journal of Sociology*, 55: 335–355.

Innes, M., Abbott, L., Lowe, T., and Roberts, C. (2007) *Hearts and Minds and Eyes and Ears: Reducing Radicalisation Risk Through Reassurance-oriented Policing*, Cardiff: Universities Police Science Institute.

Irish News (2009) 'Farset employee invites minister to "come see the work we've done"', *Irish News*, 1 May.

Jamieson, R. and McEvoy, K. (2005) 'State crime by proxy and juridical othering', *British Journal of Criminology*, 45: 504–27.

Jamieson, R., Shirlow, P. and Grounds, A. (2010) *Ageing and social exclusion among former politically motivated prisoners in Northern Ireland: Report for the Changing*

Ageing Partnership, Belfast: Institute of Governance, School of Law Queen's University Belfast.

Jarman, N. (1992) 'Troubled images', *Critique of Anthropology*, 12: 133–165.

Jarman, N. (1997) *Material Conflicts: Parades and Visual Displays in Northern Ireland*, Oxford, Berg.

Jarman, N. (2002) *Human Rights and Community Relations: Competing or Complementary Approaches in Responding to Conflict?*, Belfast: Institute for Conflict Research.

Jehn, K. and Mannix, E. (2001) 'The dynamic nature of conflict: a longitudinal study of intragroup conflict and group performance', *Academy of Management Journal*, 44: 238–251.

Jenkins, P. (2003) *Images of Terror: What We Can and Can't Know about Terrorism*, New York: Aldine de Gruyter.

Johnstone, G. (2002) *Restorative Justice: Ideas, Values, Debates*, Devon and Oregon: Willan Publishing.

Jordan, G. (2001) *Not of This World? Evangelical Protestants in Northern Ireland*, Belfast: Balckstaff Press).

Journal of Prisoners on Prisons (1996–1997) 'Special Issue – Loyalists Prisoners of War', 7.

Juergensmeyer, M. (1997) 'The limits of globalization in the 21st century: nationalism, regionalism and violence', *SPIRIT Discussion Paper Series*, 1: 1–16.

Justice Oversight Commissioner (2004) *Second Report of the Justice Oversight Commissioner*, Belfast : JOC.

Justice Oversight Commissioner (2005) *Third Report of the Justice Oversight Commissioner*, Belfast : JOC.

Kaldor, M. (2001) *New and Old Wars: Organised Violence in a Global Era*, Cambridge: Polity Press.

Karanga, M. (2000) *Race, Ethno-sectarianity and Multiculturalism: Issues in Domination, Resistance and Diversity*, Sankore: University of Sankore Press.

Kaufman, J. (ed.) (2002) *Loss of the Assumptive World: A Theory of Traumatic Loss*, London and NY: Brunner-Routledge.

Keen, D. (2001) 'War and peace – what's the difference?', in A. Adebajo and C. Sriram (eds) *Managing Armed Conflicts in the 21st Century*, London: Frank Cass.

Keith, M. and Pile, S. (1993) 'Introduction part 2: the place of politics' in M. Keith and S. Pile (eds) *Place and the Politics of Identity*, London: Routledge.

Kellerman A. (1996) 'Settlement myth and settlement activity: interrelationships in the Zionist land of Israel', *Transactions of the Institute of British Geography*, 21: 363–378.

Kennedy. L. (2001) *They Shoot Children Don't They? An Analysis of the Age and Gender of Victims of Paramilitary 'Punishments' in Northern Ireland*, Belfast: Queens University.

Kigma, K. (2001) *Demobilisation and Reintegration of Ex-Combatants in Post-war and Transition Countries*, Eschborn: Deutsche Gesellschaft für Technische Zusammenarbeit.

Kingsley, P. (1989) *Londonderry Revisited: A Loyalist Analysis of Civil Rights Controversy*, Belfast, Belfast Publications.

Kong, L. (1993) 'Political symbolism of religious building in Singapore', *Environment and Planning D: Society and Space*, 11: 23–45.

Kriesberg, L (1982) *Social Conflicts*, New Jersey: Prentice Hall.

Laclau, E. and Mouffe, C. (1985) *Hegemony and Socialist Strategy: Towards a Radical Democratic Politics*, London and New York: Verso.

LaFree, G., Dugan, L. and Korte, R. (2009) 'The impact of British counter terrorist strategies on political violence in Northern Ireland: Comparing deterrence and backlash models', *Criminology*, 47: 501–530.

Langhammer, M. and Young, D. (1987) 'The UDA plan: opening for dialogue or sectarian fix?', *Fortnight*: 4.

Lawyer's Committee for Human Rights (2002) *Beyond Collusion: The UK Security Forces and the Murder of Pat Finucane*, Washington: Lawyer's Committee for Human Rights.

Lederach, J. (1997) *Building Peace: Sustainable Reconciliation in Divided Societies*, Washington, DC: United States Institute of Peace Press.

Lederach, J. (2005) *The Moral Imagination: The Art and Soul of Building Peace*. New York: Oxford University Press.

Lister, D. and Jordan, H. (2003) 'The downfall of Mad Dog Adair', *The Observer*, 5 October, www.guardian.co.uk/theobserver/2003/oct/05/features.magazine7 (last accessed 21 November 2011).

Loftus, B. (1994) *Mirrors of Orange and Green*, Berlin, Picture Press.

Longley, E. (1997) 'What do Protestants want?', *The Irish Review*, 20: 104–120.

MacGinty, R. (2004) 'Unionist political attitudes after the Belfast Agreement', *Irish Political Studies*, 19: 87–99.

Martí, S., Pilar D. and Pedro I. (2007) 'Democracy, civil liberties, and counterterrorist measures in Spain', in A. Brysk and S. Gershon (eds) *National Insecurity and Human Rights: Democracies debate Counterterrorism*, Berkeley, CA: University of California Press.

Massumi, B. (1993) *The Politics of Everyday Fear*, Minneapolis: University of Minnesota Press.

McAuley, J. (1996) 'From loyal soldiers to political spokespersons: a political history of a Loyalist paramilitary group in Northern Ireland', *Etudes Irlandaises*, 21: 1.

McAuley, J. (2000) 'Many roads forward: politics and ideology within the Progressive Unionist Party', *Etudes Irlandaises*, 25, 1: 173–192.

McAuley, J. (2002) 'The emergence of new loyalism', in J. Coakley (ed.) *Changing Shades of Orange and Green*, Dublin: University College Dublin Press.

McAuley, J. (2003) 'Unionism's last stand? Contemporary Unionist politics and identity in Northern Ireland', *Global Review of Ethnopolitics*, 3: 60–75.

McAuley, J. (2004) '"Just fighting to survive": Loyalist paramilitary politics and the Progressive Unionist Party', *Terrorism and Political Violence*, 16: 522–543.

McAuley, J. (2005) 'Whither new loyalism? Changing Loyalist politics after the Belfast Agreement', *Irish Political Studies*, 20: 323–340.

McAuley, J. and Hislop, S. (2000) '"Many roads forward": politics and ideology within the Progressive Unionist Party', *Etudes Irlandaises*, 25,1: 173–192.

McAuley, J., Tonge, J. and Shirlow, P. (2010) 'Conflict, transformation, and former Loyalist paramilitary prisoners in Northern Ireland', *Terrorism and Political Violence*, 22: 22–40.

McConkey and Marks v Simon Community [2009] UKHL 24.

McCormick, J. and Jarman, N. (2005) 'Death of a mural', *Journal of Material Culture*, 10: 49–71.

McCubin, H., Dahl, B., Lester, G. and Ross R. (1975) 'The returned prisoner of war: factors in family reintegration', *Journal of Marriage and the Family*, 17: 471–478.

McDonald, H. (2000) 'Revealed: Nazi roots of the thugs who threaten peace', *The Observer*, 27 August, www.guardian.co.uk/uk/2000/aug/27/northernireland.henrymcdonald1 (last accessed 20 October 2011).

McDonald, H. (2001) 'UDA creates martyr to spur the vengeance of its teenage army', *The Observer*, 18 November, www.guardian.co.uk/uk/2001/nov/18/northernireland (last accessed 20 October 2011).

McDowell, J. (2001) *Godfathers: Inside Northern Ireland Drugs Racket*, Dublin: Gill and Macmillan.

McDowell, L. (2009) 'Are we in danger of losing the plot?', www.belfasttelegraph.co.uk/opinion/columnists/lindy-mcdowell/lindy-mcdowell-are-we-in-danger-of-losing-the-plot-over-violent-past-14450285.html#ixzz12F5vobP6 (last accessed 20 October 2011).

McEvoy, K. (2001) *Paramilitary Imprisonment in Northern Ireland: Resistance, Management and Release*, Oxford: Oxford University Press.

McEvoy, K. and Eriksson, A. (2006) 'Restorative justice transition: ownership, leadership and "bottom up" human rights' in D. Sullivan and L. Tift (eds) *Handbook of Restorative Justice: A Global Perspective*, London: Routledge.

McEvoy, K. and Mika, H. (2001) 'Punishment, policing and Praxis: restorative justice and non-violent alternatives to paramilitary punishments in Northern Ireland', *Policing and Society*, 11: 359–38.

McEvoy, K. and Mika, H. (2002) 'Restorative Justice and the Critique of Informalism in Northern Ireland', *British Journal of Criminology*, 42: 534–562.

McEvoy, K. and Shirlow, P. (2009) 'Reimaging DDR: ex-combatants, leadership and moral agency in conflict transformation', *Theoretical Criminology*, 13: 31–59.

McEvoy, L. (2007) 'Beneath the rhetoric: policy approximation and citizenship education in Northern Ireland', *Citizenship and Social Justice*, 2: 135–157.

McEvoy, L., McEvoy, K. and McConnachie, K. (2006) 'Reconciliation as a dirty word: education in Northern Ireland', *Journal of International Affairs*, 60: 81–107.

McGarry, J. and O'Leary, B. (1995) *Explaining Northern Ireland: Broken Images*, London: Blackwell.

McGovern, M. and Shirlow, P. (1997) 'Counter-insurgency, deindustrialization and the political economy of Ulster loyalism', in P. Shirlow and M. McGovern (eds) *Who Are 'The People'? Unionism, Protestantism and Loyalism in Northern Ireland*, London: Pluto Press.

McGrattan, C. (2009) 'Order out of chaos: the politics of transitional justice', *Politics*, 29: 164–172.

McIlheney, A. (1985) 'Arbiters of Ulster's destiny? The military role of the Protestant paramilitaries in Northern Ireland', *Conflict Quarterly*, Spring, 5: 33–40.

McIntosh, G. (1999) *The Force of Culture: Unionist Identities in Twentieth-Century Ireland*, Cork: Cork University Press.

McIver, M. (1987) 'Ian Paisley and the reformed tradition', *Political Studies*, 35: 359–78.

McKay, S. (2000a) 'My unit conspired in the murder of civilians in Ireland', *Sunday Herald*, 19 November, www.patfinucanecentre.org/fru/fru12022k1a.html (last accessed 20 October 2011).

McKay, S. (2000b) *Northern Protestants – An Unsettled People*, Belfast: Blackstaff.

McKeown, M. (2009) *'Remembering': Victims, Survivors and Commemoration Post-Mortem Database and Documents*, http://cain.ulst.ac.uk/victims/mckeown/index.html (last accessed 20 October 2011).

McKittrick, D. (2001) 'Finucane murder suspect shot dead by Loyalist gang dead in Belfast', www.independent.co.uk/news/uk/home-news/finucane-murder-suspect-shot-dead-by-Loyalist-gang-dead-in-belfast-620001.html (last accessed 20 October 2011).

McKittrick, D. (2002a) 'What makes the Loyalists angry is seeing the other side doing so well', *The Independent*, 17 January.

McKittrick, D. (2002b) 'Trust drains away', *The Independent*, 6 October.

McKittrick, D. (2007) 'Murdered while police turned a blind eye: the truth about the Troubles', www.independent.co.uk/news/uk/this-britain/murdered-while-police-turned-a-blind-eye-the-truth-about-the-troubles-433354.html (last accessed 20 October 2011).

McKittrick, D., Kelters, S., Feeney, B. and Thornton, C. (1999) *Lost Lives: The Stories of the Men, Women and Children who Died as a Result of the Northern Ireland Troubles*, Edinburgh: Mainstream Publishing.

McMichael, G. (1999) *Ulster Voice: In Search of Common Ground in Ireland*, Boulder, CO: Roberts Rinehart Publishers.

McMichael, J. (1987) 'Common eense realities', *Fortnight*: 12.

McPhilmeny, S. (1999) *The Committee: Political Assassination in Northern Ireland*, New York: Roberts Rinehart Boulder.

Memmi, A. (1990) *The Coloniser and the Colonised*, London: Earthscan Publications.

Messerschmidt, J. (2000) *Nine Lives: Adolescent Masculinities, the Body, and Violence*, Jackson, TN: WestviewPress.

Mezirow, J. (1989) 'Transformation theory and social action: a response to Collard and Law', *Adult Education Quarterly*, 39: 169–175.

Mezirow, J. (1995) 'Transformation theory of adult learning', in M. Welton (ed.) *In Defence of the Lifeworld*, New York: SUNY Press.

Miall, H. (2004) *Conflict Transformation: A Multi-Dimensional Task, Berghof Handbook for Conflict Transformation*, Berlin, Berghof, Berlin.

Mika, H. (2002) *Evaluation: Greater Shankill Alternatives 1998–2001*, Belfast: Alternatives.

Mika, H. (2006) *Community Based Restorative Justice in Northern Ireland*, Belfast: Institute of Criminology and Criminal Justice, Queen's University Belfast.

Mika, H. and Zehr, H. (2003) 'A restorative framework for community justice practice', in K. McEvoy and T. Newburn (eds) *Criminology, Conflict Resolution and Restorative Justice*, Basingstoke: Palgrave.

Mikulincer, M. and Florian, V. (2000) 'Exploring individual differences in reactions to mortality salience – does attachment style regulate terror management mechanisms?', *Journal of Personality and Social Psychology*, 79: 260–273.

Miller, D. (1978) *Queen's Rebels: Ulster Loyalism in Historical Perspective*, Dublin: Gill and Macmillan.

Miller, D. (1994) *Don't Mention the War: Northern Ireland, Propaganda and the Media*, London: Pluto.

Miller, D. (2004) 'The Propaganda Machine', in D. Miller (ed.) *Tell Me Lies: Media and Propaganda in the Attack on Iraq*, London: Pluto Press.

Mills, A. and Codd. H, (2008) 'Prisoners' families and offender management: mobilizing social capital', *Probation Journal*, 55: 9–24.

Miranda, A. (2004) 'Women as agents of political violence: gendering security,' *Security Dialogue*, 35: 447–463.

Mitchell, C. (2002) 'Beyond resolution: what does conflict transformation actually transform?', *Peace and Conflict Studies*, 9: 1–23.

Mitchell, C. (2003) 'Protestant identification and political change in Northern Ireland', *Ethnic and Racial Studies*, 26: 612–631.

Mitchell, C. (2008) 'The limits of legitimacy: former Loyalist combatants and peace-building in Northern Ireland', *Irish Political Studies*, 23: 1–19.

Mitchell, N. (2004) *Agents of Atrocity: Leaders, Followers, and the Violation of Human Rights in Civil War*, New York: Palgrave Macmillan.

Moerings M, 1992, 'Role transitions and the wives of prisoners', *Environment and Behaviour*, 24: 239–259.

Moloney, E. (2000) 'Security forces created UDA' www.nuzhound.com/articles/moloney2000/mal81-27.htm (last accessed 20 October 2011).

Moloney, E. (2001) 'Criminality dominates Loyalist paramilitarism', *Sunday Tribune*, 7 January.

Moran, J. (2004) 'Paramilitaries, "ordinary decent criminals" and the development of organised crime following the Belfast Agreement', *International Journal of the Sociology of Law*, 32: 267–278.

Morrill, C., Mayer, N., Zald, K. and Hayagreeva, R. (2003) 'Covert political conflict in organizations: challenges from below', *Annual Review of Sociology*, 30: 391–415.

Morris, P. (1964) 'The problem of after-care: III. After-care and the prisoner's family', *British Journal of Criminology*, 4: 347–353.

Morrow, D. (1997) 'Suffering for righteousness' sake? Fundamentalist Protestantism and Ulster politics', in P. Shirlow and M. McGovern (eds) *Who Are 'The People'? Unionism, Protestanism and Loyalism in Northern Ireland*, London: Pluto Press.

Morselli, C. (2009) *Inside Criminal Networks*, New York: Springer.

Mullin, J. (1998) 'Death squad conspiracy: army link to UDA assassinations', *The Guardian*, 30 March.

Murray, J. (2005) 'The effects of imprisonment on families and children of prisoners', www.fcnetwork.org/reading/Murray_Prison_Effects_Chapter_17.pdf (last accessed 21 November 2011).

Murray, R. (1998) *State Violence: Northern Ireland 1969–1997*, Belfast: Beyond the Pale.

Murtagh, B. (2001) 'Partnerships and policy in Northern Ireland', *Local Economy*, 16: 50–62.

Mythen, G. and Walkate, S. (2006) 'Criminology and terrorism which thesis? Risk society or governmentality?', *British Journal of Criminology*, 46: 379–398.

Nasar, J. and Fisher, B. (1993) 'Hot spots of fear of crime: a multiple-method investigation', *Journal of Environmental Psychology*, 13: 187–206.

Nelson, S. (1984) *Ulster's Uncertain Defenders: Loyalists and the Northern Ireland Conflict*, Belfast: Appletree Press.

Neria, Y., Solomon, Z., Ginzburg, K., Dekel, R., Enoch, D., and Ohry, A. (2000) 'Posttraumatic residues of captivity: a follow up of Israeli ex-prisoners of war', *Journal of Clinical Psychiatry*, 61: 39–46.

New Ulster Political Research Group (1979) *Beyond the Religious Divide*, Belfast: New Ulster Political Research Group.

Newman, E. and Richmond O. (eds.) (2005) *Challenges to Peacebuilding. Managing Spoilers During Conflict Resolution*, New York: United Nations University Press.

Newman, E. and Richmond, O. (2006) 'Peace building and spoilers', *Conflict, Security and Development*, 6: 101–110.

Newsletter (2007) 'CTI funding "may go to other Loyalist projects"', *Newsletter*, 9 October.

Ni Aolain, N. (2000) *The Politics of Force: Conflict Management and State Violence in Northern Ireland*, Belfast: Blackstaff.

Nic Craith, M. (2002) *Plural Identities: Singular Narratives: the Case of Northern Ireland*, Oxford: Berghahn Books.

Nieburg, H. (1962) 'The threat of violence and social change', *American Political Science Review*, 56: 865–873.

Nordstrom, C. (1995) 'Contested identities/essentially contested powers', in K. Rupesinghe (ed.) *Conflict Transformation*, New York: St. Martin's Press.

Nordstrom, C., Martin, J. and Martin J.M. (1992) *The Paths of Domination, Resistance and Terror*, Santa Barbara, CA: University of California Press.

Northern Ireland Affairs Committee (2002) *The Financing of Terrorism in Northern Ireland*, London: HMSO.

Northern Ireland Affairs Committee (2006) *Organised Crime in Northern Ireland*, London: HMSO.

Northern Ireland Prison Service (2003) *Resettlement Strategy*, Belfast: HMSO.

Northern Ireland Prison Service (2010) *Accelerated Release Scheme*, www.niprison service.gov.uk/index.cfm/area/information/page/earlyrelease (last accessed 20 October 2011).

O'Brien, B. (1997) *A Pocket History of the IRA from 1916 Onwards*, Dublin: The O'Brien Press.

O'Callaghan, M. and O'Donnell, C. (2006) 'The Northern Ireland government, the "Paisleyite Movement" and Ulster Unionism in 1966', *Irish Political Studies*, 21: 203–222.

O'Halpin, E. (2007) *The British Joint Intelligence Committee and Ireland, 1965–1972*, Dublin: IIIS.

O'Malley, P. (1983) *The Uncivil Wars: Ireland Today*, Belfast: Blackstaff Press.

Office of the Police Ombudsman (2007) *Report on the Police Ombudsman's Investigation into Matters Surrounding the Death of Raymond McCord Junior*, Belfast: OPONI.

OFM/DFM (2005) *A Shared Future – Policy and Strategic Framework for Good Relations in Northern Ireland*, Belfast: Community Relations Unit.

OFM/DFM (2007) *Recruiting People with Conflict-Related Convictions, Employers' Guidance*, Belfast: OFM/DFM.

OFM/DFM (2010) *Programme for Cohesion, Sharing and Integration: Consultation Document*, Belfast: OFM/DFM.

O'Kane, E. (2010) 'Learning from Northern Ireland? The uses and abuses of the Irish "model"', *British Journal of Politics and International Relations*, 12: 239–256.

Østergaard-Nielsen, E. (2006) *Diasporas and Conflict Resolution: Part of the Problem or Part of the Solution*, Copenhagen: DIIS.

Parkinson, A. (1988) *Ulster Loyalism and the British Media*, Dublin: Four Courts Press.

Patterson, H. (1982) 'Paisley and Protestant politics', *Marxism Today*, January: 26–31.

Payne, B., Conway, V., Bell, C., Falk, A., Flynn, H., McNeill, C. and Rice, F. (2010), *Mapping Restorative Justice in Northern Ireland*. Available at www.law.qub.ac.uk/schools/SchoolofLaw/NewsandEvents/filestore/Filetoupload,2 16022,en.pdf (last accessed 21 November 2011).

Pepinsky, H. (1991) 'Peacemaking in criminology and criminal justice', in H. Pepinsky and R. Quinney (eds) *Criminology as Peacemaking*, Bloomington, IN: Indiana University Press.

Persic, C. and Bloomer, S. (2001) *The Feud and the Fury: The Response of the Community Sector to the Shankill Feud*, Belfast: Springfield Intercommunity Development Project.

Pickering, S. (2001) 'Undermining the sanitized account: violence and emotionality in the field in Northern Ireland', *British Journal of Criminology*, 41: 485–501.

Pile, S. (1997) 'Opposition, political identities and spaces of resistance' in S. Pile and M. Keith (eds) *Geographies of Resistance*, London: Routledge.

Pochrass, R. (1987) 'Terroristic murder in Northern Ireland: who is killed and why?', *Terrorism: An International Journal*, 9: 195–213.

Police Service of Northern Ireland (2003) *Report of the Chief Constable 2002–2003*, Belfast: PSNI.

Poole, D. and Rénique, G. (1992) *Peru: Time of Fear*, London: Latin America Bureau.

Popper, K. (1994) *The Myth of the Framework: In Defence of Science and Rationality*, London: Routledge.

Pranis, K. (2001). 'Restorative justice, social justice, and the empowerment of marginalized populations', in G. Bazemore and M. Schiff (eds), *Restorative Community Justice: Repairing Harm and Transforming Communities*, Cincinnati, OH: Anderson.

Principles of Loyalism (2002) *The Principles of Loyalism: An Internal Discussion Paper*, Belfast: UVF/PUP.

Progressive Unionist Party (1981) *Presentation to the Secretary of State of Northern Ireland*, Belfast: PUP.

Progressive Unionist Party (1985a) 'Agreeing to differ for progress', May, Belfast: PUP.

Progressive Unionist Party (1985b) 'Sharing responsibility', September, Belfast: PUP.

Progressive Unionist Party (1996a) *Manifesto for the Forum Election*, Belfast: PUP.

Progressive Unionist Party (1996b) 'Dealing with Reality', press statement issued by Billy Hutchinson, 31 March, Belfast: PUP.

Progressive Unionist Party (1996c) 'Support the Progressive Unionists', forum election communication, Belfast: PUP.

Progressive Unionist Party (2001) *Election Manifesto*, June, Belfast: PUP.

Progressive Unionist Party (2003a) *2003 Election Manifesto*, Belfast: PUP.

Progressive Unionist Party (2003b) 'How long are you prepared to wait for benefits to our community', election communication, Belfast: PUP.

Progressive Unionist Party (no date) *Breaking the Mould*, Belfast: PUP.

Public Records Office (2004) *Subversion in the Ulster Defence Regiment, by British Military Intelligence (1973)*, http://cain.ulst.ac.uk/publicrecords/1973/subversion_in_the_udr.htm (last accessed 21 November 2011).

Purvis, D. (1998) 'North West Freedom Address', Gay Pride North West, Progressive Unionist Party, copy held by author.

Purvis, D. (2011) *Educational Underachievement and the Protestant Working Class: A Summary of Research, for Consultation* www.dawnpurvis.com/wp-content/uploads/2011/03/EDPWC-Research-Summary-Dec10.pdf (last accessed 20 October 2011).

Quinney, R. (2000) 'Socialist humanism and the problem of crime', in K. Anderson and R. Quinney (eds.) *Thinking about Erich Fromm in the Development of Critical/Peacemaking Criminology*, Urbana, IL: University of Illinois Press.

Racioppi, L. and O'Sullivan See, K. (2007) 'Grassroots peace-building and thirdparty intervention: the European Union's special support programme for peace and reconciliation in Northern Ireland', *Peace and Change*, 32: 361–390.

Rankin, A. and Ganiel, G. (2008) 'DUP discourses on violence and their impact on the Northern Ireland Peace Process', *Peace and Conflict Studies*, 15: 116–135.

Redpath J. (1983), 'No murals here', *Circa*, 8: 20–21.

Relatives for Justice (1995) *Collusion 1990–1994, Loyalist Paramilitary Murders in North of Ireland*, Belfast: Relatives for Justice.

Relatives for Justice (2008) 'Security forces created Shankill UDA', www.relativesforjustice.com/security-forces-created-shankill-uda.htm (last accessed 20 October 2011).

Richmond, O. (2006) 'The linkage between devious objectives and spoiling behaviour in peace processes', in E. Newman and O. Richmond (eds) *Challenges to Peacebuilding: Managing Spoilers During Conflict Resolution*, New York: United Nations University Press.

Ritchie, M. (2007) 'Statement by Margaret Ritchie MLA, Minister for Social

Development to the Northern Ireland Assembly on the future of the CTI'. Northern Ireland Executive press release, 16 October.

Robson, T. (2000) 'Northern Ireland: community relations and community conflict', *Development*, 43: 66–71.

Robson, T. (2001) 'The co-option of radicalism: conflict, community and civil society', *Critical Sociology*, 27: 221–245.

Roche, D. (2001) 'The Evolving Definition of Restorative Justice', *Contemporary Justice Review*, 4: 341–353.

Rolston, B. (2000) *Unfinished Business: State Killings and the Quest for Truth*, Belfast: Beyond the Pale.

Rolston, B. (2003) 'Changing the political landscape: murals and transition in Northern Ireland', *Irish Studies Review*, 11: 3–16.

Rolston, B. (2003) *Drawing Support: Murals and Transition in the North of Ireland*, Belfast: Beyond the Pale.

Rolston, B. (2005) '"An effective mask for terror": democracy, death squads and Northern Ireland', *Crime, Law and Social Change*, 44: 181–203.

Rolston, B. (2006) 'Dealing with the past: pro-State paramilitaries, truth and transition in Northern Ireland', *Human Rights Quarterly*, 28: 652–675.

Rolston, B. and Tomlinson, M. (1986) 'Long-term imprisonment in Northern Ireland: psychological or political survival?', *Working Papers in European Criminology*, 7: 162–183.

Romens, A. (2007) *Re-Imaging Communities or Re-Imaging Heritage? A Look at Northern Ireland's Latest Transformation Program*, www.saic.edu/pdf/degrees/pdf_files/aap/2007_Anne_Romans.pdf (last accessed 20 October 2011).

Rose, R. (1971) *Governing Without Consensus: An Irish Perspective*, London Faber and Faber.

Rosenbaum, H. and Sederberg, P. (1976) *Vigilante Politics*, Philadelphia, PA: University of Pennsylvania Press.

Rowthorn, B. (1981) 'Ireland's intractable crisis', *Marxism Today*, December: 26–35.

Ruane, J. and Todd, J. (1996) *The Dynamics of Conflict in Northern Ireland*, Cambridge: Cambridge University Press.

Rummel, K. (1994) *Death by Government*, New Brunswick, NJ: Transaction Publishers,

Sack D. (1998) *Homo Geographicus: A Framework for Action, Awareness and Moral Action*, Baltimore, MD: Johns Hopkins Press.

Sageman, M. (2008) *Leaderless Jihad*, Philadelphia, PA: University of Philadelphia Press.

Santino, J. (2001) *Signs of War and Peace: Social Conflict and the Use of Public Symbols in Northern Ireland*, New York: Palgrave.

Sappington, A. (1996) 'Relationship among prison adjustment, beliefs and cognitive coping style', *International Journal of Offender Therapy and Comparative Criminology*, 40: 54–62.

Schmalleger, F. (1996), *Criminology Today*, Englewood Cliffs, NJ: Prentice Hall.

Schmid, A. (2004) 'Framework for conceptualising terrorism', *Terrorism and Political Violence*, 16: 197–221.

Schroeder, T. (2007) 'Reflection, reason and free will', *Philosophical Explorations*, 10: 77–84.

Shephard, R. (1997) *Aging, Physical Activity and Health*, Champaign, IL: Human Kinetics.

Shirlow, P. (2000) 'Fundamentalist loyalism: discourse, resistance and identity politics', in R. Gold and G. Revill (eds) *Landscapes of Defence*, Harlow: Prentice-Hall.

Shirlow, P. and McEvoy, K. (2008) *Beyond the Wire: Former Prisoners and Conflict Transformation in Northern Ireland*, London: Pluto Press.

Shirlow, P. and McGovern, M. (eds) (1997) *Who Are 'The People'? Unionism, Protestantism and Loyalism in Northern Ireland*, London: Pluto Press.

Shirlow. P. and Monaghan, R. (2006) *Forward to the Past? Interpreting Contemporary and Future Loyalist Violence*, Unpublished ESRC report (RES-000-22-1013).

Shirlow, P. and Murtagh, B. (2006) *Belfast: Segregation, Violence and the City*, London: Pluto Press.

Shirlow, P., Tonge, J., McAuley, J. and McGlynn, C. (2010) *Abandoning Historical Conflict? Former Political Prisoners and Reconciliation in Northern Ireland*, Manchester: Manchester University Press.

Shirlow, P., Graham, B., McEvoy, K., hAdhmaill, F. and Purvis, D. (2005) *Politically Motivated Former Prisoner Groups: Community Activism and Conflict Transformation*, Belfast: Northern Ireland Community Relations Council.

Silber, L. and Little, A. (1995) *The Death of Yugoslavia*, London: Penguin Books.

Silke, A. (1998a) 'The lords of discipline: the methods and motives of paramilitary vigilantism in Northern Ireland', *Low Intensity Conflict and Law Enforcement*, 7: 121–156.

Silke, A. (1998b) 'In defense of the realm: financing Loyalist terrorism in Northern Ireland – part one: extortion and blackmail', *Studies in Conflict and Terrorism*, 21 (4): 331–361.

Silke, A. (1999) 'Ragged justice: Loyalist vigilantism in Northern Ireland', *Terrorism and Political Violence*, 11: 1–31.

Silke, A. (2000) 'Drink, drugs, and rock'n'roll: financing Loyalist terrorism in Northern Ireland – part two', *Studies in Conflict and Terrorism*, 23: 107–127.

Sinnerton, H. (2002) *David Ervine: Uncharted Waters*, Dingle: Brandon.

Sluka, J. (1996) 'The writing's on the wall: peace process images, symbols and murals in Northern Ireland', *Critique of Anthropology*, 16: 381–94.

Sluka, J. (2000) '"For God and Ulster": the culture of terror and Loyalist death squads in Northern Ireland', in J. Sluka (ed.) *Death Squad: The Anthropology of State Terror*, Philadelphia, PA: University of Pennsylvania Press.

Sluka, J. (2007) 'Silent but still deadly: guns and the peace process in Northern Ireland', in C. Fruehling (ed.) *Open Fire: Understanding Global Gun Cultures*, Oxford: Berg.

Smith, A. (2003) 'Citizenship education in Northern Ireland: beyond national identity?', *Cambridge Education Journal*, 33: 15–32.

Smooha, S. (2002) 'Types of democracy and modes of conflict management in ethnically divided societies', *Nations and Nationalism*, 8: 423–431.

Social Democratic and Labour Party (2008) *The Issues Explained in a Nutshell*, Belfast: SDLP.

Soja, E. (1996) *Thirdspace: Journeys to Los Angeles and Other Real-and-Imagined Places*, London: Verso.

Soja, E. (2000), *Postmetropolis: Critical Studies of Cities and Regions*, Oxford: Blackwell.

Southern, N. (2005) 'Militant Protestantism: an analysis of the theology of political resistance and its impact on Northern Ireland', *Religion*, 35: 65–77.

Southern, N. (2007) 'Britishness, "Ulsterness" and Unionist identity in Northern Ireland', *Nationalism and Ethnic Politics*, 13: 71–102.

Southern, N. (2008) 'Territoriality, alienation, and Loyalist decommissioning: the case of the Shankill in Protestant West Belfast', *Terrorism and Political Violence*, 20: 66–86.

Spencer, G. (2004) 'Constructing loyalism: politics, communications and peace in Northern Ireland', *Contemporary Politics*, 10: 37–55.

Spencer, G. (2008) *The State of Loyalism in Northern Ireland*, Hampshire: Palgrave Macmillan.

Stedman, S. (1997) 'Spoiler problems in peace processes', *International Security*, 22: 5–53.

Stedman, S. (2000) 'Spoiler problems in peace processes', in P. Stern and D. Druckman (eds) *International Conflict Resolution after the Cold War*, Washington, DC: National Research Council Press.

Steenkamp, C. (2008) 'Loyalist paramilitary violence after the Belfast Agreement', *Ethnopolitics*, 7: 159–176.

Stevens, J. (2003) *Stevens Enquiry Overview and Recommendations (3)*, www.madden-finucane.com/patfinucane/archive/pat_finucane/2003-04-17_stevens_report.pdf (last accessed 20 October 2011).

Stevenson, J. (1996) *'We Wrecked the Place'*: *Contemplating an End to the Northern Irish Troubles*, London: The Free Press.

Sutton, M. (1994) *Bear in Mind these Dead: An Index of Deaths from the Conflict in Ireland 1969–1993*, Belfast: Beyond the Pale.

Tara (1973) *Proclamation*, http://cain.ulst.ac.uk/othelem/organ/docs/tara73.htm (last accessed 20 October 2011).

Taylor, P. (2000) *Loyalists*, London: Bloomsbury.

Till, K. (1999) 'Staging the past: landscape designs, cultural identity and *Erinnerungspolitik* at Berlin's Neue Wache', *Ecumene*, 6: 251–283.

Todd, J. (1987) 'Two traditions in Unionist political culture', *Irish Political Studies*, 2: 1–26.

Turk, A. (1982) *Political Criminality: The Defiance and Defense of Authority*, Beverley Hills, CA: Sage Publications.

Turk, A. (1984) 'Political crime', in R. Meier (ed.) *Major Forms of Crime*, Beverley Hills, CA: Sage Publications.

Ulster Democratic Party (1987) *Common Sense: Northern Ireland-An Agreed Process*, Belfast: Ulster Democratic Party.

Vannais, J, (2001) 'Postcards from the edge: reading political murals in the North of Ireland', *Irish Political Studies*, 16: 133–60.

Vasquez, J. (1993) *The War Puzzle*, Cambridge: Cambridge University Press.

Vasquez, J. and Mansbach, R. (1984) 'The role of issues in global co-operation and conflict', *British Journal of Political Science*, 14: 411–433.

Vayrynen, R. (ed.) (1991) *New Directions in Conflict Theory*, London: Sage Publications.

Walker, G. (2004) *A History of the Ulster Unionist Party: Protest, Pragmatism and Pessimism*, Manchester: Manchester University Press.

Ward, T. and Gannon, T. (2006) 'Rehabilitation, etiology and self-regulation: the Good lives model of sexual offender treatment', *Aggression and Violent Behaviour*, 11: 77–94.

Ward, T. and Maruna, S. (2007) *Rehabilitation: Beyond the Risk Paradigm*, London: Routledge.

White, B. (1995) 'A Loyalist's view from the hub', *Belfast Telegraph*, 5 October.

White, J. (2003) *Terrorism: An Introduction*, Belmont, CA: Wadsworth.

Whitfield, D. (1987) 'Gusty Spence – heretic on the Shankill', *Morning Star*, 7 February.

Whyte, J. (1991) *Interpreting Northern Ireland*, Oxford: Clarendon Press.

Whyte, J., (1983) 'How much discrimination was there under the Unionist regime 1921–68?', in T. Gallagher and J. O'Carroll (eds) *Contemporary Irish Studies*, Manchester: Manchester University Press.

Wilson, C., Gutiérrez, F. and Chao, L. (2003) *Racism, Sexism and the Media: The Rise of Class Communication in Multicultural America*, 3rd edn, Thousand Oaks, CA: Sage

Wood, I. (2006) *Crimes of Loyalty: A History of the UDA*, Edinburgh: Edinburgh University Press.

Woodworth, P. (2001) *Dirty War, Clean Hands: ETA, the GAL and Spanish Democracy*, New Haven, CT: Yale Nota Bene.

Wootton, A. (1988) *Erving Goffman: Exploring the Interaction Order*, Cambridge: Polity Press.

Zakin, G., Solomon, Z. and Neria, Y. (2003) 'Hardiness, attachment style, and long term psychological distress among Israeli POWs and combat veterans', *Personality and Individual Differences*, 34: 819–829.

Zarkov, D. (2001) 'The body of the other man; sexual violence and the constructions of masculinity, sexuality and ethnicity in the Croatian media', in C. Moser and F. Clark (eds) *Victims, Perpetrators or Actors? Gender, Armed Conflict and Political Violence*, London: Zed Books.

Zartman, W. (1989) *Ripe for Resolution: Conflict and Intervention in Africa*, Oxford: Oxford University Press.

Zoellner, L., Alvarez-Conrad, J. and Foa, E. (2002) 'Peritraumatic dissociative experiences, trauma narratives, and trauma pathology', *Journal of Traumatic Stress*, 15: 49–57.

Index